HOW NOT TO BE A BOY

Don't cry; love sport; play rough; drink beer; don't talk about feelings. But Robert Webb has been wondering for some time now: are those rules actually any use? To anyone? Looking back over his life, from schoolboy crushes (on girls and boys) to discovering the power of making people laugh (in the Cambridge Footlights with David Mitchell and Olivia Colman), and from losing his beloved mother to becoming a husband and father, Robert considers the absurd expectations boys and men have thrust upon them at every stage of his life. *How Not To Be a Boy* explores the relationships that made Robert who he is as a man, the lessons we learn as sons and daughters, and the understanding that sometimes you aren't the Luke Skywalker of your life — you're actually Darth Vader.

SPECIAL MESSAGE TO READERS

THE ULVERSCROFT FOUNDATION
(registered UK charity number 264873)
was established in 1972 to provide funds for
research, diagnosis and treatment of eye diseases.
Examples of major projects funded by
the Ulverscroft Foundation are:-

- The Children's Eye Unit at Moorfields Eye Hospital, London
- The Ulverscroft Children's Eye Unit at Great Ormond Street Hospital for Sick Children
- Funding research into eye diseases and treatment at the Department of Ophthalmology, University of Leicester
- The Ulverscroft Vision Research Group, Institute of Child Health
- Twin operating theatres at the Western Ophthalmic Hospital, London
- The Chair of Ophthalmology at the Royal Australian College of Ophthalmologists

You can help further the work of the Foundation
by making a donation or leaving a legacy.
Every contribution is gratefully received. If you
would like to help support the Foundation or
require further information, please contact:

THE ULVERSCROFT FOUNDATION
The Green, Bradgate Road, Anstey
Leicester LE7 7FU, England
Tel: (0116) 236 4325

website: www.foundation.ulverscroft.com

HOW NOT TO BE A BOY

ROBERT WEBB

ISIS
LARGE
PRINT

First published in Great Britain 2017
by
Canongate Books Ltd

First Isis Edition
published 2018
by arrangement with
Canongate Books Ltd

*A catalogue record for this book is available
from the British Library.*

ISBN 978 1 78541–522–7 (hb)
ISBN 978–1–78541–528–9 (pb)

Published by
F. A. Thorpe (Publishing)
Anstey, Leicestershire

Set by Words & Graphics Ltd.
Anstey, Leicestershire
Printed and bound in Great Britain by
T. J. International Ltd., Padstow, Cornwall

This book is printed on acid-free paper

For Abigail

Contents

Overture

"If I get this right, Tess Rampling will definitely want to have sex with me." The idea slouches through my fifteen-year-old brain and disappears before I've had time to ask it exactly why a sixth-former of Rampling's cosmic beauty would want to have sex with a GCSE pit-sniffer like me.

I take Rick Astley's "Never Gonna Give You Up" out of its paper bag and gaze at his pink face. "Oh dear, Rick Astley, you're not 'gonna' like this. You really have no idea what's about to happen to you." Gently, I lift the lid of Great-Auntie Trudy's wooden gramophone to reveal the record turntable within.

The gramophone used to be in Trudy's bedroom, and when I was chin-high to its wooden lid (about four years old) we would happily listen to Terry Wogan on Radio 2 while she brushed her hair and "put her face on". Or sometimes, she'd play a favourite LP like the soundtrack to *The King and I*. The first track of that record was called "Overture" and seemed to be a non-singing medley of some of the other songs. I liked the "Overture": a friendly invitation and a promise of what was to come. Some of the best tunes were missing, but I guessed that was to keep them as a surprise.

It's not big, my room. The gramophone is among the wooden hand-me-downs that sprout from the walls and nearly meet in the middle. Here's a chest of drawers and a little bookshelf that Mum gave me recently. Here's the wardrobe that never yielded to Narnia no matter how faithfully I reached for the cold air.

The bedroom walls are pale green: pock-marked with Blu-Tack scars from sci-fi posters now replaced with Van Gogh prints from Woolworths. They have "Vincent" written under them in swirly writing. Recently, and with great solemnity, I took down the huge *Empire Strikes Back* poster — the picture of Darth Vader offering his hand to Luke. "Come with me," he says to his defeated son.

There's a Greenpeace picture of a boat cleaning a polluted sea by magically drawing a rainbow in its wake. I get the point it's trying to make, but even I can see the thing has all the truth and beauty of Lester Piggott narrating his tax return. Anyway, it's there to show that I mind about the ozone layer or something. Similarly, there's a line drawing of a defiant-looking African boy against a horizontal tricolour which I vaguely associate with the ANC. In the impossible event that Tess Rampling ever sets foot in this room, she will instantly see that a) I disapprove of apartheid; b) I disapprove of pollution; and c) I now prefer post-impressionists to *Star Wars*. The first two parts are even true.

We live next door to RAF Coningsby. They've finally supplied us with double glazing to make up for the familiar scream of the Tornados. The condensation I used to draw pictures in now occurs between the panes rather than on the inside, like an itch you can't scratch. Thanks, lads. Still, the room retains its own unique and homely smell which I really like. It will be many years before someone points out that this smell has a name: "damp". Occasionally my step-dad Derek loses an argument about turning on the central heating and the smell turns into what I would call the equally comforting "grilled dust".

Here, in 1987, it feels wrong to be using the gramophone in an enterprise even vaguely connected with sex, like trying to make erotic art out of Fuzzy-Felt. But then, extreme measures are sometimes necessary when it comes to the sublime person of Tess Rampling. Apart from being the Most Beautiful Girl Who Ever Smiled and Frowned at the Same Time and Tossed Her Auburn Hair Out of Her All-Forgiving, World-Comprehending Eyes, Tess is also two years above me at school and therefore a figure of demoralising maturity. I see her walking between classes, having intellectual-sounding conversations with male teachers who look very pleased to be able to help. I want to help her too. My God, I want to help her brains out. I want to help her like we just invented helping.

I take the shiny record from its sleeve and savour the smell of the vinyl even though I dislike this song with some energy. There was a nervous moment in Woolworths when I picked it up for the first time to check the back of the sleeve: "Please let the B-side be just an instrumental. Surely it's just an instrumental!" And lo — Stock, Aitken & Waterman did not let me down. I impale "Never Gonna Give You Up" on the central upright of the record player and the B-side wobbles down onto the turntable. This is sweet. Tess Rampling is surely going to want to have sex with me when she sees the way I stick it to Rick Astley.

What I'm doing here in my teenage bedroom is planning an end-of-term, school-hall sketch show. My form teacher, Mrs Slater, says that the correct term is "revue", but I don't much like the word: it sounds square and not something you would see on the telly. I can't imagine Rik Mayall saying "revue". At a pinch, Stephen Fry might say it, but there are limits to how much I get to copy Stephen Fry without attracting peer group ridicule. Bad enough that I've started to pronounce "grass" to rhyme like a southern "arse" rather than a native Lincolnshire "lass". No, it's a sketch show. I write a dozen sketches, cast myself in all the best parts, with friends taking up the feed-line slack, and then put on a show in the main hall at lunchtime. The ostensible value of this is to encourage team-spiritedness and raise money for charity. The actual reason, of course, is to get Tess Rampling to want to have sex with me.

The sketches this time include "The Price is Slight" (TV game-show parody), "Glue Peter" (children's TV show parody), "The GAY-Team" (parody of children's TV action drama, also apparently watched by American adults) and, of course, my lethal take on "Never Gonna Give You Up" in which I will mock Rick Astley's dancing while lip-synching to rewritten lyrics of the song which I'm about to pre-record over the instrumental.

Some of these sketches are less than fully formed, both technically and morally. "The GAY-Team", for example, is currently no more than the desire for four of us to jump out in front of the curtain in Hawaiian shirts, brandishing hairdryers. What happens after that is currently anyone's guess, but I'm pretty sure I'm going to draw the line at doing "the gay voice". I suspect the other boys in the team will want to do "the gay voice", but in my sophisticated opinion, doing "the gay voice" has no place in the comedy of 1987, even in Lincolnshire where literally no one is meant to be gay.

Obviously I will get Matthew Finney to "black up" to play B. A. Baracus. That's different. Finney is very short and even weedier than me. So he really only has to stand there wearing dark-brown make-up and say "Murdoch, you crazy fool" or possibly "Murdoch, you crazy homosexual" and we're on to a winner. I see no reason why this might cause offence: although it's possible that there are gay people in Lincolnshire, it is not possible that anyone is black. Apart from my brother's friend, "black Steve". (I mean, there are a lot of Steves so what *on earth* else could they call him?) And black Steve won't be watching, so obviously there's no problem.

5

I look out of the bedroom window and think about Matthew Finney. I foresee that Finney will resist the make-up for some reason. Probably because he's a shocking little racist who didn't even go on the Drama trip to see *Woza Albert!* Yes, that's it. I turn from the window and start to punch an invisible Finney in the face for being such a racist. "No, you don't like that, do you, Finney? You can dish it out but you can't take it!" I get into quite an involved fight with Finney, who is surprisingly agile and keeps head-butting me in the ear which is really annoying. He throws me to the ground and grabs me by the throat. Desperate for breath, I seize an old Rubik's Cube from under the bed and gash Finney in the eye with an unsolved corner. He reels back and —

Mum knocks on the door and pops her head round. "Everything all right?"

It's good that she's started knocking, but she hasn't yet got into the habit of waiting for an answer.

I look at her from the floor, panting and slightly aglow. "Yeah, fine thanks."

"I heard . . . choking sounds."

"Yeah, Matthew Finney was trying to strangle me."

"Righto." She adopts a relaxed smile and it takes her half a second to scan the room for evidence of actual danger as opposed to "Robert doing that thing he does". She has a word for it.

"Pretending?"

"Yup."

She nods and makes to leave, and then: "Fish fingers!"

"Brill."

She glances at the Rubik's Cube I'm still holding and then goes, closing the door slightly too casually.

Buoyed by the thought of fish fingers for tea and grateful that this was a mere "pretending-intrusion" rather than a full-scale "wank-intrusion", I get up and turn back to the gramophone.

It can't be easy for Mum, I think. Pretending is not Normal. Normal boys have real fights, not pretend fights. Nor are they virgins at fifteen. Nor do they write comedy sketches or keep a diary. And if they did keep a diary, they probably wouldn't write things like:

Slater said in MS today [Media Studies] that
Wogan is going to be on 3 nights a week instead
of 1. I said "he must be feeling under-exposed".
She really laughed but no one else did. They
think I'm just up her arse. Tess didn't hear it,
obviously. Thing is — if he does it 3 nights a
week he might be bored of it by the time I'm
famous so I get to be interviewed by Anneka
fucking Rice or something. I'm joking but it's a
real worry.

Massive weird thing. Last night Mum was
going out and coz I was going to be left alone
with Derek, everything was suddenly horrible.
She asked me why I looked all massively sad and
I said "nothing" for a bit and then completely
lost it and cried my eyes out like a baby. Like a
fucking BABY. We went in here and she gave me
a cuddle, rocking me sort of from side to side

7

and it was boring but also good really. She asked me again and I just said I didn't want her to go and Derek would just be watching his nature programmes about clubbing baby seals to death and that it was stupid of me and not to worry and all that jazz. She went out anyway but Christ knows why I went so mental.

I load a portable tape recorder with a blank cassette and press "Play", waiting for the leading hiss to turn into the regular hiss, then "Stop". If I'm honest, I can't be sure if the recording quality of a boy singing in his bedroom over the instrumental version of a single played through a 1960s gramophone into the tiny external microphone of a cheap tape recorder and then eventually played through the speakers of a cuboid school hall is going to be — pristine. Neither, if I gave it a moment's thought, am I necessarily as good a singer as the inter-national recording star Rick Astley, especially with my zero interest in singing and my recently broken voice which I still can't get the hang of. Why does it have to be so fucking *deep*? Dad's fault. Still, what I lack in technical expertise will, I feel sure, be more than made up for by stupid dancing. Everyone likes my stupid dancing. And then there's the new lyrics which have an undeniable verve, if not sophistication. I look at the chorus:

> First I'm gonna swing my hands
> Then I'm gonna twist my feet
> Then I'm gonna turn around:
> I'm quiff-ey!

Then I'm gonna burst my zits
Then I'm gonna shake my bits
Like I've got the shits:
I'm getting a stiff-ey.

I frown at these last two lines. I mean, it's brilliant —
obviously it's all brilliant — but I just worry a little that
the logic of having the shits and getting a stiffy doesn't
really follow. Am I saying that Rick Astley is aroused by
diarrhoea? Is that *really* what I want to say? But no,
surely it's the way that he shakes his "bits" that makes
him look like he's "got the shits" and his "stiffy" is the
effect produced by the whole performance. That's fine
then. I press "Pause" and then "Play" and "Record" on
the cassette player. There again, "shits" is going to be
quite difficult to get past Mrs Slater. What could Rick
Astley have, if not the shits? Wits, mits, fits, pits —
PITS! "Then I'm gonna smell my pits". There's
definitely a move he does in the video involving one
arm being raised above his head in a sort of
half-hearted circle that I could easily turn into a
pit-sniff. "Then I'm gonna sniff my pits." Excellent.
And that should become the second line, moving "bits"
down to line three so that it's the shaking of his bits
that gives him the stiffy. Perfect.

I shove a can of Insignia up my INXS T-shirt and
spray my own pits. Looking in the mirror, I wonder
how long it will be before I need the brand-matching
shaving foam and aftershave. Does Tess Rampling
approve of Insignia? She surely doesn't approve of Rick
Astley, but what if she doesn't like the way I smell? If

she ever gets close enough to smell me. What if she sees the show and thinks it's crap? What if she doesn't even come? The appalling possibility sinks in. I look carefully in the mirror to see what happens to my face when an appalling possibility sinks in. Oh, it does that.

It's fine. There's the funny dance. When in doubt, do a funny dance. I already feel sorry for Mum who's going to have to listen to "Never Gonna Give You Up" coming from behind this door about seventy-four times as I practise the dance. First, the words. I clear my throat, set the record turning and release the Pause button on the tape. This needs to be good. This needs to be better than it needs to be.

The dance isn't perfect, but I get through it just fine. Despite all the practice, this is the first time I've done it from start to finish without stopping. Moments before I went out on stage, someone in the wings had said, "We reckon about seven million viewers." I see. I wonder if Tess Rampling is one of them. The year is 2009 and this is *Let's Dance for Comic Relief*. I've just done my version of the audition scene from the eighties movie *Flashdance*.

Tall, Welsh and handsome, the presenter Steve Jones beckons me over and says, "I'm almost speechless, what the hell just happened?"

"Something," I say, trying to catch my breath, "very intense." Co-presenter Claudia Winkleman randomly says, "I actually love you." The audience are still making a huge racket. Right . . . so it went better than I thought. Be cool. Steve Jones turns to the judges.

Anton Du Beke says, "It's a complete thing of beauty." Baby Spice Emma Bunton says she thinks I must be a trained dancer. That leaves Michael McIntyre, whom for some reason I identify as a threat. Naturally, I lean an elbow on Steve Jones's shoulder and glare at McIntyre as if I'm about to kill him. I imagine this looks like Han Solo leaning against Chewie, except this is Han Solo in a black leotard with a massive curly wig. Michael blinks and then starts saying something about how he used to have a French girlfriend. The audience likes this, so I soften up and try to give him a sweet smile. I cross my hands over my crotch: now that the dance is over and I've dropped the lunatic aggression, I'm suddenly just a bloke dressed as a woman. Even if Tess Rampling isn't watching, I know that Dad is.

McIntyre has been listening to the audience too and senses that he's under-doing it. He ends with a shower of compliments and I nod gratefully to him, even though part of me still wants to head-butt him in the ear à la Matthew Finney. This is, after all, a charity event. So it's no time to be "minty". I had a "minty moment" earlier which I now regret.

The term "minty" is used for that precious moment in the life of an actor where he or she is in possession of a complaint about the way they feel they're being treated but haven't yet expressed that complaint. Try it now: keep your mouth closed while running your tongue over your front teeth — savouring that *minty* freshness — while rolling your eyes at the ceiling with long-suffering patience. It's safe to try this at home, but

I wouldn't recommend doing it in public or you may be mistaken for Trevor Eve.

I was as frightened before the dance as I feel shy now. Michael gets cartoon super-aggression; the make-up artist just got passive-aggression. Either way, the solution, apparently, was aggression.

Earlier, in the make-up room, Roxy had driven another hairpin through the curly wig and the sensation was like a Smurf ice-skating on my scalp. She might as well have been using a staple-gun. "I think it's probably quite well fixed on now," I say as I try to relax my grip on the arms of the make-up chair, "you can probably stop now, if you like."

"No, darling, just need a few more," she says. I've known Roxy, the TV make-up lady, for about eight minutes and this isn't going well. Young, distracted and phenomenally good-looking, she's the kind of girl who wouldn't have given me the time of day at school. She doesn't look like Tess, but she has a Tess-like aura. I try not to hold this against her, despite the fact that she keeps stabbing me in the head. She's blithely reaching for another kirby grip and I suddenly know what it's going to be like when we have androids for dentists.

"It's just — it's on so tight already that I've got a massive headache. I'm a bit worried that if my head hurts this much I won't be able to remember the dance." Roxy is only half listening. In the next chair along, Les Dennis is discussing the terms of his mortgage in bitter detail. Another pin makes a forced landing into the back of my neck, strafing three layers of skin on the way. The room judders. "The thing is, Rocky —"

"Roxy."

"Yeah, the thing is, I know it's a big wig, but I'm really, really sure that you can give it a rest with the pins now."

Ooh, that came out a bit minty.

The tone I'm aiming for is suave and avuncular, a professional gravitas which may or may not be undermined by the fact that I am currently wearing a sparkly leotard and a padded bra. I've also attracted some attention. Les Dennis has broken off from his mortgage monologue and sips his coffee in the mirror with studied nonchalance.

Roxy hesitates. "If it falls off during the dance, I'll get the sack."

"I promise you it won't fall off. Even if it did, I will make sure that everyone knows that it was my fault and I promise you won't get the sack."

The fear, the adrenaline, the headache, the thing the bra is doing to my chest and the thing the "dancer's support garment" is doing to my testicles all contribute to the following: "I promise it won't fall off. I swear *on the grave of my dead mother* that it won't fall off."

I say it with enough emphasis to make half a joke of it, but I know that this is a low move. In any argument, the "dead mum" card is the one you play as a last resort. It doesn't change anyone's mind, but it usually embarrasses them into a more receptive mood. This is cheap. I want the dance to go well, but it's always important to remember that there's a very fine line between being a perfectionist and being a minty fuckwit.

I cross one bare leg over the other. Roxy obviously thinks I'm nuts. "OK, Robert, I won't put any more in and I'll take a couple of the top ones out." She says this loudly and slowly, as if to an old geezer in a care home who just complained about the exact number of baked beans on his toast. An old geezer in a leotard. "That would be great, thanks." I look across at Les Dennis. He gives me a smile and a wink, which is nice of him but now I feel even worse.

Not long after, I'm in the back seat of a car on the way home from Ealing Studios. I didn't forget the *Flashdance* routine. And twenty-two years earlier, I didn't forget the Rick Astley one either.

I check my phone: on Twitter, a man who used to be very important to me has said something kind. And I have a voicemail from another man who is even more important who has been even kinder. These two messages will change things, and my reaction to them informs this book. But the journey will be a slow one. That night, I'll get back to the flat to find a bunch of friends who came round to watch the show with my wife Abigail, who is pregnant with our first daughter. And after everyone has left and Abbie has gone to bed, I'll sit in our little garden and drink another two bottles of red wine and smoke about thirty Marlboro Lights. Tomorrow I'll do something similar — but in the pub in the middle of the day. This behaviour won't change when our daughter is born, and the moment will come when Abbie will tell me about these months and say as she looks at me steadily: "You let me down."

I don't know what I'm doing. I haven't got the first clue what I'm doing. In the car, the London streetlights liquefy as I cry all the way home. I think of my fifteen-year-old self in his bedroom practising that other dance in what feels like that other lifetime.

15: Bit self-indulgent, isn't it?
43: What?
15: This. You, talking to yourself.
43: You were expecting to grow out of it?
15: I wasn't "expecting" anything. Christ.
(*Pause*)
43: Can you please stop that?
15: Stop what?
43: Looking at my hair. It happens.
15: Sorry. Just a bit of a shock. I mean, what the fuck —
43: It just fell out, OK?
15: Right.
43: Look, there's good news, all right? I came to give you the good news.
15: Like Jesus?
43: If you like.
15: Like Jesus with a massive bald patch?
43: Mate, get over it. I have.
15: Really?
43: No, not really. But look, I'm a TV star!
15: Oh my God.
43: Good, isn't it?

15: No, I mean "Oh my God — what a penis".

43: Well —

15: Hark at cunty. "My name's Robert Webb and I'm a TV star!" Is that how you talk?

43: Look, if you're just going to be horrible —

15: How big?

43: What?

15: How big a star?

43: Erm, well, I don't really think about it in those terms.

15: Like fuck you don't. Bigger than John Cleese?

43: No.

15: Bigger than Rik Mayall?

43: Er, no, not really.

15: Well, it doesn't sound very fucking —

43: Nigel Planer.

15: What?

43: I'm about as famous as Nigel Planer, if you must.

15: (*Considers this*) Right. Well, I suppose that's —

43: Actually, Rik Mayall didn't have a sketch show, so —

15: Yes he did! He was in *A Kick Up the Eighties*.

43: Oh yeah, I forgot that.

15: You FORGOT *A Kick Up the Eighties*!?

43: Look, a lot's happened, all right? A lot of good things. I'm married with two children.

15: Oh, OK.

43: You pleased?

15: Yeah, course I'm pleased. I mean, I get to have sex at least twice, right?

43: Well, yes, that's one way of looking at it.

15: Oh, Mr Mature, Mr Fucking VICTOR MATURE isn't bothered about all the sex. I suppose you have sex all the time.

43: No, not really. I suppose 21 might turn up later; he's at it constantly.

15: I like the sound of 21.

43: I think he's a bit of a wanker.

15: Sounds like he does less wanking than you.

43: Right, I'm going.

15: No, sorry, hang on. Sorry.

(Pause)

15: I like your accent.

43: My accent?

15: You sound quite posh.

43: Ah yes. Well, that was your idea. You want to sound like Stephen Fry, don't you?

15: What's wrong with that?

43: Nothing. I mean it's a bit —

15: Look, I just don't want to sound like fucking Dad, all right? I want to be the opposite of Dad.

43: You've just said two different things and the second one is impossible.

15: Worth a try.

43: Waste of time. Close your eyes and don't think of a pink elephant.

15: What?

43: Close your eyes and don't think of a pink elephant.

15: OK . . . *(Closes eyes)*

43: What are you thinking of?

15: A pink elephant.

43: You've got — you can open your eyes now — you've got this idea of Dad as an abrasive northern male with an overdeveloped sense of adventure who takes women for granted and drinks too much. And you're about to spend twenty-five years trying to be "not that".

15: So?

43: So you're screwed.

15: So I should just give in and be a macho bullshit arsehole like other blokes.

43: Other blokes aren't all like that. Listen, a few years ago, I did this charity dance thing on TV and it went really well. Lots of people said kind things but there were two messages that really mattered. One was from Stephen Fry and the other was from Dad. It was the one from Dad that was the most important by a long way. You want his approval and you're much more like him than you th —

15: What did Mum say?

43: What?

15: This dance thing. What did Mum say?

43: Mum, she . . .

15: She liked it too, right?

(Pause)

43: Yes.
(*15 looks at 43*)
15: What's the matter?

A year or so before *Let's Dance*, I'm driving a car for the first time since getting married. It's a smart navy-blue Audi A3, given to Abigail by her dad. I'm alone but in a mysteriously good mood. What, I wonder, has gone so right? Is it the free car? The free car certainly helps. Abbie's dad had just retired and says he doesn't need it any more. Yes, the free car is a bit of all right; an absurdly big engine for a little car and much sportier than the second-hand Datsun Cherry ("Chesney") that I blew my inheritance on when I was seventeen. But no, it isn't that. What is it? What's that noise?

Tap. Aaah . . . there you are. Abbie and I have been married for a while but this is the first time I've driven a car whilst wearing a wedding ring. Every time I change gear I hear the tap of the ring on the gearstick. And suddenly I'm seven again and sitting on the back seat, and Mum is driving us between the golf club where my grandparents (and Auntie Trudy) work in the kitchen and our new bungalow in the next village. It's a journey we make many times a week and that *tap* is one of the happiest sounds of childhood. It means that I'm alone with Mum.

"Quiet boy", "painfully shy", "you never know he's there": these are some of the phrases I catch grown-ups using when they talk about me. But not here, not in the car with Mum. And definitely not when "Sailing" by

Rod Stewart comes crackling over the MW radio. The gusto of our sing-a-long is matched only by the cheerful lousiness of my mother's driving.

"We are SAAAAILING" (tap, second gear), "we are SAAAAILING" (tap, into third), "cross the WAAAATER, tooo the SEEEA" (tap, stall, as she tries to take a left turn), "we are sail —" (tap, handbrake, ignition), "we are s —" (tap, ignition, choke, window-wipers), "to be NEEEAR you" (triumphant re-start, cancel window-wipers, tap, crunch into first), "to be FREEE!".

I like it here. There are no men, and there are no other boys. I don't seem to be very good at being a boy and I'm afraid of men.

One man in particular.

"Hello, boy, only Dad. You're probably already in the pub. I watched y'dance on the box. Your, erm Comic Relief . . . spectacular. Huh! Bloody well done, mate. Bloody well done. I saw you being interviewed and worrying what I'd think. Dressed like that. Cobblers, mate! You looked *good*! You looked bloody marvellous, on that stage. I couldn't stop laughing. I'm proud of you, boy. I probably don't say it enough. You know me, silly old sod, I go me own way and I'll probably die on me own. Haha. *[brief pause]* Proud of you, Rob. *[another pause]* I'm sorry I wasn't much of a family man when you was a little boy. Couldn't help it, mate; couldn't help it. *[voice cracking]* All right, boy, I'll let you go. Have a pint for me. You know how I feel about you. Cheerio, boy. Cheerio."

* * *

I didn't call him back. When I first heard that message, I didn't know what to do.

I know what to do now. Come with me.

ACT ONE

CHAPTER
ONE

Boys Can't Get Enough of Dad

"What is a history teacher? He's someone who teaches mistakes."

Graham Swift, Waterland

"Pass it to Webb!" shouts Pete Garvey, "Webb hasn't had a kick yet!" It's 1984 and this is the first Games lesson at grammar school. Pete has known me for nearly a week and although it was kind of him to say "pass it to Webb", he cannot know that he is making me, at best, a complicated offer.

He doesn't know what happens when someone tries to pass me a football or what happens when I try to kick one. He comes from a different primary school and so wasn't there when I was consistently the second-to-last boy to be picked for any team; the last being Mark Sharpe, who had cerebral palsy. No, Pete (or rather "Garvey" because at this school girls keep their given names while boys won't hear theirs again for years) is a kindly Top Male who wants to help. I wish he didn't.

"Why, you'll be charging about like Bryan Robson!" Auntie Trudy had said once she'd finished sewing

"Webb" labels into my new kit. The severity of the "Webb" was at odds with the loving neatness of her stitches. Bryan Robson, I think. Yes, I've heard of that one. And Luther Blissett: that's another one. What teams do they play for? England. I'll just say they play for England and pretend I'm making a joke. And this top — blue with a white collar — what team is that? Definitely not England. Everton, then? Newcastle Rovers? Denmark?

As it happens, I'm not even wearing the top. It's a warm afternoon in early September and the Games teacher, Mr Leighton, has divided us into "shirts" and "skins"; i.e. the boys on the skins team are topless. Great. What happened to coloured armbands? What happened to those coloured sash things that you wore over one shoulder at junior school to show what team you were on? No, just shorts and boots now, apparently. It's all a bit fucking Hitler Youth if you ask me. I'm running around with my arms weirdly by my sides so that my ribs don't stick out so much. Aged eleven, my body makes an average garden rake look like it just had a great Christmas and could do with a nap.

It's a long pass and I welcome the sight of the ball arching towards me in the same way that a quadriplegic nudist covered in jam welcomes the sight of a hornet. The ball is going to take a horribly long time to arrive because I have "found a space". This is the football skill at which I excel. Oh, I can "find a space" all right. Show me an empty patch of games field and I'll stand in it. Or rather, I'll hop around in it, looking desperately alert. My alertness is based on the knowledge that, at any moment, the empty patch could suddenly close up and fill with other players; that I might be made to come into contact with a football. I usually manage to avoid this. When the empty patch moves, I move.

But today my negative-space triangulation has gone wrong and I've found not just a "space" but a "great space". The ball is over halfway towards me and I note wretchedly that it's an excellent pass. The bloody thing is going to drop at my feet like a gatepost swinging onto a latch. I have just enough time to look left and right as if checking for an interception from an opposing player. Actually, I'm looking left and right in the *frantic hope* of an interception from an opposing player. But no. No one is near enough. It's just me, the ball, the good faith of Pete Garvey, and everyone watching.

Most of my concentration goes into fighting the urge to put my arms up to protect my nipples. Simultaneously, I extend my right foot up and forward in an attempt to trap the ball, which of course bounces straight under it and goes off the pitch. To complete the demonstration, I lose my balance and fall on my arse.

The consolation of this is that while getting up I can make sure I get muddy knees like the other boys. This will save me the usual bit of admin where I fall onto them deliberately when no one is looking. The general laughter isn't especially cruel and Garvey yells, "Football isn't really your game, is it, Webby?" I muster the Wildean response "Not really!" and notice the sound came through my nose. It's his kindness that makes me nearly cry. Obviously I do nothing of the sort. That would be like showing an interest in poetry or getting a stiffy in the showers.

Communal showering is a fresh hell that concludes every Games lesson the way an awkward exchange of details concludes a car crash. At home, the bathroom door is always locked and, "bath night" aside, I never change the top half and bottom half of me at the same time. I am, in short, a never-nude. In the changing room, I just about get from the bench to the shower without having a heart attack, watching my bare feet step daintily over the stud-punctured turf clods on the tiled floor. I also manage not to physically flinch at the echoed shouts from my fellow eleven-year-olds and the acrid smell of Ralgex and Right Guard which some of them are optimistically wafting about. I'm very proud of the fine sprinkling of pubic hairs I've managed to grow, although that area in general looks like the head of a ninety-year-old woman recently returned from a perm too many at the hairdresser's. The hairs keep a discrete distance from each other and the essential baldness beneath catches the light. We are all, of course, surreptitiously checking each other out. I'm relieved to find that I have neither a small penis nor an unsettlingly large one. But in general I'm hopelessly skinny and I'm still recovering from the No. 2 hit that year, "So Macho!", in which Sinitta made her feelings about what was required very clear: "I don't want no seven stone weakling/Or a boy who thinks he's a girl . . ."

On the field, following another mortifying screw-up, Mr Leighton had approached for a bit of referee/Games coach banter: "Good gracious me, Webb. Did your mother drop you on your head when you were a small child?" He delivers this with the well-practised air of a teacher's catchphrase and his good humour beams out of him. It's actually the friendliest thing I've heard all week. I smile back.

"But then, if she did, you probably wouldn't remember!" he adds, supplying the punchline which I will spend the next hour wishing I'd thought of.

As it happens, Mr Leighton, I do remember. Nobody dropped me on my head, but I did fall down a flight of stairs. As earliest childhood memories go, this is satisfyingly dramatic. My mother was there at the bottom and so was my father, your ex-pupil, Paul — the other Webb. The one who was very good at football, as well as all the other sports you taught him.

Not that Dad ever boasted about that kind of thing. One of the good things I can say about him is that he was no show-off. And there are plenty of other good things to say about Paul Webb at his best. But first, dear reader, I think it's about time we had a look at the place I've so far managed to avoid, the place where we find Paul Webb, to put it mildly, not at his best. Time to go to the beginning.

"Purple," I thought, as I bounced down the last few steps. It's unlikely that I actually *said* "purple" — that would have been madly precocious for a two-year-old. And anyway, I wouldn't have had time to say "purple" because I was otherwise occupied screaming the house down. It's the stairs that were purple, you see: hard, steep, and with a fraying carpet of purple. On the way down I'd had a pretty good look at them, as well as a pretty good feel of them as they made contact in rapid succession with my knees, elbows and head. They fanned round in segments at the bottom, dropping me neatly into the living room where Mum instantly materialised to scoop me up. Consoling, checking for cuts or breaks, she was making the kind of sympathetic noises I would make if my own two-year-old fell down a flight of stairs. I was soon aware of another noise, though, the noise Dad was making. He was laughing. "Poor old boy," he said, chortling through his moustache, "poor old boy, ha ha ha."

Seventeen years later, I put a suitcase down in the same room and notice the stairs have been re-carpeted: they're now a kind of old-folks-home blue. Delia, the woman that Dad painfully refers to as his "lady-friend", catches my look.

"I suppose coming back here must bring back some memories," she says carefully. I don't mind Delia. Dad had various "lady-friends" while still married to my mum, but Delia wasn't one of them. That didn't stop my mother constantly referring to her as "Delilah" and noting she was always getting lipstick on her teeth.

"I remember falling down those stairs when I was two," I say.

"Oh dear," says Delia, alarmed. And then, "How do you know you were two?"

"I must have asked Mum about it."

The mention of my mother is unfair. It's like reminding Gok Wan that I used to hang out with Prince. Delia inspects her shoes for a second, but then looks up with a kind smile.

Dad bustles through and has been listening. "I don't remember the stairs, boy," he says cheerfully.

"No."

"I was probably pissed!"

"Yes."

"Ha ha ha. Well, you're 'ome again now, mate."

Delia isn't sure if this last remark is the diplomatic success Dad seems to think it is. She smiles again. I try not to look at her teeth.

"Yeah," I say.

The house was called Slieve Moyne and was my first home as a staircase-bopping toddler, and then my third home as an oh-so-watchful young man in his late teens. What happened in between is a happy story with a sad ending, or, from where I'm typing, a sad middle with a happy present. But let's not get ahead of ourselves.

Lincolnshire is a large and largely ignored county on the east coast of England, sufficiently far north to be considered Northern, but somehow not Professionally Northern in the manner of, say, Yorkshire or Tyneside. From where I grew up, it takes about an hour to get to a major road, the A1 — also known as "the Lincolnshire bypass" — and it's this sense of isolation that gives the place some of its character and beauty, as well as some of its problems.

Slieve Moyne was in the village of Woodhall Spa. Growing up, I was given the impression that Woodhall was one of the "nicer" villages in the area. Certainly the Conservative Club, the Golf Club, the Tea House in the Woods and the Dower House Hotel — a stately procession of mock-Tudor buildings with horse-brassy fireplaces — lend the place an impregnable air of Tory respectability. In my first few years, I thought this was not just desirable but typical. England was the most normal part of Britain, Lincs the most normal part of England and Woodhall the most normal part of Lincs. In a few years, I would think of the place as Tatooine, the planet Luke Skywalker imagines to be furthest from the bright centre of the universe. But for now, it *was* the universe and one with which I was perfectly content. There was just one problem. When we first meet Luke on Tatooine, he has an issue with his mysteriously absent father. My father, on the other hand, was all too present. And his name might as well have been Darth Vader. Actually it was Paul. It's a silly comparison of course. Dark Lords of the Sith aren't constantly wasted.

"You shouldn'ta come back, Obi-Man! *[hic]* When last we met, I wuz just an old boy *[belch]* Now I'm the master and you're a fucky old bastard. Oh bollocks, I just cut me thumb off. Bloody light sabre needs a new fuse."

Here we go then. It's the mid 1970s and I live with Mum, Darth and my two older brothers Mark and Andrew.

Imagine a child's drawing of a house. This one would show three bedrooms upstairs, the little one with Rupert the Bear wallpaper for me, the middle one for the grown-ups and the one at the other end containing Mark and Andrew wearing denim waistcoats and walloping each other with skateboards (because that's what Big Brothers do). There is smoke coming out of the chimney, as it should in all drawings of this kind; in this case provided by Darth holding double pages of the *Daily Mail* against the fireplace to encourage the flames. Sometimes he gets distracted while doing this because he's shouting at James Callaghan on TV, and the paper catches fire. He has to throw the lot into the fireplace, which of course sets fire to the chimney.

He has laid the fire using the logs and sticks that he chopped up with the chainsaw left leaning against the back door, the one he uses for his job as a woodsman on the local estate (my Daddy is a woodcutter). The Mummy will be in the tiny kitchen, standing over an electric hob (because that's what Mummies do) and stirring Burdall's Gravy Salt into a saucepan of brown liquid.

It's a static picture, of course, so we can't see that the Mummy's hands are shaking because she knows that the Daddy has spent all afternoon in the pub and has come home in one of his "tempers" (because that's what Daddies do). If, during tea, one of the Big Brothers speaks with his mouth full or puts his elbows on the table, the Daddy has been known to knock him clean off his chair. The Mummy will start shouting at the Daddy about this, but of course she can't shout as loud as the Daddy. No one can shout as loud as the Daddy or is as strong as the Daddy which is why the Daddy is in charge. The Little Brother will start crying at this point and will most likely be told to shut up by the Big Brothers who are themselves trying not to cry because that's another thing that they've learned doesn't go down well with the Daddy.

On the rare occasions the subject of Dad's behaviour came up over the following years, the fixed view was that "Robert got away with it" and that Mark and Andrew (six and five years older than me respectively) were mainly the ones in harm's way when Dad ran out of words. This in turn was held up to be some kind of hippy crèche compared to the treatment Dad received from his own father, Ron.

So I was lucky. Still, I remember the summer's day when I was watching the Six Million Dollar Man battling with Sasquatch and the following moment I was being lifted an impossible number of feet into the air and thrashed several times around the legs with a pair of my own shorts that had been found conveniently nearby. Dropped back on the settee, I looked at those navy-blue shorts with a baffled sense of betrayal. They were *my* shorts. My navy-blue shorts with the picture of Woody Woodpecker on the pocket. And he's just hit me with them. Maybe in the seconds before I was watching Steve Austin, I'd spilt something or broken something. Maybe I'd got too close to the fire or the chainsaw. Who knows? Actually telling a child why he was being physically punished was somehow beneath the dignity of Paul's parenting style.

34

* * *

There are happy early memories from Slieve Moyne too, of course. Singing along with Mum whenever her beloved Berni Flint appeared on *Opportunity Knocks*; the thrilling day the household acquired its first Continental Quilt (a duvet), which my brothers and I immediately used as a fabric toboggan to slide down the purple stairs; playing in the snow, playing in the garden — all the sunlit childhood fun you'd expect from times when Dad was out.

And, to be fair, there were moments when he was affectionate. For example, if he was in a good mood he might crouch down in front of me, put his massive fist under my nose and say in a joke-threatening way, "Smell that and tremble, boy!" For years I wasn't quite sure what this phrase meant — "smellthatandtremble" — it was just a friendly noise that my dad made when he was trying to make me laugh. Oh, and I laughed all right. I mean, you would, wouldn't you?

But in general, I'm afraid my memories of those first five years in that house tend towards the nature of a bad dream. To avoid *real* bad dreams, the trick was to make sure there was a gap in my bedroom curtains. If those brown curtains opposite my bed were closed shut, then the Curtain People appeared. They were the silhouettes of four or five grown-ups who would materialise in the curtains to have silent conversations about what kind of bad dream I was going to have that night. Leaving a gap deterred them for some reason, and some of the worst nightmares could be avoided. But the real problem was not avoiding the night-time imaginings but the daytime reality. Not the Phantom, but the Menace. And he was unavoidable.

A classic of this sci-fi/horror genre was the episode called "Do an eight, do a two". This family favourite has me, aged five, sat in the living room with a pencil and paper, being yelled at by Dad to "DO AN EIGHT! DO A TWO!" It had come to his attention that I wasn't doing very well in my first year at primary school and that, in particular, I was unable to write the numbers "8" or "2". Actually, I could write an "8", but I did it by drawing two circles, a habit which Mrs Morse of St Andrew's Church of England Primary School found to be lacking calligraphic rigour. Anyway, the rough transcript of "Do an eight, do a two" goes like this.

Dad: DO AN EIGHT! DO A TWO!

Mum: He's trying! There's no point shouting!

Dad: JUST DO AN EIGHT!

(Five-year-old, sobbing, does an eight with two circles)

Dad: NOT LIKE THAT! DO A PROPER ONE!

(Five-year-old dribbles snot onto the paper and does some kind of weird triangle)

Dad: WHAT'S THAT MEANT TO BE? DO AN EIGHT!

Mark: Or a two!

(Eleven-year-old Mark, desperate for any rare sign of approval from Dad, has joined in)

Dad: WHY CAN'T YOU DO ONE? JUST DO AN EIGHT!

Mark: Or a two if you like, Robbie! Why not do a
    two, probably?
(Mum takes five-year-old on her lap. Five-year-old
    thinks it's over)
(Comedy pause, titters from the studio audience)
Mum: Try and do a two, darling.
(Five-year-old freaks out. Then somehow manages
    a wobbly two)
Dad: DO A TWO!
Mum: HE'S DONE A BLOODY TWO!
Dad: DO ANOTHER ONE!
Mark: Or an eight!

Next week on *At Home with the Pillocks*, Daddy
Pillock cuts his own thumb off by going out to work
with a chainsaw following an afternoon session in the
pub. He gets most of it sewn back on. Mind that light
sabre, Darth!

Where Andrew was during this fun-packed interlude,
I don't know. Probably upstairs listening to Abba. I
don't blame either Mum or Mark, by the way. You
might be thinking "this is *nothing*" compared to your
own experiences with a domestic hard-case. Or maybe
you're wondering how my mother put up with it for an
instant. The truth is, we were all terribly afraid of him.
In any case, Mum was probably just biding her time at
that point. She had already made her plans. Before the
end of that first school year, she divorced him and he
moved out.

★   ★   ★

Hell hath no fury like an angry son with a book deal. Actually, I'm trying to be fair. I come not to bury Darth, but to understand him. If this account of my father's mistakes is starting to look sadistic, then I suppose the make-over had better begin with my saying that Paul was no sadist. He laughed when I fell down the stairs because he was trying to teach me to treat pain lightly. It's a hard world and what you do with pain — if you're a man like Paul — is shrug it off. He was trying — ineptly and far too early — to "toughen me up". At a stretch I could even say that he was trying to protect me.

Poor old Dad: there he is with his three small boys and his insufficiently compliant wife; with his dangerous job and his lonely role as breadwinner (a role he insists on, is expected to insist on) and his drink problem which, by the standards of the day, is no problem at all. He is doing what he's supposed to do. He works hard, he drinks like it's going out of fashion (he has a point) and he keeps his boys in line. He can't quite keep his wife in line: when he puts up a Conservative election poster in their bedroom window in 1974, Mum puts a Labour one in the window of the room next door (my bedroom).

What a disappointment. Did she not promise in that church to "obey" him? It's not a promise she can keep. Especially when he's broken a few promises of his own.

"It would be in the seventies, I'd say. And I told him I was going to Woodhall Spa and the bloke said, 'Well, if you're going to Woodhall, look up Paul Webb. You won't find anyone better for drinking, fucking and fighting.'"

This is said to me in 1992, when I'm nineteen and living with Dad again; when I've put my suitcase down and the purple stairs have turned blue. I'm in a local pub and I've been chatting to a random bloke of Dad's age who is pleased to tell me about Paul's reputation in the seventies. The man knows I'm Paul's son — everyone knows I'm Paul's son — and he doesn't seem to mind that Paul's "reputation" signals to me a world of terrible shit. I listen, nodding. He offers to buy me a drink: "Anything for the son of Paul Webb!" I accept. And nod, and listen.

Dad's reputation for living the pub life in the *high style* was one with which I'd been acquainted for years before I met this guy. It was — at the risk of tabloid overkill — "legendary". And even the most dubious legends are seductive (see "religion"). Listening to this idiot in the pub, drinking his booze, I feel strangely proud of Dad. At least he's famous. Famous for being a brawl-magnet, tit-prospector and piss-artist, but, y'know, at least he's . . . well, he's really made that his own, hasn't he? I mean, that's what all his friends and contemporaries were licensed to do, that's what many of them tried to do, but my dad did it best! So that, I suppose to myself, aged nineteen — four pints down, looking for a connection with my living parent — is sort of good, really, isn't it?

It's April. She died two years ago this week.

Dad was in a different pub tonight. I guess I'll mention this bloke to him as a funny story when I have another lager in front of the telly. As I wobble home, I find that I'm quite looking forward to that. And then, as I get closer to Slieve Moyne, I start to wonder. I don't wonder about telling him what I heard. I wonder about whether this is really going to be the father-son bonding exercise that I'm looking for. There's no doubt that he'll like it. We get on best when we're both drunk. Why wouldn't he like it? That was his whole fucking thing, wasn't it? Starting (and finishing) fights, cheating on Mum . . . Ooh, mind that drain in the pavement, it sticks out a bit. Hic. Here comes another car in the dark; oh, he's dipped his lights because he didn't want to dazzle a pedestrian. People are nice, really, aren't they? Some people. Wobble.

And there he is when I get in, watching the boxing on the TV.

"All right, Rob? Just watching a bit of boxing on the box. D'you 'ave a good night?"

"Yes thanks, mate!" I say this loudly and confidently: you have to be loud because years spent cutting down trees with no ear protection has rendered him half deaf. I say it confidently because that's how he wants me to be. It's how I want to be, too. Especially tonight.

"Who d'you see in the pub, boy?"

I help myself to a beer from his fridge and come into the living room, the "do an eight, do a two" room, the Woody Woodpecker room. This is the room where Mum tried to protect us from him; the room where we weren't big enough to protect her from him. Our lovely Mum . . . it seems now that I'm moving quite slowly and deliberately. Vaguely, I wonder why this might be.

And why is my heart thumping so hard? Probably the walk home.

He sits with one leg crossed over the other on one of the straight-backed dining-room chairs, an elbow resting on the table where we eat. (I see you've got your elbows on the table; didn't you used to have quite strong views about elbows and tables?) I move round him, looking at the neatly combed brown hair on his head, and take a seat opposite. He's forty-eight and still strong. Wiry and fast. But not as fast as he was. I look at him steadily while he watches the TV.

I say, "Yeah, just the usuals — Will, Dave. Oh, and some bloke. He was talking about your reputation, back in the day."

Dad keeps his eye on the fight. "Who's this, boy?"

"Didn't catch a name. Sorry. He said that you used to be the most fun for drinking, fighting and fucking women. I suppose that would be around the time you were married to Mum."

I feel the blood in every vein. His attention darts from the TV to my face. His body doesn't tense. Even if it did, it would be hard to tell — his body is already a rusting corkscrew of guilt and anxiety. But, like all tough guys — or once-tough guys — he has an acute sense of another man coming to a simmer. He checks my expression. Yes, Robert is thinking about having a go. The boy doesn't quite know it, but he's about ready to kick off. Just like his brothers. Good old boy: typical Webb.

"No, no, no, mate," he says, slowly uncrossing his leg, stubbing his fag out, "I don't know about that."

He's embarrassed. Or he has the grace to look embarrassed. Or he has the sense to look embarrassed because he intuits correctly that if he shows the first sign of pride in this description, in his "reputation", I'm going to climb across the table and try to kill him. I wait, looking at him still. I've never been in a fight in my life, but if I'm going to have one, it'll be this one. The Freudian Counterfuck, the Return of the Jedi, the Attack of the Implacable Hiccupping Teenager. It's a stupid idea but I'm hammered.

He turns back to the boxing. After a moment he says, "Y'mum and me had some hard times, son . . ." I break my stare and follow his gaze to the boxing now. The pissed-up rage drains away in an instant. "Hard times" is not just a blanket phrase; I know he's using it as a euphemism for something very particular. In fact, for a particular person. "But we had some bloody good times too." His eyes redden; I won't say that they "well up" because he won't allow them to get that far. He sniffs his snot up and passes the back of a hand — the one with the sewn-on thumb — across his nose and briefly across his eyes. I see the heavy pulse in his throat, the throat that I just imagined being able to strangle. And I notice that I love him. And that Mum once loved him. I could reach across the table and touch his arm. I could say, "Dad, I'm sorry about Martin." But I don't. I don't mention Martin.

Darth on the deck, his mask off for a second, and neither of us can really bear it. I watch the boxing with him for what I think is a decent interval and then I say,

"Night, Dad" and he replies "Night, boy" and that's that.

You see, the childhood drawing of Slieve Moyne, the one with the two grown-ups and the three boys, the one we started with — that picture is incomplete. It's the house that I remember, but if I showed that drawing to Mum, Dad, Mark or Andrew, they would look at it for a long time. They would see that someone is missing.

In Auntie Trudy's bedroom, at one end of the gramophone, is a picture box. It's a Perspex cube holding six photographs. The one that she keeps facing upwards, so that she can always see it, is of a cherubic boy with light brown hair, wearing his St Andrew's School uniform. This is Martin John Webb, my eldest brother, who died of meningitis when he was six years old.

One way of imagining life is that it's a competition between love and death. Death always wins, of course, but love is there to make its victory a hollow one. That's what love is for. When the worst came for Mum and Dad in 1971, there was nothing they could do to soften the blow. But they had enough remaining love to make a reply. I can't help liking their reply.

My brother died and I was born ten months later.

If something terrible happens to you, and you're lucky enough to have supportive friends, there will be a period when you hear a version of this several times a week: "And if you need to talk, I'm right here. I mean, just talk. Because I'm here. For a talk. And if you don't want to talk, maybe think about talking. Talk."

There are times when we're all grateful to hear this, and other times when we experience it as pressure. And although I've no doubt that there are many women and girls who have that second reaction, I think it's men and boys in particular who get into trouble here. We feel grateful for the kindness, but helpless and frustrated. "Talk about what? What's to talk about? Talking won't *change* anything, will it?" Suddenly we're surrounded by well-meaning people encouraging us to talk about our feelings. The problem is, talking about our feelings is something we've been specifically trained not to do.

What are we saying to a boy when we tell him to "man up" or to "act like a man"?

At its most benign, we might just be saying: do the thing that needs doing even if you don't want to do it.

But more often, when we tell a boy to "act like a man", we're effectively saying, "Stop expressing those feelings." And if the boy hears that often enough, it actually starts to sound uncannily like, "Stop *feeling* those feelings."

It sounds like this: "Pain, guilt, grief, fear, anxiety: these are not appropriate emotions for a boy because they will be unacceptable emotions for a man. The skills you need to be your own emotional detective — being able to name a feeling and work out why you're feeling it — you don't need to develop those skills. You won't need them."

It sounds like a good deal. The great thing about refusing to feel feelings is that, once you've denied them, you don't have to take responsibility for them. Your feelings will be someone else's problem — your mother's problem, your girlfriend's problem, your wife's problem. If it has to come out at all, let it come out as anger. You're allowed to be angry. It's boyish and man-like to be angry.

I do it. I notice it more often these days, but I still do it. I express anger when what I'm actually feeling is shame. Or I get angry when I'm afraid; angry when I'm feeling uncertain or anxious; angry when I'm in grief. I bet you can think of men who even get angry when they fall in love. And probably have angry sex.

And yes, women do it too — of course they do. The difference is that they haven't been encouraged since childhood to wear a total lack of self-awareness as a badge of pride. On the contrary, the message they've been getting is that they are "intuitive". They are "nurturers" and "good listeners". They're there to intuitively tell men to go to the doctor and to nurturingly sort out the laundry. Luckily, they can also "multi-task", so they can do both at the same time, as well as booking their kids' dental appointments and making a lasagne. Sadly, men can't "multi-task" apparently, which must be the reason we tend to take a step back from all that.

And yet, when people saw Dad walking down the street in Woodhall Spa, they did not think: "Ah, there goes Paul Webb, a walking powder-keg of repressed grief."

Paul's public face was beloved by more or less the entire village. Generous with his time, charismatic, cheeky, cajoling and straightforwardly kind, he didn't so much live in that village as *host* it. He would walk into a pub and I would watch the whole room subtly adjust itself in his direction and settle itself in for a treat. They adored him. But then, they didn't have to live with him.

Mum did. She had been through the same loss and put up with Dad's domestic reaction until she couldn't put up with it any longer. Her name, by the way, was Pat (she hated "Patricia") and if kicking Dad out of the house was brave, what she did next was heroic.

CHAPTER
TWO

Boys Aren't Shy

"Were we closer to the ground as children, or is
the grass emptier now?"

Alan Bennett, *Forty Years On*

"It is a truth universally acknowledged that a woman of
thirty with three sons and no income must be in want
of a husband." I'm pretty sure that's how *Pride and
Prejudice* begins. Something like that.

But it's fair to say that, had one of Jane Austen's
penniless heroines, in Derbyshire say, in the early
1800s, found themselves in Pat's situation in
Lincolnshire in 1977, they would probably come to a
similar conclusion. Austen's women can be shockingly
dry-eyed when it comes to marriage: yes, it would be
preferable to marry for love, but love is only one of the
reasons to marry. They are "accomplished ladies" with
no formal education; Pat is a working-class woman
who's certainly clever, but not clever enough to avoid
getting knocked up before finishing her A levels, bless
her. For Austen's heroines to sign on to the dole was
impossible; for Pat, socially unthinkable. She has always
had a part-time job — as a school secretary, a hotel

47

secretary, a bar-worker — but she's just as likely to "retrain" or "get a BTEC from Loughborough" as Elizabeth Bennet is to split the atom. Lizzie can't rely on the support of her parents because they are genteel but broke. Pat can't expect long-term help from Nan and Dada because their gentility runs to an aspiring regard for the *Daily Mail*, but not to having any spare cash whatsoever. And Austen's ladies won't receive maintenance payments from their errant husbands to provide for their children. And neither will Pat. At least, not for a long time.

Dad treats maintenance payments with the same baffled incredulity that his generation will soon adopt when told that wearing car seat belts is now the law. It's as if he can't believe the dumb literalism of it: what, *every* month? The full amount? On time? Seriously? He has to be threatened with a court appearance before he starts supporting his family with anything like the same rigour with which he previously buggered it up.

So yes, we've come a long way: Mum concludes that she needs another husband. I'm not saying that's the decision every woman in her position would have made, but it's the one she made and I respect it.

Anyway, she doesn't have to find Mr Darcy. She just has to avoid another bloody Heathcliff.

She's down to her last two cards: her diffident charm and (it's only an opinion but what son could say less?) considerable beauty. It'll be enough.

The helpless target is Derek Limb.

They meet at a village ball at the Golf Hotel. He is not the only man offering to buy her a drink that evening, but he's the one who looks sufficiently grateful and claims to own a racehorse, which is a start. Derek is not exactly Sacha Distel: eight years older than Mum, he has a colourless wart on his top lip and a paunch which presages a future rendezvous with Fat. Fat is coming for Derek, Fat will have its day. There again, Mum is on the pull and not wearing her glasses.

More to the point, Derek is teetotal and mild. Winningly, there is nothing in his demeanour to suggest an interest in screwing other women or hitting children. For Mum, this makes him a veritable prince amongst men.

It's not so much a courtship as an *Anschluss*. She marches peacefully into Derek's heart and plants a flag. Not the Nazi flag, you understand. I don't know what Mum's flag would be, but I imagine it would feature the singer Elkie Brooks holding a bottle of Gordon's gin and looking whimsical. In any case, they marry.

We all move into "the new house", which is a three-bedroom bungalow in Coningsby, a village about ten minutes down the road from Woodhall but less leafy. On return from their honeymoon in the Lake District (the first time Derek has left Lincolnshire), we begin to learn more of Derek's fascinating habits.

He smokes forty Consulate menthol cigarettes a day and his (according to Derek, totally unrelated) "cough" is treated by his "cough medicine". The medicine comes in an endless series of large brown bottles from

49

the chemist on a repeat prescription that Derek's GP wrote shortly before he died. Derek self-medicates by up-ending the bottle into his mouth and counting to twenty.

Once a week he buys himself half a pound of aniseed balls which he keeps loose in his trouser pockets, along with his small change and the keys to his glamorous "Pacer X" American car which he can't afford to drive very often because "it drinks petrol". When he gets to the seed of an aniseed ball, he's in the habit of taking it out and leaving it on any convenient surface. The only time he gets cross is if my brothers or I talk over the racing results when he's trying to listen to them on the radio with the 5mm aniseed nucleus stuck to the top of the Radio 2 knob. It's fascinating to watch the speed and efficiency with which he can fill in those results on the racing page of the *Daily Mirror*.

Derek has inherited an agricultural spare parts business from his late father. Essentially, he buys tractors and takes them to pieces. This would be a good business for someone who was there to do it but Derek is mainly not there. Derek is at the bookies'. He has a low-level gambling addiction which means that when "customers" turn up, we know what number to call. I know the bookies' phone number off by heart before I'm eight years old. A quarter of an hour later, the Pacer X makes its stately return: sometimes the customer is still there, sometimes he isn't.

In short, Mum has married another prize turkey. She's swapped Darth Vader for Jabba the Hutt. That is, if you can imagine Jabba not so much as a dangerous gangster but more as a silly bugger picking his nose and watching *Bullseye*.

The search for a likeable father figure goes on: a man who is gentle without being docile, dynamic without acting like a psychopath. I wonder to myself if such a man really exists.

Well, there's always Dada (pronounced "dar-dar"). This is Mum's dad, John. He and Grace (Nana and Dada) are the steward and stewardess of the kitchen at Woodhall Spa Golf Club. Grace's sister Trudy (Auntie Tru) works in the kitchen too. The three of them live in a little house which you get to from the kitchen by running across a field, although for some reason they prefer to walk (what is it with grown-ups and all this "walking"?).

I stay with them every weekend and for about half of any school holiday. One day in the distant future, Derek will express disappointment that people in the village tell him my Wikipedia page says that I grew up in Woodhall Spa, when in fact I lived with him and Mum in Coningsby for fourteen years. I tell him truthfully that I don't have anything to do with that page. What I don't say is that this impression has certainly come from the answers I've given in interviews.

"Where did you grow up?"

"Woodhall Spa."

Or, more accurately, the kitchen, grounds and gardens of Woodhall Spa Golf Club. That's where I grew up. And in front of the TV. That's the other place. Buck Rogers, Michael Knight, Zorro, Dick Turpin, Bo and Luke, Jon and Ponch, Steve Austin, the Doctor, Thomas Magnum, Hannibal Smith, Colt Seavers, Captain Kirk, Commander Koenig, Dr David Banner, Mr T, Tucker Jenkins, Roj Blake, Flash Gordon, Logan, Monkey, Steel, Starbuck, Stringfellow Hawke, and Robin Hood. What a great bunch of guys and not a father among them. Not one.[1] And according to most of them, there are few problems in life that can't be solved by punching someone quite hard in the face. These are my alternative role models. We're off to a terrific start.

Dada is hammering a wooden stake into the earth and I blink with every strike. I'm going to use his name, John, from now on because "Dada" is annoyingly close to "Dad" and we can do without the confusion. John's a big man in his early sixties, with grey hair kept neatly in check with a steel comb. His moustache is grey too, more bristly but somehow friendlier-looking than Dad's. He has some extra weight these days, but carries it with the upright economy of a soldier, which is of course what he was. They all were. Trudy and Grace were in the ATS and the Wrens respectively (the women's branches of the Army and Navy). The kitchen crosstalk is peppered with wartime idioms like "Ooh,

---

[1] Sci-fi pedants, stand down. The Doctor becomes a sort of father in the David Tennant era, but not in the time we're talking about. And yes, it turns out Kirk is a dad, but again, in a later movie, and he's been completely absent from his son's life anyway, so who cares.

stand by y'beds!" or "Do we think it's time for a NAAFI break?"

I'm here because I've been encouraged by Nan and Tru to "go and help Dada with the greenhouses". Since I'm not much taller than your average tomato plant or stronger than one of its stems, it's not so much a matter of "helping" as of "watching". But I quite enjoy these trips to the greenhouses with John. On the way we have "slow bike races" down the back lane, seeing who can go slowest on his bike without falling off. He never seems to be in much of a hurry and that's the main thing I like about him — no sudden moves. Currently, I tend to win the slow bike race because my little red Raleigh still has stabilisers, although I'm perfectly capable of overbalancing and falling off anyway.

As well as the kitchen steward, John is also one of the club gardeners. In my memory, the greenhouse itself is this vast glass menagerie of flowers and shrubs, roughly the size of The Crystal Palace. I suppose it was actually just a fairly big shed with a mouldy glass roof. He would find the greenhouse key, the one with the blue string kept under a flowerpot. And then I'd follow him inside, my nostrils suddenly accosted by the chlorophyll funk of tomato plants. I could just about manage one of the smaller watering cans, so he could make that one of my "jobs".

Outside, John is banging in those wooden posts. He'll use them to stretch a taut string down the line of carrots and then tie on the "bird scarers". These are rectangles of coloured foil that flutter in the wind as if we are growing a patch of Willy Wonka's Golden Tickets.

There's not much "helping" I can do here, so John takes a hoe and — a little optimistically — tries to show me how to break up the soil in a nearby bit of the garden. He hands me the massive wooden pole with a slab of rusting iron on the end and gets back to his work. I wield the hoe with the panache of Fred Astaire dancing with his cane. Except in this case, Fred's lost his cane and his friend Mike, who is a professional pole-vaulter, has lent Fred his vaulting pole and Fred is trying to twirl and spring around with that instead. On his return, John watches my efforts for an amused moment and then says, "Yeh, y'getting in your own way, mate." He takes the hoe as if it's made of polystyrene and expertly turns the soil, slashing weeds and flicking unwanted stones onto the gravel path with all the untroubled grace of Zorro using a bullwhip to extinguish a candle at twenty paces.

He's a kindly grandparent, my Dada, but not exactly a born teacher. I watch the display of manly competence and feel my infant pride being gently compressed into a pancake.

Back in the kitchen, Nan lets me run a finger around the bowl of the delicious scone mix that she's just made, and Auntie Trudy supplies me with a ham sandwich the way I like it — quartered diagonally with the crusts cut off. I take the sandwich, hoping that John won't notice the absent crusts. He is a strong advocate of what seems to be the male consensus that the crusts on sandwiches are "the best bit", as is the fat on ham, the rind on bacon, the runny surface of a fried egg, the stalk of any vegetable and the skins on sausages. All of this is "the best bit", a view which I think insane but I'm clearly in the minority.

Tru: Were you helping Dada?
Me: (*Nods*)
John: Ooh, he was 'elping all right! He was 'elping me like mad! (*Winks at me*)
Tru: I bet he was!
John: Every time I turned round, there was Rob, 'elping his head off!
Nan: Course he was, a big strong lad like him!

John checks his watch and moves to the oven, taking one of the vast beef joints out and setting it on the table. The meat crackles in its juices at my eye level. He takes his bone-handled carving knife in one hand and a sharpening steel in the other, and flashes the blade against the steel with scarcely credible speed and power. I eat my sandwich, watching.

Outside, I play on my own whenever I can, which is almost always. Mark and Andrew are so much older and they do their own thing. To me, this seems to consist mainly of going to Jubilee Park with their friends in order to fall out of trees. I can hardly picture my brothers from those days without one of them with his arm in plaster.

I take a more cautious approach to the outdoor life and I don't do it with other children. Unless, of course, you count the Guy-Buys. The Guy-Buys are my imaginary gang of friends. I am the Captain of the Guy-Buys, obviously, and they are my twelve — yes, twelve, like the apostles — men.

One day, my wife will put this together with what she knows of my sexual history and come up with one of her favourite ways of taking the piss.

"What were they called again, your imaginary friends? The Gay Boys?"

"The Guy-Buys."

"The Gaybo's?"

"The Guy-Buys."

"Not the Bi Guys."

"No, dear. Not the Bi Guys, the Guy-Buys."

Let me tell you, there is nothing gay about the Guy-Buys. If there were girls in the Guy-Buys, that would be different and, indeed, gay. If I understand two things about masculinity at the age of seven, it is a) the Sovereign Importance of Early Homophobia, and b) the Paramount Objective of Despising Girls. Nobody wants to be a gay and only gays play with girls — this much has been made clear. As I hold the door open for the Guy-Buys and count them into the kitchen, I remind them that to play with girls would be lunacy.

Generally, we go around on our bikes, fighting crime. Actually, I go around on my toy tractor with pedals or, for a while, on an apple box which I've tried Sellotaping to Andrew's skateboard. But basically, we range around the whole of the Golf Club, acting out scenarios from TV shows. Sometimes I'm Zorro, sometimes one of the wisecracking traffic cops from *CHiPs*, and always heavily armed with a selection of my favourite plastic swords and guns.

Of course, like Steve Austin and Buck Rogers, I am also an expert in karate. I get used to the quizzical looks on the faces of golfers as they walk by observing the seven-year-old kicking and chopping the teeth out of some invisible villain. Occasionally a golfer will mime a quick-draw and say something inscrutable about "Buffalo Bill" and chuckle to himself. I just stare back, waiting for him to go away.

Spend any amount of time with middle-class, liberal parents (and, speaking as a middle-class, liberal parent, I find these cunts impossible to avoid) and sooner or later you'll find yourself talking about gendered play. You'll hear a version of the following . . .

"I mean, we gave India a Star Destroyer for her birthday but she just dressed it in a nightie and put it to bed," or "I mean, we *tried* to get Huckleberry to play with a couple of dolls but he just tied them together with string and turned them into Nunchucks."

Some people can't get enough of stories like these. Imagine trying to get a girl to play with a spaceship! A-hahahahaha! See how fashionable liberal attitudes get slammed face-first into a wall of timeless biological reality! It's PC gone mad! A-hahahaha!

Actually, it's timeless biological reality gone mad. In children, it's about as easy to find conclusive evidence of a "male brain" or "female brain" as it is to find conclusive evidence of an immortal soul. As imaging technology improves, it becomes clearer not only that every brain is unique, but that they simply do not neatly divide into two groups based on sex.[1] I'm only citing one study here — and in general you're not going to find this book very "citey". Other people have covered this ground much better than I could — what with being scientists — and so this would be a good moment to recommend *Delusions of Gender* by Cordelia Fine and *Pink Brain, Blue Brain* by Lise Eliot. But the point stands: if Huckleberry doesn't like the colour pink, he wasn't born with that idea in his head — somebody put it there.[2]

In the above-mentioned *Delusions of Gender*, Cordelia Fine cites a study from 2000 in which . . .

> Mothers were shown an adjustable sloping walkway, and asked to estimate the steepness of the slope their crawling eleven-month-old child could manage and would attempt. Girls and boys differed in neither their crawling ability nor risk-taking when it came to testing them on the walkway. But mothers underestimated girls and overestimated boys — both in crawling ability and crawling attempts.[3]

---

[1] *Science* magazine, 30 November 2015: http://www.sciencemag.org/news/2015/11/brains-men-and-women-aren-t-really-different-study-finds.

[2] And quite recently: for the first half of the twentieth century the colour pink was associated with boys and blue with girls. See *Pink and Blue: Telling the Boys from the Girls in America* by Jo B. Paoletti (Indiana University Press, 2012).

[3] *Delusions of Gender* (Icon Books, 2011), pp. 198–9.

I'm sure that most of those mothers would be horrified to hear that their gender assumptions had leaked into their behaviour like that — but, to put it mildly, there's a lot of it about. Other studies have shown that when parents place birth announcements in newspapers, they are more likely to express "pride" if it's a boy and "happiness" if it's a girl. Indeed, if it's a girl, they are marginally less likely to make the announcement at all. Going even further back along the timeline of a child, research has found that parents look forward to having their baby for gendered reasons — fathers citing the fun they're going to have teaching their son sports, and mothers showing higher expectations of personal intimacy with their daughters. (Some hope — but hey lads, don't worry about forgetting Mum's birthday: you've been off the hook since you were *in utero*.) Expectant mothers who know the foetus is male are more likely to report foetal movement as "violent".

So the odds are that Huckleberry, compared to India, is expected to be more independent, more aggressive, more outward-facing and less interested in personal relationships since *before he was born*. With the best will in the world, bunging him a Barbie when he's five years old isn't really going to cut it.

There I am, the Captain of the Guy-Buys, hopelessly unsocialised and massively into my swords and guns. It's the most normal thing about me. So I prize it highly.

★   ★   ★

In between shoot-outs, chases and swordfights, the Guy-Buys and I retire to one of our dens to make repairs and plan the next massive punch-up. I have about five dens in various locations around the club. They are not difficult to "build". What you do is, you snap a couple of branches in a conveniently thin part of a rhododendron bush and then just step inside. Some of the bushes are literally the size of a house.

Inside, the sunlight dapples the carpet of dirt and leaves and I look up to the canopy and listen. There's a blackbird singing on a branch of a nearby horse-chestnut tree. Autumn's coming — must ask Auntie Tru for a Tupperware box; those conkers won't just collect themselves. And in September, a new school — Coningsby Junior School — where you're seven till eleven. Bigger boys. And some of the teachers are men. WH Smith's have already put their "Back to Skool" signs up. Why do they spell it the easy way that's wrong, instead of the hard way that's right? Maybe they're just trying to be nice. Nobody really likes this time of year, do they? Just one long Sunday teatime.

What's that sound? Miles away, probably. One of the Vulcans? No, not deep enough. A Phantom, that's the one. Auntie Edna, who works in the kitchen with the others, says it's good that Coningsby has Vulcan bombers because: "If it happens, Robbie, it'll be over so quick we won't know anything about it." They say on the news that America has more nuclear missiles than Russia, so I suppose it's good that our team is winning.

A Phantom jet up there, way up there, beyond the roof of my leafy cathedral.

43: Hey there, little buddy!

(7 *draws his sword*)

7:   Friend or Foe!?

43: Friend. So . . . how's it going, dude?

(*Silence*)

43: Sorry, erm. Hello. You might not recognise me but . . . I'm 43.

7:   Pardon?

43: I'm 43.

7 (*Pause*): I'm 7.

43: Yes! Exactly. How are you doing?

7:   Pardon?

43: How are you?

7:   I'm very well, thank you.

43: Good.

(*Silence*)

43: Yup. You see I'm writing this book and I wondered if you could help me.

(*Silence*)

43: (*Looking around*) Great den. One of the bigger ones, I think.

7:   Not the biggest.

43: No. Of course not. There's the one near the old railway line.

(7 *looks at 43*)

43: You have to be quite brave to get in it, jumping over the dyke and through the gap.

7:   I can do it!

43: I know you can.

7:   I do it all the time.

43: Yes, mate, I know.

(Pause)

43: Any Guy-Buys around at the moment or can we talk privately?

7: The Guy-Buys aren't real.

43: No, course not. But play-real.

7 *(Slowly putting his sword back in his snake belt):* Yeah, they're play-real.

43: Real in the story.

7: Yeah.

43: Sometimes more real than real life.

(Silence)

7: Is that what your book's about?

43: Well, the themes of memory, fantasy —

7: Is your book about the Guy-Buys?

43: Oh! Er, no, not really.

7: Oh.

43 *(Pause):* It's about the Captain of the Guy-Buys.

(7 smiles)

7: What happens?

43: He has adventures.

7: What sort of adventures?

43: Oh, this and that. Wouldn't want to give the game away.

(7 nods, imagining)

43: Well, I'll be off, leave you in peace.

7: You said you wanted me to help.

43: You've helped already. It helps me that we've talked, if only for a bit.

7: Right.

43: Will you be OK here, on your own?

(7 draws his sword again)
43: Yep, dumb question. Anyhow, take it easy.
7:   Wait. Are you from America?
43: Er, no, we all talk like this now.
7:   That's a bit rum.
43: Isn't it!
(43 makes to leave)
7:   Will I see you again?
43: Yeah . . . when you're 15.
7:   Who will you be?
43: I'll still be 43.
7:   You stay the same?
43: No, I change. But I'll always be 43 in the story. Stories are like that.

Alone. Safely, invincibly alone.

I don't want attention. Attention hurts. Yes, there are twelve Guy-Buys, but they're not disciples and they are certainly not my boyfriends.

They're bodyguards.

It's not like I don't have real friends, not quite. And my last year at Coningsby Infant School (across School Lane from Coningsby Junior School) is going quite well. At the birthday parties of friends I wait for the moment when someone's mum clears away what's left of the Angel Delight and says plaintively, "I wish they were all like you, Robert." Which is to say, "I wish they were all as quiet as you, Robert." I'm almost indignant if I don't get that compliment at some stage. But then, I'm also uneasy, because I know that boys are not supposed to be quiet. Boys are supposed to be "cheeky", like my brothers.

And like Roger Baxter. Roger is my Best Friend. Matthew Tellis, Michael Key and I follow Roger around during playtime. Roger is obviously the leader. Bradley Hooper used to be the leader, but his dad was in the RAF and they moved to Cyprus. So Roger, being the Avon to Bradley's Blake (don't worry if you never saw *Blake's 7* — I just mean the spikier, more interesting second-in-command finds himself suddenly in charge), is elevated in a way he doesn't enjoy. "Blummin' 'ell, I can't even have a wazz in peace," says the seven-year-old Roger as the three of us follow him into the boys' loo to watch him urinate. While I pretend to have my own wee (having a real one is impossible unless completely alone), I can't help being fascinated by the way Roger pulls his whole foreskin back on these occasions. It's not something I've been inclined to try for myself yet, just in case it's only my foreskin that's keeping the whole thing in one piece. I have visions of the round bit on the end just falling off. You can't be too careful about this kind of thing.

You also have to be careful about girls. They're everywhere. At playtime, someone usually starts a game by striding round the playground chanting, "All join up for playing . . ." and then whatever the game is. Any boy who wants to play links up and chants along, so you might get six boys walking about the playground with their arms around each other's shoulders, shouting, "All join up for playing . . . War. NO GIRLS!" or maybe, "All join up for playing . . . Star

Wars. NO GIRLS!" It was a remarkable girl who tried to join in, but she would literally be pushed away. It was, of course, unthinkable that we would join in with whatever the girls were doing. Unless you count the pitiless destruction of anything they were trying to build, like a snowman.

Because how dare they? I mean, it's not called a "snow-woman", is it? A seven-year-old in pursuit of the Paramount Objective of Despising Girls finds it all conveniently laid out for him: the culture, the language — it's really no effort. And if you're especially frightened and insecure, as I was at that age, or as Donald Trump is now, then membership of the in-group is best secured by showing the maximum contempt for an out-group: in this case, girls.

Two years earlier, my recently divorced mum had brought me in to meet my new teacher, Mrs Walker. This was during the brief moment after Dad had been kicked out but while we were all still living at Slieve Moyne. I would wake up most mornings in Mum's bed — the nightmares took their time to get the memo that the danger had passed — and Mum would stretch and yawn and say, "Well, this won't do." Maybe she just liked the company: I guess she hadn't slept alone for a long time.

One afternoon, we sing along to Rod Stewart's "Sailing" on the way over to the new school, but then as soon as we're in the company of Mrs Walker, the world's friendliest primary school teacher, I, of course, turn into Mutey McMute-Child, Professor of Total

Silence at the University of No Sounds At All. "He's just very shy," explains my embarrassed mum. I hear that word a lot. "Shy" is my defining characteristic. Everyone tells me I'm shy so I must be.

But then, what is Mum supposed to say? "He's just mildly traumatised by all the domestic argy-bargy. He and particularly his brothers were subjected to a level of physical admonishment which in future, more civilised decades, will be quite reasonably described as 'abusive'. His father scares the living Christ out of him, I'm afraid. And even though I divorced that guy's sorry ass months ago and permanently kicked him into touch, the thoughtless durr-heart still haunts Robert's dreams like an Avenging Demon from Planet Shit. So, y'know, Rob doesn't talk much."

No, that would be unladylike. So I'm "shy". Mrs Walker finds a book with which to assess my reading. When we don't get very far, she tries another book, and then another. Eventually, we try the kind of book that you give babies to test their gums on. Mrs Walker is making a good job of not looking surprised, but I can sense that this isn't going swimmingly and I feel embarrassed.

After a couple of quiet years in the bungalow I'll become an unusually good reader, so I won't pretend to you that this was all my fault. Mum, on the other hand, watching one book being swapped for another, is dying a thousand deaths of shame. But the shame doesn't belong to her either. She's carrying it for someone else.

I'm not sure where Dad was that day, but it was about four in the afternoon so I could hazard a guess.

At the Golf Club, I find a bumblebee on the ground. It looks all wrong because the ground is not where large bees are supposed to be. He's alive (bees are always a "he") and moving his wings slowly, somehow testing them. We're on a large, gravel concourse in between the kitchen and the first tee. Golfers wander back and forth. The sky is grey and it's getting dark.

I think my bee might be dying. He's trying to crawl but not really getting anywhere. Maybe he was struck by a lethally big raindrop. Or maybe he just stung someone. I've heard that bees only have one sting and they die when they use it. This makes them just as scary as wasps, but much more wise and noble. Stupid, stinger-happy wasps. No, my bee is in bad shape for some reason. I extend a finger, wanting to stroke it, but don't dare. That's the other difference with wasps, of course — bees look sort of furry: they remind us of mammals. I can smell the moisture in the air and know that it's about to rain again. That won't help. I build up a circle of tiny stones around the bee to offer it some protection, and then wonder if I'm just trapping it, so I make a little gap in the circular wall in case the bee needs to get out. The rain starts to fall and I go inside.

In the kitchen I look through the window towards my bee in his roofless castle. But the lights are on and I can only see my reflection. Why am I Robert? Why is my name Robert Webb and why do I have curly blond hair? Do other people feel "me" the way I feel "me"? It seems unlikely. And why am I crying? I mean, it's only a bee.

I try to dry my eyes before anyone notices. I'm not going to tell anyone about this, not even Nan or Tru or Mum. They would be nice about it, of course, but I know the truth about my bee.

I wasn't supposed to look after it. I was supposed to stamp on it.

CHAPTER
THREE

Boys Love Sport

"The thing about football — the important thing about football — is that it is not just about football."

Terry Pratchett, *Unseen Academicals*

I pick my nose, not knowing whether to laugh or cry. There's no point trying to deny it: these are *girls'* socks. It's Auntie Tru's fault, I think, as I bitterly compress a bogey between upper and lower incisors . . . I mean, how could she do this to me?

Roger Baxter sits on the low school wall next to me. "Cheer up, Robert. I mean, y'right, they do look a bit like girls' socks but . . ." Roger is being kind but also smiling broadly as he looks down at the offending socks, "I must say, it's not as bad as all that."

I shake my head and mutter, "It's the story of my life." I don't really know what this phrase means but I've heard Mum say it quite often and it seems to convey the depth of my world-weary sophistication.

"Bloody 'ell, Robert, you don't 'alf come out with some grown-up things, you." I like the sound of this

69

and make a mental note to come out with as many grown-up things as possible in future.

It's Sports Day. I've been at the junior school for two years and I'm nine. I don't play with the Guy-Buys any more, but I've tried to write stories about them. One of them is entitled "Fallen Hero", in which the Captain of the Guy-Buys is isolated from his gang and being hunted through a forest by the baddies. Wounded and exhausted, our hero somehow makes it back to his base, whereupon the Guy-Buys see that he needs help. They charge out and slaughter the baddies without mercy. It's a massacre. The End.

Why didn't I say something in the clothes shop? Suddenly, the new rule about Sports Day PE kit is that everyone has to wear white socks. It fell to Trudy to take me to the shop in Coningsby. It's the kind of place where you ask for something and then the shop assistant turns to one of the ten thousand little drawers behind her and hands over the right thing.

Except this is not the right thing. I look up sceptically as the socks are passed across the counter. They're certainly white but . . . something is wrong. I've seen white socks before. They tended to rise no higher than the beginning of your shin and feature a couple of stripes at the top, like the ones John McEnroe or Jimmy Connors might wear. These are different: they are long and they are patterned. And not just a pattern that is somehow drawn on — no, they are *made* of pattern. If you hold one up to the light, there is as much hole as sock. These are . . . these are girls' socks.

The shop assistant tells Trudy the price and there's a moment I've witnessed before when Trudy registers this as roughly three times the money she was expecting to pay. She rummages in her huge red purse with a polite smile and panicking fingers.

So it seems rude to moan to Tru about this. Instead, I wait until Mum and Tru have had the usual battle — the one where Mum tries to give Tru money for what she's spent on me and Tru refuses to accept — and then with Trudy safely in Derek's car, being taken back to the Golf Club, I whine at Mum for about half an hour. She tries several tacks but eventually says, "Oh for crying out loud, Robert, it doesn't matter whether they're girls' socks or boys' socks! Socks are socks!"

I've never heard such an outrageous lie in all my born days. I can see from her irritation that she regrets not getting the socks herself. Yes, she knows perfectly well that Auntie Trudy has fucked up. Fucked up big-time. Who on *earth* is she trying to kid? She might as well send me onto that playing field in a bloody tutu.

My plan is to run so fast that no one will notice the socks because my legs will be a blur of light. But this is not much of a plan. The whole school is already changed for Sports Day and I do some experimental running around the playground, trying to casually glance down at my legs in the hope that they have basically disappeared. But no, the socks remain, bulging like Day-Glo bagels now that I've rolled them down to my ankles. And anyway, it's already too late. It's not the parents lining the track on the playing field that will be

71

the problem; it's the other kids in the playground right now.

Especially the boys. The ones who love football. There they are, every Games lesson, lining up with their hands on their hips, listening to the Games teacher while frowning very seriously at the ground and spitting. They're practising for the future when they'll adopt the same pose when surveying the meat counter in a supermarket. Spitting is no longer required, but hands remain on hips and the new action is to walk backwards into a passing woman.

Matthew Tellis in particular is being a dick. I don't like Tellis anyway — he cheats at marbles. "Look at Robert! Good socks, Robert! Ha-ha Haha-ha! My name's Robert and I'm a girl!" Some other boys are starting to circle. This is bad.

"Shurrup, Tellis, y'wassock," says Roger, "it's not his fault, it's his auntie!" Some of the others mutter "auntie" and quietly scoff. But as ever, I'm emboldened by the intervention of a male with a leading part. Tellis doesn't enjoy being chastised by Roger, and while he's still recovering I go in for the kill. "Maybe they'd look better if my legs were covered in shit, Matthew."

Roger explodes with laughter, as do the other boys. I've just referred to an incident which Matthew Tellis will never live down. A couple of weeks ago, he put his hand up and asked to go the toilet. Our teacher, Mrs Benson, must have been having a bad morning because her impatient response was, "If you're not back by the time I've counted to twenty, you're in big trouble."

This turned out to be an unwise threat. Because Matthew, being an obedient boy, started his own countdown. He ran to the loo, pulled his pants down, pushed out half a turd, and then, knowing that he was running out of time, pulled his pants back up and returned to the classroom. The stink was enough to make James Ryan, who was sitting next to Matthew, throw up in a cloakroom. Mrs Benson, however, was not one to admit a mistake on this scale. It was time for PE.

Have you ever seen a nine-year-old boy who's just shat himself doing star jumps in a white PE kit?

I have.

Poor, blameless Matthew had been getting away with it until now. It's fragile, and you wouldn't want to found a major religion on it, but there is a level of honour among schoolboys. There are some places we know we just shouldn't go.

Unless, that is, one of us is cornered and has just been called a girl. Then all bets are off.

Tellis is doing his best to laugh off the shit comment, but he's still looking at my socks and trying to think of something to come back with. Oh no you don't.

"I'll not take clothes advice from Mr Shittylegs!" I almost shout. I'm annoyed with myself because I think "fashion advice" would have been better than "clothes advice", but it won't matter. The business end of the insult is obviously "Mr Shittylegs" and that will do nicely. Tellis begins to stalk towards me and the look in his eyes isn't so much one of anger as of fear. He knows that, as humiliating nicknames go, "Mr Shittylegs" has the potential to — well, stick. I mean, it has legs. I mean, it could run and run. Oh dear. Sorry, everyone. And especially sorry, Matthew Tellis.

Roger is still laughing as he steps in front of me and blocks Matthew's advance. The others are hooting and falling around, yelling "Mr Shittylegs". Michael Key starts jogging on the spot, lifting his knees as high as he can and blowing a short, loud raspberry every time his feet hit the ground. "Pwpbpbpb . . . Pwpbpbpb . . ." This is getting out of control — someone else thinks it's time for a song: "Oh, they call me Mr Shittylegs. They call me Mr Shittylegs. Yes, they call me Mr Shittylegs. Coz my legs are covered in shiiiiiiiiit!"

Rather magnificently, Tellis just says "Yeah, yeah . . ." and drifts away with a kind of resigned ennui, as if Magnum has just tolerated a group of kids taking the piss out of his moustache. He'll be back.

I'm exhilarated. But now there's a new problem. Lisa Proctor has been watching. Lisa used to sit next to me in class in our first year at this school, and although I made an outward show of discomfort, theatrically pushing her pencil case back to her if it strayed a millimetre onto my half of the desk, for example (you can't be too careful about "girl fleas"), the truth was that I liked Lisa. In fact, when I thought no one was looking, Lisa and I got on really well.

She approaches and speaks to me in worryingly measured tones. "That wasn't very nice, Robert. That wasn't very nice at all. I didn't think you were like the others, but you are, aren't you?"

I don't have anything to say.

"You're just like the others." The boys standing around do some obligatory snorting and eye-rolling. Lisa walks off with her friend Cathy.

I want to tell her that this was self-defence, that Tellis started it. And that, no, I'm not "just like the others". Because the one thing I hate hearing more than "You're not like the others" is "You're just like the others". Confusingly, the others don't seem to think that they're the others either.

Guys, hands up who are "the others"? None of us are the others. Except for when we are. But that — please understand — that's only because of the others. We're the nice ones, you see. The problem is those others.

Anyway, I think to myself, it's all very well for Lisa. What would happen if she had to wear boys' socks? Nothing. At worst, she might get called a "tom-boy". Big deal. Compared to being a girl that's a promotion.

One of the more alarming novelties of junior school was the presence of male teachers. This included the Headmaster, Mr Morgan, a bald, strong-looking man with stern glasses. In the first assembly, he welcomed us new arrivals with an avuncular smile but then quickly stiffened up when it came to the School Rules.

"Rules," he says in a projected baritone that could bounce off the back of a hall twice the size, "to be obeyed!" Oh God, another hard case. Corporal punishment is still with us here in 1980, and it is rumoured that Mr Morgan uses a slipper. Another teacher, Mr Duke, on the other hand, keeps a yellow wooden stick on his desk which he has nicknamed "The Yellow Peril". He seems amiable enough, Mr Duke, telling the class his "bad jokes", although I'm nervous of his Englishman, Irishman and Scotsman jokes because the punchline always seems to be about Irish people being stupid. I think these jokes should be avoided since I consider them the main reason why the IRA on the news are so cross and keep blowing things up. I have no evidence that "The Yellow Peril" is there for deterrent purposes only. For all I know, this guy could at any moment stop telling jokes and just come at me with a fucking *stick*.

If that happened, the Guy-Buys couldn't protect me and neither could Roger. Mark, maybe. If my biggest brother Mark saw someone coming at me with a stick . . . yes, Mark would have an opinion about that.

Mark pulls up a bar stool and clears his throat. It's 2009 again, the "Let's Jump Up and Down in a Leotard for Comic Relief" year, and I'm making a documentary about T. S. Eliot. The BBC have commissioned four vaguely familiar TV faces to make an hour-long programme each about their favourite poems, and how poetry in general has affected their lives. For my episode of *My Life in Verse*, I've chosen "The Love Song of J. Alfred Prufrock". I have a brilliant director/producer in Ian McMillan and we're in the Angel pub in Horncastle, Lincolnshire.

This was the pub where you could reliably get a pint of "snakebite and black" from about the age of sixteen onwards. This beverage, in case you've managed to avoid it, consists of half a pint of cider in the same glass as half a pint of lager, topped off with a squirt of blackcurrant cordial. The cordial is there for people who prefer their vomit purple. Needless to say, I didn't like snakebite and black. I liked Bacardi and Coke — the alcoholic drink that most approximates to a bag of sweeties.

The programme has a biographical element and Mark has turned up to be interviewed about my childhood. Ian thanks him for helping me with the film and Mark says lightly, "No problem, I'd do anything for him." If anyone bats an eyelid at this, I'm not one of them. It's obviously true. It's Mark.

Ian opens with the question, "What was Rob like when he was growing up? I mean, if you had to think of one word, then . . ."

"Spoilt."

"Sorry?"

"Spoilt, I'd say." Mark glances at me. I'm looking at a beer mat and have raised two eyebrows in mock innocence. But this rings a loud bell. Ah yes, I think: that was the other one. Not just "Robert is shy" but "Robert is spoilt".

Nan and Trudy didn't just cut the crusts off my sandwiches. They also skinned my sausages and took the pips out of grapes. From more distant relations, Mark and Andrew sometimes got joint Christmas cards, while I never had to share so much as an Easter egg, never mind a bedroom. It's inexplicable to me now that as teenagers my brothers were still sleeping in the same room, while I had one to myself, but that's the way it was.

And it feels like I got more treats. The Golf Club days I looked forward to the most were in the holidays when Nan, John and Tru all had a day off. That might mean a trip to the second-best place in the world (after Skegness) — Lincoln! This glittering metropolis was a forty-minute drive away in John's white Granada and on warm days he would even wind the sun roof open. I would go around the Cash & Carry with him, trying to push the industrial-sized trolley through the transparent plastic curtains into the massive fridge room (the whole room was a fridge) and help (watch) John load up with breeze-block cuboids of cheddar and Red Leicester. Then we'd catch up with "the girls" in Marks and Spencer and Trudy would take me to a bookshop and treat me to a *Doctor Who* paperback or two. Finally, saving the best till last, we would proceed like kings towards the unsurpassed glamour of lunch at the Berni Inn. A rump steak (fillet was for birthdays) for Little Lord Fauntleroy, followed by another attempt to sip Nan's extraordinary coffee-with-the-cream-on-top without seriously scorching my whole mouth.

How did Mum feel about all this "spoiling"? She kept an eye on it, but an indulgent one. She would occasionally pick me up on a decline in my manners after a weekend at the Golf Club; or for helping myself to biscuits without asking. But that's about it.

In any case, she saved my most outrageous spoiling for herself: from when I was about five up until seven years old, she would read me bedtime stories. With her other boys, she never had the time or freedom. Now she did. *The Lion, the Witch and the Wardrobe, The Jungle Book* and, my favourite because she did an accent from the American South for the characters, *The Adventures of Tom Sawyer*. I don't know if I grew to love reading because it reminded me of time with Mum, or if I grew closer to Mum because she was the one who read me these great stories.

It doesn't matter. We talk a lot about privilege these days and I'm always eager to try to acknowledge my own: an able-bodied white male who has never had any serious brush with physical or mental illness and who is (now) educated, middle class and paid well to do a succession of jobs that I really like. Part of the reluctance to type that last sentence (and I could have gone on) is a reasonable fear of seeming boastful. But the thing is, I'm not boasting because I'm not responsible for virtually any of it. Most of it was luck.

Privilege is just a posh word for luck. Maybe you remember Martin. Obviously, I do. As we saw, it's more than likely that, for me to be born in the first place, someone else had to die. So I think I know a thing or two about luck. I could dedicate this book to Martin but that would be the point at which a quiet gratitude turns into posturing sentimentality. There were nights in my late teens, wandering home from the pub when I lived with Dad, when I would look up at the stupefying beauty of a cloudless Lincolnshire night sky and thank the stars . . . thank my luckiest star — Martin.

But then, I was pissed. Sentimentality is a real emotion, plus something unhealthy: in this case, five

79

pints of Carling Black Label. The truth is I didn't know the poor kid, and he had no intention of dying. I thank him anyway.

So — the thing or two I know about luck. Thing number one: you should do your best to notice luck so that you don't accidentally take credit for it. Thing number two: luck is not your fault.

And when it comes to colossal strokes of good fortune (and there's a whopper coming up at the end of this chapter), it starts here — it starts with having a family who loves you and someone who inspires you to read. Not because reading makes you smart, although it helps, but because to involve yourself in a story is to imagine what it's like to be someone else. Generally, boys aren't much encouraged to do that.

Susan and Lucy in grief for their dead king, the great lion; Charlie, eking out his year-long ration of Wonka Bar; Emil, alone on a train (before he meets his detectives), pricking his finger on the safety pin; the Doctor, losing his mind on Castrovalva; his companion Tegan, longing for home; Luke Skywalker, looking for adventure in a twin sunset — together with Mum or alone in my bedroom, stories were a way to reach distant places. But also, and without my noticing, a way to reach distant people. That's where I really caught a break. I don't mean I suddenly had miraculous powers of empathy; I just mean that empathy had a chance.

Martin and stories — my lucky stars, my twin suns.

I walk to junior school on my own. It's only about ten minutes and Derek shows me a back way which avoids crossing most of the roads. This suits me because I now get to avoid Derek giving me one of his sloppy kisses when he drops me off. One day, one such car-based farewell was witnessed by a friend (Tellis again, in his pre-Shittylegs pomp). As Derek's Pacer X departed, Matthew said, "I know who your girlfriend is, Robert — y'dad!!!" This was annoying not just because I knew it was unusual (and shameful) for any dad to be physically affectionate, but also because Derek was not my dad. It never occurred to me to call him anything other than "Derek", or sometimes "Des".

That's not exactly what he wanted. I said earlier that Mum had only two cards to play: her charm and beauty. That's not quite right. When it came to our Derek, I think it's safe to say that she had a third card: me.

Why? Because I was bloody gorgeous, that's why.

Derek had always wanted a little girl, and I was the next best thing. Quiet, polite, with wide blue eyes and a mass of curly, white-blond hair, I was Little Lord Fauntleroy in a tank top. Mum asked if I wanted to start calling him "Daddy" and I said "no, thank you". She asked if I wanted to change my name from Webb to Limb and I said "no, thank you". My name was Webb and that was that. Also, the offer of adoption was not extended to Mark and Andrew and I didn't want a different name to my brothers. I remember it being said quite often, by Mum's friends, and later by Mark and Andrew themselves: "There's not many blokes who would have taken on three boys." That may be true, but that's not quite what Derek did. He took on two boys, a wife that bowled him over and a placid little cherub that he doted on. He was loving and gentle and we all liked him. I didn't mind his cuddles, but I did wish he'd give it a rest with the constant snogging.

At the other end of the spectrum, granddad John had just called time on any snogging at all. I was about seven when one night at the little house at the Golf Club, I went to give him a kiss goodnight. He was watching *The Two Ronnies* with a cold meat supper on his lap. I leaned awkwardly across one of his massive legs and, overbalancing, ended up putting a hand in his stuffed chine (relax — it's a food) while head-butting him in the belly.

"Yeh, now you're a grown man and all, Rob, we probably don't need to bother with the goodnight kiss." It had all been getting a bit embarrassing for a while, so this came as a relief.

"Righto."

"G'night, my boy."

"N'night, Dada."

As for my father, well . . . the vexed issue of physical affection was avoided altogether because I hardly ever saw him. By the time I was a student he would say hello and goodbye with a firm handshake. I was well into my thirties before I'd had enough of this handshake bullshit and gave him a hug.

"Oh, come here, y'prat."

"Oh, righto, boy. We're hugging now, are we?"

"Yes, we are."

"Heh! Righto, mate." He was surprised and pleased.

Oh. So it was that easy, was it? And it only took thirty-five years. Well done, everyone.

Mark and Andrew also got a bit more huggy (with me, if not each other) as we got older and the Sovereign Importance of Early Homophobia had started to recede. But as boys, it didn't happen, except once . . .

I'm seven again and we're at home in Coningsby. It's one of those rare nights that Mum has persuaded Derek to take her out and early enough that they leave before my bedtime. This makes Mark — nearly fourteen — the man of the house, or rather, the teen of the bungalow, and Mum has asked him to tuck me in. I get my pyjamas on and get into bed.

"Right then, Bobs, what's the drill?"

"Pardon?"

"What does Mummy normally do now?"

Mark has that parental knack of taking the first-person perspective of the child — he doesn't usually call Mum "Mummy", but he knows that I do. I appreciate this. I tell him the routine: "She tucks the sheets and blankets in, but not the top thing, and then reads to me for a bit and then she says, 'Goodnight, God-bless, sweet dreams and see you in the morning', and then I say 'I 'ope so!', and then she gives me a kiss and leaves the door a bit open so I can see the light from the hall."

For some reason, a flicker of doubt crossed my brother's face about halfway through this speech. I wonder if he's got a headache or something.

"Mummy reads to you?"

"Yep."

He clicks his fingers and claps his hands together cheerfully. I must have been imagining things. It is, after all, impossible to hurt Mark because Mark is both The King and The Fonz.

"Right then, I've not quite got time for a story, Bobs, but I'll do the rest."

He does the tucking in and then, born actor that he is, leans in and softens his voice. "Night night, Robbie, God-bless, sweet dreams and see you in the morning."

"I 'ope so!"

To my amazement and delight, he gives me a light kiss on the lips. Then he goes, leaving the door ajar as requested.

I adore both of my brothers. But it's fair to say that, growing up, Mark was to me not only The King and The Fonz, but also Tucker Jenkins and Han Solo. Not forgetting the lead singer of Showaddywaddy, who I thought was cool. Dark, with brown eyes like Mum, rather than pale and fair like me and Andrew (and Dad, before the outdoor work and indoor booze turned his own complexion to mahogany), Mark seemed to me to be everything a boy was supposed to be.

For a start, he had brown, straight hair. How was I supposed to compete with that? He played the lead in school plays and seemed to be in the first XI of everything. He was captain of real teams, not imaginary ones. He was in the Cadet Corps, he could play the guitar, he could draw and paint, he seemed — like The Fonz — to have a girlfriend for each day of the week.

He and Andrew had been sent to Gartree Secondary Modern School (Lincolnshire — then and now — is one of those places that still does selection at eleven). And there, sadly, was where they both had to acquire a new skill: that of being "hard". Andrew was pretty "hard", but Mark was the "hardest". Years later, there was a day at school — another school — where I was in serious danger of being bullied, by which I mean beaten up, by a couple of much older kids. A third intervened: "I wouldn't — that's Mark Webb's little brother."

And that, I can tell you, did the trick. It was as if an attack on Little Lord Fauntleroy was an attack on The King himself. Mark's writ reached down through school years and across towns and villages. My tormentors backed away as casually as they could manage. One of them, over his shoulder, offered an apology for the misunderstanding.

No one with any sense enjoys being written about. I include myself and I'm doing the writing. But getting me wrong is my problem — with everyone else . . .

A memoir is a story, and to turn a person into a character is an act of simplification, even if the author is your brother and the character is drawn with love. So I'll be more than averagely careful here because, these days, Mark is one of the most respectable blokes you're ever likely to meet. A proud father himself, he coaches the local kids' football team and he's the managing director of a large agricultural supplier. He's always been funny but, in terms of straightness and probity, he makes most policemen look like Super Hans. He drives an Audi.

But at the time, well . . . obviously you don't get a reputation like that — the sort that scares the hell out of people when you're not even in the room — without having demonstrated on well-timed occasions a capacity for sudden and overwhelming violence. A willingness to be more like "those others" than "those others".

"Troubled" is the word I've heard Mark use to describe himself as a teen and a young man. And "borstal" is a term I've heard to describe Gartree School in the 1970s and 80s. Mark and Andrew became tough as a survival requirement of a lousy and uncaring system. They worked hard and did well, despite how little Gartree expected of them. They were only supposed to be boys.[1]

It's incredible, the way we stereotype girls and boys. Do it with race or religion and people would rightly look at you as if you were out of your mind.

Try this. Let me condense some of the stuff I've heard said about boys by parents, friends, grandparents and even the odd teacher. Wherever you see the word

---

[1] See Rebecca Asher on the low expectations placed upon schoolboys in Chapter 2 of her excellent *Man Up* (Harvill Secker, 2016). Generally, this is also a class problem, a race problem and a special educational needs problem. Not much of that is relevant to Gartree, however, since they were all white, all working class and special educational needs hadn't been invented. They still thought dyslexia was caused by witches.

"boy" or "boys", substitute the word "black" or "blacks".

"Leo, of course, is a typical boy. He can't sit still. Yes, I know boys can enjoy reading but it doesn't come naturally. You know where you are with a boy — they're so straight-forward, aren't they? Emotionally uncomplicated. After all, boys will be boys."

Are we having fun yet? Try this for girls. Substitute Muslim or Muslims.

"Girls love flowers, don't they? I know it's unfashionable to say so, but if you can't get a girl interested in cookery then you're doing something wrong. It's just that girls know, in their heart of hearts, that all they really need to do is sit around looking pretty. Ha! I'm joking, of course: some girls want to have a career and quite right too."

I didn't have to witness any of it, my brothers being the tough guys. I got the other guys: the ones who taught me to whistle (Mark), taught me to ride my bike without stabilisers (Andrew), taught me to tie my shoelaces (Mark), took me to the pictures to see *The Empire Strikes Back* (Andrew), encouraged me to sing without embarrassment (Mark), showed me how to get a high score on *Space Invaders* (Andrew), taught me how to fire an air rifle safely (Mark), played with me at bailing out a sandcastle when the tide was coming in (Andrew), taught me how to dial a number on an analogue phone by tapping it out on the receiver (Mark), taught me to drive (Andrew), taught me how

87

to laugh at myself (Andrew), taught me how to laugh at Mark (Andrew), gave me a kiss goodnight (Mark).

Yes Marky, yes Andy — "spoilt" is about right. Mum, Trudy and Nan spoiled me rotten.

But those women had help, my dearest lads, my bruised old fruits. They had your help.

It's bedtime. I'm eleven and she doesn't read to me any more because I want to read on my own, at my own speed — reading backwards and forwards, skipping and rewinding, burrowing wormholes in time — putting present people next to distant people. It's becoming a habit.

And I'm just old enough to object to being "tucked in". But Mum still comes into the bedroom to wish me goodnight and do some absent-minded clearing up. I think she likes it in here. She's looking thoughtful and I wonder if I'm in trouble.

"I talked to Mr Morgan today," Mum says.

Oh blimey, this could be bad. But there was no Parents' Evening tonight, was there? Sometimes she comes home from them inexplicably pleased with me; sometimes quite stern and telling me I need to "pull my socks up".

Socks. She's got a nerve.

She knows Mr Morgan quite well: when he was headmaster of a different school, Mum was his secretary. This gives me access to the priceless but scarcely credible knowledge of his first name: Jim. I've tried to share that around but no one believes me. Jim Morgan. I mean "Jimmy Hill! Chinny reck-ON!!"

"He phoned me about your eleven-plus results."

Oh OK, so they spoke on the telephone. Hang on, my eleven-plus what?

Everyone has been talking about the eleven-plus exam for a long time. I know that this result will make the difference between whether I go to Gartree or Grammar. The only thing is, I have no idea that I've already taken it.

Every now and then Mrs Benson would hand out sheets of paper containing "tests". They were weird but sometimes quite fun and mainly seemed to involve puzzles where you had to work out which shape wasn't like the other shapes. All very peculiar, but better than doing maths or football. I suppose the tests had been past papers. And then one day, without mentioning it, she just handed out the present paper. Not necessarily a bad approach but a bit of a surprise all the same. So, I've taken my eleven-plus. Interesting news.

"Mr Morgan says that you're borderline."

"Borderline," I repeat, cluelessly.

"He says that you'll either do well at Gartree or struggle at the Grammar School."

This seems about right. Relative to the rest of the class, I've settled at the disappointing end of clever or the hopeful side of dim. Mrs Benson has devised four groups for spelling and maths. The sets are: "Felicity Bryan", "Group A", "Group B" and "Brains of Britain". Felicity is in a genius league of her own and gets bespoke questions. I quickly realise they're never going to put me in Felicity Bryan, which is probably just as well. I very nearly cope in Group A, and Group B get slightly easier questions and then . . . oh dear. There are three boys who all live on the local caravan site. They're quite often in trouble and they don't smell too good. Mrs Benson is willing to encourage them where possible, but I'm not sure that, these days, giving them their own set and calling it "Brains of Britain" would be considered best practice.

She has her favourites, Mrs Benson, and I've lately become one of them. She's been impressed with my stories in "Creative Writing". Sometimes she gets me to read them out to the class, which is nerve-racking until I get to the funny bits. It's not so bad when my classmates laugh. The more they laugh, the less frightened I am.

"So . . . where am I going to go?" I ask. Mum has finished her desultory tidying and sits on the side of the bed. She pushes her glasses up the bridge of her nose and looks at me.

"I thought I'd let you decide."

I see. Righto. Grammar or Gartree, Grammar or Gartree . . . tough one. Well, the Grammar boys wear burgundy blazers as opposed to Gartree's black ones. Burgundy is surely closer to pink, so that's a negative. And you hear about Grammar school people being called "snobs". I'm not completely sure what this word means but it seems to have something to do with posh people being unpleasant. And although we live in a bungalow, not a caravan, we're certainly not posh in our family, so maybe I don't belong at the Grammar school. I scan my mother's face, but for some reason she's now looking down at her knees and breathing very calmly.

There again, Mark and Andrew didn't make Gartree seem like the kind of place I would much like. I've looked up the word "borstal" in Derek's one-volume encyclopaedia — the one he uses for the crossword — and I didn't like what I found. Of course, girls go to both schools but . . . there's something about Gartree that seems more "boy-like". But I ought to want that, really, oughtn't I? I ought to want to be with the tough boys.

And wouldn't it be better to do well there than to "struggle"? It feels like I do plenty of struggling as it is. And the Grammar school is a bus ride away, whereas I could just walk to Gartree. Bit of a conundrum all round really, isn't it? I look at Mum again. What does she want me to do? What's the right answer?

"I think I'd rather struggle at the Grammar school," I say.

Her dark hair has fallen in front of most of her face, but I can see her lips as they compress into a faint smile. They relax again and her neutral expression is back when she looks up and meets my gaze. Her head is incredibly still when she asks: "Sure?"

I nod vigorously. "Yep. Sure."

"Good idea," she says and then breaks into a big smile. "Anyway, it might not be as difficult as all that if you work hard! Which I know you will."

Crikey, what have I got myself into?

"Night night, God-bless, sweet dreams, see you in the morning."

"I 'ope so!"

I think I said the right thing. I'll know for sure if she puts a record on in the kitchen. Early Beatles or Cliff for nostalgia or general cheerfulness. Elkie Brooks for everything from vague whimsy to outright misery. Something up-tempo by the Bee Gees if she's more excited or hopeful. For a moment there's a heaviness to her movements as she pauses at the door. Then she glances back and gives me a playful wink.

Queen Elizabeth's Grammar School, then. The posh one. From down the hall, I hear the familiar disco introduction to "Stayin' Alive". I check the curtains for shadows and wonder what Dad will say about this. I'll find out when I see him at Christmas.

Well, you can tell by the way I use my walk
I'm a woman's man: no time to talk.

CHAPTER
FOUR

Boys Are Brave

"I promised you, Dad, not to do the things you've
    done
I walk away from trouble when I can
Now please don't think I'm weak, I didn't turn the
    other cheek,
And Papa, I sure hope you understand.
Sometimes you gotta fight when you're a man."
                Kenny Rogers, "Coward of the County"
(written by Roger Bowling and Billy Ed Wheeler)

"Soo noi," begins Mr Jennings in an accent which
reminds me of the times when my heart would sink as I
realised the TV show *Why Don't You?* would be coming
from the Belfast studio, "on Monday we asked the
quessjen, 'What is Phezzecs?' and on Tuesday we asked
the quessjen, 'What is Biolojay?' and soo . . .", he pauses
meaningfully, "what d'yeh thank Am gonna ask ye noi?"

I have no fucking idea what he's going to ask me
now. He might as well be talking Spanish. Xenophobia
is too grand a word for it: teetering on adolescence, I'm
still basically alarmed by the sound of anyone who
doesn't sound exactly like me.

Actually I do know what he's going to ask, because it says on my timetable that this is "Chemistry". Shall I put my hand up? But what would be the point? It's obvious that I'm going to hate this science subject as much as the other two. We're in the General Lab. As opposed to the Science Lab, the Biology Lab, the Chemistry Lab, the Domestic Science Lab, the Physics Lab or the Maths Lab. The sudden eruption of Labs in my life is deeply unwelcome.

Mr Jennings has eased himself onto a bench, one plump buttock at a time, and is dangling his legs playfully while he waits for someone to answer his stupid question. Why, I wonder, have they bothered turning science into three different subjects if all three are going to be taught by this prat? I mean, he seems nice, but science now is a galaxy away from science fiction. When are we going to talk about rockets? Little Nerd Fauntleroy is peeved.

The Maths Lab, at least, is just a classroom. Unfortunately, what it lacks in farty gas taps, red-hot gauzes and lethal glassware, it more than makes up for by being full of Maths. This teacher, Mr Bandeen, has barely introduced himself before he's crouching next to me for a remedial one-to-one about the cruel mysteries of long division. It's an infinitely quieter and more patient "do an eight, do a two", but the old panic is still there. Mr Bandeen's breath and I become so well acquainted over that first term that I can tell you with confidence that he takes sugar in his coffee.

It's a mixed school, but it's the rest of the boys that seem to look forward to Maths. The freaks. Or, more accurately, the "normal boys". I'm the freak. I'm the frightened, ungrateful, resentful freak and I've already decided that Bunsen burners and decimal points have been sent to destroy me.

Seven of us from that year of Coningsby Junior School have passed our eleven-plus. Or to put it another way, seven out of about thirty of us have managed to attain a sufficiently high score in a random quiz based on a meaningless version of an IQ test which in 1984 had already been discredited for over twenty years. We are split into the three forms in the first year and mixed with other Apparently Magnificent Sevens or Eights from the other primary schools in the area.

My form teacher is Mrs Brockley, who also teaches us French. She pins her short hair with a severe-looking grip and I suppose she's somewhere in her forties. As her bright blue eyes range over the class and fix us one at a time, she makes it clear without quite spelling it out what she requires from Form 1B: respectful silence when she's talking, cheerful replies to light-hearted enquiries, thoughtful answers, intelligent questions. These are the rules. They are good rules. But deviate from them too widely and those blue eyes will nail you into your chair and you will receive a five-minute monologue detailing exactly why you have let yourself down. You don't mess with Mrs Brockley.

League-of-her-own superstar Felicity Bryan has naturally made the cut, and I start to notice something about at least half of these other grammar-school kids. They sound like Felicity. They sound like people on the news rather than people in Lincolnshire watching it. They pronounce the "a" in "fast" to rhyme with "farce". They talk about something at home called a "bed-ruhm", rather than a "bed-room". After lunch, they put their knives and forks together at an angle, with the handles resting at 7 or 8 o'clock rather than straight down towards 6. They don't seem all that worried about what's happened to Zammo because they don't watch *Grange Hill*. Wilbur Chatterton has been to Tuscany. It is rumoured that Felicity Bryan has a piano at home. They are the first people with their hands up. They aren't always the smartest, but they are always the most talkative. And the more they talk, the smarter they get. Who are these people?

Carl Billingham is one of them. He sits next to me and won't shut up. He has freckles and nobody likes him, but that only seems to make him even more irrepressibly chatty and irritating. He draws on my hand when I'm not looking. I try ignoring this, but if I ignore it for too long then he gets to finish his doodle and I've got a Nazi swastika on my hand. I haven't yet fully absorbed the Bad News about the Nazis but I understand a swastika on your hand is not a good look. This is a whole new level of annoying: Tellis would have just drawn a cock or maybe some boobs. You knew where you were with Tellis, but he's at Gartree.

I see lots of Carl Billingham because I obey the strange law that says you're supposed to hang out with the person you sit next to. At morning break, most of the 1B boys end up milling around in the main hall watching sixth-formers doing their shit breakdancing.

Carl Billingham can do a passable "caterpillar", which wins everyone's grudging respect for a couple of minutes, but then he rejoins us for the main business of staring listlessly at the sixth-form boys trying to spin on their heads. We do it every morning. We don't know why.

One of the boys will have taped the Top 40 and some songs will be more breakdance-appropriate than others. Chaka Khan's "I Feel For You", for example, seems to work much better than "No More Lonely Nights" by Paul McCartney. Some of the sixth-form breakdancers carry on regardless, like they can't hear the difference. You don't stop breakdancing just because the music's wrong: that would look queer.

At home, my brothers have reacted to my new QEGS (Queen Elizabeth's Grammar School) status about as well as I expected; which is to say, Mark is proud and pleased and Andrew takes it as a personal affront. Generally, the dynamic between Mark (seventeen), Andrew (sixteen) and me (eleven) is like a *Tom and Jerry* cartoon. Tom the cat (Andrew) chases Jerry the mouse (me) all around the place until the bulldog Spike (Mark) makes an unexpected appearance to give Tom a thump.

One teatime, I manage to tear a slice of bread into five jagged pieces by trying to butter it straight from the fridge.

Andrew is thrilled. "Grammar-school education and he can't even butter a slice of bread!"

I feel like pointing out that they don't actually teach us how to butter bread, and that I was exactly this much of a klutz last August and it didn't seem to bother him then, but — I don't. I don't give Andrew witty retorts because a) I'm not that witty, and b) he still towers over me and you never know what he's going to do. He would never hurt me but I try to avoid earning one of his "hard stares". Also, if I'm sitting at the kitchen table, he's incapable of passing behind without tapping me on the head. This can be quite a light tap or, at the other end of the scale, he just pushes my whole face into a bowl of Ready Brek.

Most of the time we get along well enough, and I look forward to Tuesday teatimes when we go into his and Mark's bedroom and watch *Monkey* or *The Water Margin* on their portable black and white telly. Andrew used to have a big poster of Abba standing in front of a helicopter on his side of the room, but he's replaced that with the rather less amiable prospect of Sid Vicious. There's also a diagram of a man in his underpants with the various karate strike points and vulnerable spots helpfully labelled.

After *Monkey* has finished, Andrew will usually turn to me and say "Time for Beeeeeatings!", and we have some kind of play-fight which usually ends with me hitting my head on a chest of drawers and trying not to cry.

I don't mind the occasional bump on the head but the grammar-school thing is clearly going to be a permanent pain in the arse. "He can't even butter a slice of bread" is the opening line in a show that will

98

run and run. It's called "Clever Boys Don't Have Any Common Sense". Andrew has a lead part in the original cast but he's hardly alone. Dad (who seems to have forgotten he went to the same school), as well as Derek, Nan, John, colleagues from part-time jobs, some of Mum's friends and even Mum herself, will all join the chorus at various times.

Teasing Clever Boys for being impractical is part of a wider ambivalence around boys and education. All through our primary-school years we are aware of the stereotype: that "boys will be boys"; that we can't sit still; that we're loud and cheeky and unruly and disruptive; that we have "too much testosterone" to concentrate; that we don't like reading as much as girls and are much happier with a football than with a book.

I think it's quite likely that these beliefs affect the academic life of boys. And that some boys duly live down to those expectations and can hit their GCSEs still thinking that maleness and studying is an awkward fit and that reading is still basically for gaylords.

Even at QEGS, where we were constantly told we were super-duper and tremendously lucky, a boy and a girl who came top of their class would each need a different excuse: if accused of intelligence, the girl would be expected to shrug it off and say that she just worked very hard. If accused of diligence, the boy would be expected to claim that it was all done at the last minute and he just happens to be quite good at that particular subject. It's OK as long as you didn't make an effort. It's not OK to be a "girlie" swot.

In my case, it's not like I had much to talk down. My average exam score that first summer put me seventeenth in a class of twenty-four. There were two boys in the top five: Pete Garvey and Russell MacAllen. I wondered how they would handle this weird status of being Clever Boys.

They handled it bloody quietly, is how they handled it.

Mark is trying to get into the bathroom. My brothers argue all the time but are loudest on a Friday night when they're getting ready to go out. I get a vicarious thrill from the potency in the air as they separately anticipate an enjoyable evening of sex and violence at Coningsby Community Centre. The soundtrack to the row about who is taking too long in the bathroom will depend on who won the row about whose music is going to blare from their shared record player: Status Quo if it's Mark, the Sex Pistols if it's Andrew.

"Come on, Andrew, how long are you going to be, you twat?"

"Bog off, Snap, I'm washing me hair."

"I told you what would happen if you called me that again."

"Ooh, I'm scared! You won't want this water, I've just shat the whole bath."

"Right, I'm coming in."

"Get lost, you queer! I'm still in the bath!"

"Unlock this door, you poof!"

"Mum! Mum! Snap's gone queer and he's coming to rape me!"

100

Mum, from the kitchen: "Stop swearing in front of Robert."

"D'you hear that, Snap? Mum says stop fucking swearing in front of Robert."

Andrew has made himself laugh so much he'll have to come out quite soon to get to his asthma inhaler. He knows the consequence of winding Mark up like this will probably involve some kind of "slap", but in the moment he doesn't care. I suppose, in the moment, a Sex Pistol never cares about messing with the Status Quo.

The only time I hear Andrew say something nice about Mark during this period is when he tells me about the other night at the Community Centre when Mark got beaten up by a woman. She had become enraged for some (for all I know, perfectly good) reason and attacked Mark. Instead of fighting back (unthinkable) or even protecting himself (surely reasonable), he just stood there with his hands behind his back and let her beat him black and blue. "Everyone was watching," said Andrew. "Yeah, I must say that was quite good." I try to imagine the physical courage required to show that much contempt for someone and begin to grasp why Mark scares the crap out of everyone. God knows, he has a sense of theatre.

The Mark versus Andrew show can be entertaining, but as we all get older the joke starts to wear thin. Neither of them can offer a comment or ask a question without expecting a sarcastic or hostile response from the other. I doubt this is unusual for teenage brothers: it's just a pity they had to keep it up for another thirty years. A violent father didn't guarantee violence, but it didn't help. An absent father didn't guarantee very angry young men, but that didn't help either. The masculine insistence on competition and one-upmanship didn't make a genuine friendship impossible, but, to put it mildly, that really didn't help at all.

They get on much better these days, now they're both around fifty. All things considered I think that's a good effort and ahead of schedule. Some men don't recover from masculinity at all.

"Is Masculinity In Crisis?" is the title of a segment you might catch every now and again on a daytime magazine show like *BBC Breakfast* — somewhere in between "Which Compost Bin?" and a report on nude zorbing. I'm tempted to say that masculinity *is* a crisis, but that's suspiciously neat. Still, as soon as I try to rescue the word I find myself wondering — why bother? What's it for? "He has masculine qualities." Like what? Bravery? Honesty? Stoicism? That's great, but I've also seen various women exhibiting these qualities all my life. "He's proud of his masculinity." OK, well, good for him, but — what? He's got a leather wallet? He's glad he isn't a woman? He's better at doing man-things than other men seem to be? What is this word doing apart from conjuring a bunch of stereotypes about driving gloves and body odour?

And "femininity" — what is it? Having hair? I mean, long hair on your head but none on your legs, under your armpits or within a square mile of your Feminine Ladysecret. Taste in scarves? A sense of colour? The capacity to shut the fuck up when men are talking? What is this stuff?

I promise I am not being wilfully dense about this. I don't know what the words "masculinity" and "femininity" have to offer. Avoiding them, we still have a massive language of more precise words to describe individuals and their behaviour which somehow manage not to come pre-loaded with a steam tanker of gender manure from the last century.

If we want to say that David Beckham puts a lot of thought into his appearance, then we can say . . . oh, I've just done it. I didn't need to bring his sex into it. Or his attitude to his sex. I don't have to view his personality through the prism of his famously golden balls, assuming that were either possible or desirable. I could say Lily Allen's songs are full of swearwords which are at odds with her "femininity" — or I could get a life.

I don't want to spoil everyone's fun. I don't think Rudyard Kipling's poem "If —" would be improved if the last line were not, "And — which is more — you'll be a Man, my son!" but rather, "And — which is more — you'll be an unrealistic paradigm of one person's idea of human virtue, my son/daughter."

That would clearly be shit. But, however you feel about "If —" (I'm fond of it), there is nothing exclusively masculine about the virtues listed. Kipling would probably disagree, but then so would a lot of people in 1909.

So when I say that masculinity is something to recover from, I don't mean that the condition of being male is some innately fallen state. I mean that being male is terrific but comes with a load of extra baggage that is worth noticing. Because you might be carrying a load of stuff you don't need. Stuff which is getting in your own — and other people's — way.

The uncertain pleasures of the Community Centre are a long way down the line and I'm in no hurry to get there. The chief joy of Friday night is getting the hell away from communal showers, conical flasks and English.

I'd been looking forward to English. I thought it might involve more Creative Writing. But no. Box analysis of sentences plus the reading of Esther Hautzig's *The Endless Steppe*. Under the supervision of Miss Wain, a nice lady of about 108, each member of Form 1B falteringly reads another paragraph of *The Endless Steppe*. On and on we play this solemn game of tag-team recital, each of us taking another nibble at the endlessness.

Aged twelve, I hate reading out loud — it's embarrassing and I do it very badly. It's embarrassing *because* I do it very badly. I start nervously counting paragraphs to anticipate which one will be mine to read out. Clearly, while I'm doing this, I'm not listening to the story. But then it's quite hard to listen to the story anyway because it's being read out by children who are seeing the lines for the first time and don't happen to be professional actors.

Here in the twenty-first century, believe it or not, I'm a professional actor. And if you're listening to the audio version of this book, you can be pretty sure I was very familiar with this paragraph before anyone pressed "Play" and "Record".

I suppose what Miss Wain and other English teachers were doing was making sure that the book at least got read. I further suppose that everyone basically hates reading aloud and needs practice for mysterious reasons to do with confidence. This is me trying to be Tremendously Fair.

However, this method is also an excellent way of putting children off books. Particularly if it's a dull book. Which *The Endless Steppe* may well be — I don't know, I wasn't listening. I think the story had something to do with a girl and her family coping with the day-to-day problems of their exile in Siberia. Trying to be fair yet again, I can see the value in getting a bunch of cloistered Lincolnshire kids in a cushy liberal democracy to imagine other children in much worse times and places. I just think that this only works if the young readers are enjoying the book enough to actually give a shit. In my view, no matter how hard it was for Esther Hautzig, at least she didn't have to read *The Endless Steppe* by Esther Hautzig. In that respect she was laughing.

More positively, Friday is the start of the weekend. Trudy, Nan and John have just retired from the Golf Club and I miss my dens. They've moved into a three-bedroom terrace on a former RAF housing estate. It's just the other side of Coningsby and so staying there now involves something very new but surprisingly fun: playing with other boys. Roger Baxter lives on the same estate. I don't get acres of space to roam around in, but I do get some company. At twelve, I'm just about ready for the swap.

Roger was another of the Apparently Magnificent Seven and I save him a space next to me on the bus on the way to QEGS. I say "save him a space" — the bus is nearly empty at that point and no one else ever tries to sit next to me. If they did, obviously I would just stare out of the window and hope Roger didn't mind too much.

What you do in this new, "playing with real people" lark is: you get on your second-hand Raleigh Grifter (trying to remember that the right handlebar twist-grip is for changing gears and not to be disrespected as a pretend motorbike throttle since you are not actually in *CHiPs*) and "call" for a friend.

"Is Roger in?"

"Hello, Robert," says Mrs Baxter, trying not to let the dogs get out. "He's on the computer but come in."

Roger has a Commodore VIC-20 which, technically speaking, has a much smaller memory than my 48K Spectrum, but does have the advantage of actually looking like a computer. Still, I've grown to love my "Speccy" and treat it with almost religious respect. After each session with *Horace Goes Skiing, Jetpack* or *The Way of the Exploding Fist*, I carefully put the Spectrum back in the box that first revealed itself to me under the wrapping paper last Christmas Day.

"All right, Webb! Shall we call for Tellis?" Roger asks. He tosses a joystick up in the air and it instantly snaps back on its cable and clatters heavily against the VIC-20

— a machine which I'm then scandalised to see Roger is going to leave lying around on the carpet. There's something "who gives a shit?" about Roger which reminds me of one of my brothers. I quite like it.

"Yeah! Nice day for the farm," I say.

"Nice day!" he mimics, taking the piss out of my boring observation. And then, in the next instant, looks out of the living-room window. "Y'not wrong, Rob: it *is* a nice day. Let's go!"

I like it when he calls me "Rob" as he used to at Coningsby Juniors. It's strictly "Webb" and "Baxter" on the school bus. He's in a different form and I don't see him much at school. He doesn't even watch the shit breakdancing.

Matthew Tellis, on the other hand, is at Gartree and seems much nicer these days, partly, I imagine to myself, because he's glad Roger and I still hang out with him. To be honest, the fact that he lives on a farm helps. In many ways it's my Golf Club substitute, except quite often I seem to be the only one who thinks that what we're doing is unbelievably dangerous. Or maybe I'm just the biggest coward. I always have some urgent concern that I try to keep to myself but then can't: the unpredictability of the wind as we make our way through a narrow pathway between four-foot nettles; the steepness of a hill we're about to ride our bikes down; the stability of a ladder reaching up to the top of the hayloft; the wisdom of firing water pistols into this flower-bush of infuriated wasps; the way this dinghy on the river has a slow puncture and I can't swim.

Roger has somehow always understood this about me and never seems to mind. He usually offers some friendly encouragement.

"Just whack the nettles out the way with y'stick!"

"Just ride down it on your back brake, we'll wait for you at the bottom."

"I'll hold the ladder while you go up. I'll go up last."

"The Jaspers don't care about us. No waspy stings for Webby."

"There's no current today, Rob. Anyway, I'll not let you drown!"

Why can't I be more like Roger? We had the same terrifying swimming teacher at junior school — how come Roger could take his feet off the floor of the pool? Why hasn't anyone else noticed that if you put your head underwater everything goes dark and sounds weird and the water goes up your nose and tries to kill you? Why can't I save *him* from drowning?

I understood what I was supposed to think: that playing with people was better than playing with a computer. And that outside was better than inside. And that real friends were somehow healthier than imaginary ones. It's just that all this wholesomeness made heavy calls on my very limited supply of courage. How much easier to forget all this "growing" business and just stay at home getting better and better at *Jet Set Willy*.

Boys gave bravery a bad name, I thought. They wanted it for stupid stuff like swimming and wasps, nettles and fighting. And not just pretend fighting. Actual fighting.

★   ★   ★

Kenneth Gibbs was new. He wasn't a big lad but he was Scottish with spiky hair. Either of these attributes alone would have been enough to alarm me, but the combination had me lowering my head whenever I heard his voice. It was like sitting in a classroom with a punk Gordon Strachan. But he was gregarious and friendly enough and he slotted himself in quickly.

The trouble with Gibbs was that he kept pinching girls on the "erse". Mostly they just told him to get lost, but Gibbs was enjoying being the cheeky-chappie with a precocious eye for the ladies. He wouldn't stop. None of his targets wanted to be the first to make an issue of it, which was understandable. Who wants to mention their "bottom" to a teacher?

One lunch break, after witnessing yet another unwanted goosing, Carl Billingham decided enough was enough. You remember Carl — the posh freckly kid I sat next to?

"For God's sake, Gibbs, just pack it in. None of the girls wants you pinching them on the bum. Just grow up." At which point, Gibbs turned wordlessly to Carl and thumped him hard in the mouth. I'm glad to say that this kind of thing was rare enough to be shocking. Boys were forever hitting each other, but not in the face. Even Pete Garvey was shocked: "Bloody hell, Gibbs! What d'you do that for? I'm gonna report you, you little twat." Not, I'm going to kill you, mind — I'm going to report you. Boy, did I pick the right school.

It's afternoon registration and Mrs Brockley has Ken Gibbs in a rhetorical half-nelson and won't let go. She's calm but occasionally remembers how livid she is. She doesn't raise her voice; it's just that her voice is never going to stop. She's teaching. She's quite simply going to teach this kid to death.

"From what I hear, Kenneth Gibbs, you've been behaving in this offensive and disrespectful manner for some — STAND UP WHEN I'M TALKING TO YOU! — for some time. And that it isn't just Valerie and Fiona who've been subject to this appalling nuisance. Tiffany, is it true that you've been pinched as well?"

Tiffany Rampling (younger sister of the famous Tess Rampling) could have done without this, but nods. "It's everyone, really. I mean, all the girls."

"ALL of the girls!?" Mrs Brockley repeats unnecessarily — she's already been told it's all the girls. But fact-finding is not her current purpose, and she's only just getting started. "Let's see then. Hands up everyone who can honestly say they have been pinched or otherwise groped by Kenneth over the last few weeks."

Kenneth Gibbs, crimson of face, shifting his weight from foot to foot, watches wretchedly as every single female hand goes up. It happens in slow-motion and the unanimity is crushing. But there is also a vulnerability about it which haunts me — every girl checking every other girl for support. They need numbers.

Mrs Brockley's sense of drama doesn't desert her. She's quite determined that Kenneth Gibbs will never forget this. "Look around you, Kenneth. Look at the classmates that you have insulted. That you have *insulted*." She actually waits for him to do this. Gibbs

110

does his best. Then she waits even longer. He tries looking around again at the silent tableau of his accusers. This really isn't his day.

"All right, girls, thank you — you can put your hands down. And now, Kenneth, look at Carl."

Carl is next to me with a wet paper towel over his mouth. His gums stopped bleeding about twenty minutes ago and frankly he's milking the situation slightly, but I don't blame him.

Mrs Brockley is reaching her conclusion. "Carl didn't have to say anything. He could have stood idly by, while you continued to harass your fellow pupils. But he chose not to. He chose to intervene. Not because he expected to be thanked but because it was right. Carl is a gentleman."

She lets that last word hang in the air for a beat and then releases Gibbs from his stand-up misery. The subject is dropped and never raised again. Neither are the skirts of the girls of Form 1B, at least not by Kenneth Gibbs.

This won't be the last time the word "gentleman" bongs its way into my brain, making my heart race and my throat constrict. This time, it's a combination of shame and envy that is doing the bonging, throbbing and strangling. I was one of the boys who "stood idly by" while Carl, no less of a physical weed than me, stepped up. Much as I would do almost anything to avoid even the minor biffing Carl got for his trouble, it would almost be worth it, *almost* be worth it if the result was to be called a gentleman. The word contains, but is not limited to, notions of chivalry and class, that is, 1) boys should protect girls, and 2) that to be "gentle" is to aspire to "gentility" — the place where only posh people understand right from wrong.

That's not what Mrs Brockley was talking about. All she said was: boys should not disrespect girls because people should not disrespect people. They should aspire not to mere gentility, but to the greater prize: gentleness. In their manners, and in their actions. And anyone willing to do this — especially at risk of a smack in the face — is worthy of praise.

In fact, it sounded to me that to be a gentleman, you needed both manners and bravery. And that thought was horribly fascinating. Because I thought only wimps needed manners. And only tough guys were brave.

Dad turns up at the bungalow when he trusts himself to be nice — Christmas mornings or the odd birthday. And he *is* nice. I'm always glad to see him on these days, although I can't quite reconcile this new, cajoling charmer with the Darth of my memory.

He and Mum circle each other like JR and Sue Ellen, but without the oil-fields or shoulder pads. Also without the flirtation — if the atmosphere is always warm, it's warmed by sparring jokes. They're both funny, but Mum has less to prove. They know each other horribly well. It's like two countries that suffered the intimacy of being at war for years now getting on by mildly taking the piss out of each other. Mum always wins by default because she knows how the war ended. She won.

In public, and after a gin or two, her touch isn't always so light. One Sunday lunchtime, I found myself sipping another Coke in a Woodhall Spa pub with Mum, trying to follow the chat between her and her old Woodhall friends.

"The trouble is, Pat," says her friend Jeff, "that's the plain fact of the matter in Rhodesia. Or whatever they want to call it now. Everyone says the same thing about the blacks — the blacks don't *want* to work."

Mum, who has banned Cape apples from the house, purses her lips and waits until Jeff looks to the ceiling for his next insight. Then she briefly rolls her eyes at me. Jeff is one of the nicest guys around — it's just that his political views are typical of his time and place. She's slightly ahead but she's no activist or campaigner. She'll ignore Jeff's comment because it isn't worth falling out with him and spoiling her favourite afternoon. Such is village life. But it's possible that she's still angry with Jeff, or angry with herself, when Dad walks in. By the way, his middle name is Frederick and Mum has always called him Fred. I find this impressively grown up.

Dad sees her too late and has to approach, warily, and with a smile within his new beard. "Now then, Pat!"

"Fred, nice to see you. May I introduce you to Robert. He's your son."

She says it slightly louder than necessary and, in a small pub, it's enough to cause a minor stir. It doesn't take much around here for a woman to get a reputation

113

as "outspoken", but she'll take the risk when it comes to Fred.

Dad's smile remains intact as he nods at her slowly, "All right, mate, all right." He turns to me. "Now then, boy!" I'm twelve but he takes one of my ears between his thumb and index finger and gives it an affectionate wobble and squeeze. Unfortunately, it's his sewn-on thumb which has about twenty nerve endings where there ought to be a million. The experience is quite painful and I try not to wince.

"I know you, buggerlugs," he tells me in a low, friendly voice. He ruffles my hair and immediately spots someone he simply *has* to talk to. "Now, Keith! What have you done to the bloody weather?" And off he goes.

Maybe it was this public dad-shaming that brought him to the bungalow a few weeks later to take me to a fireworks display. I wish he hadn't bothered. Guy Fawkes night was always exciting at the bungalow — a few grown-up friends round, jacket potatoes in the oven, Derek in the garden with a battered tin of cheap explosives which he set off one at a time after reading the names out by the illumination of a cigarette-lighter.

But Mum has made some kind of point so I'm encouraged to go. Besides, this new, friendlier Darth is quite fun even though I never manage to string three words together in his company.

The fireworks are at the house of one of Dad's Woodhall Spa friends, Neil. He has a massive garden and the display is unbelievably good. Multiple rockets go off as Catherine wheels whir and Neil plays Handel's *Music for the Royal Fireworks* loudly through a stereo speaker poking out of an upstairs window. Neil appears to be a fair bit wealthier than most people and I start to think of him as the Village Millionaire. The fact that he and his wife are two of those rare and glamorous people who went to university, coupled with the classical music, persuades me that he is also the Village Intellectual. He's a generous host with amiable manners and I like his voice — he sounds like some of the grammar-school boys grown up. He's even been to Tuscany.

After the main event, we're left with a house party. Incredibly, the place has about three downstairs rooms, none of which are the kitchen. I'm shepherded into one of them with some noisy older kids whom I don't know. Luckily I won't have to talk to anyone because there is to be some kind of film presentation. Yes — the Village Millionaire has a video cassette recorder. The movie is called *Flashdance*.

It tells the improbable story of a young woman called Alex who works as a welder but wants to be a ballerina. I get the feeling I'm a bit young to be watching this, what with all the swearing and the regular flashes of naked breasts in the backstage scenes. Still, that audition dance Alex does at the end . . . I mean, it's not like watching Michael Jackson but it's definitely very good. Sadly, *Flashdance* is obviously a girls' film. What a pity — I nearly enjoyed that.

Afterwards, Dad sits with me on the stairs. Oh God, he's Making An Effort.

"Who've you been talking to, boy?"

"I don't really —"

"Eh?"

"I don't really know anyone so —"

"What you got there, boy, a Coke?"

"Yeah."

"Do you want some of my beer?"

"No thanks."

"I can get you a shandy if you like."

"No thanks."

"Eh?"

"No thanks."

"You don't want a shandy?"

"No thanks."

He's looking at me, smiling wryly and nodding to himself. He says, "I know you, Webby. Left to your own devices, you'd probably get yourself a beer and get pissed and go round snogging every girl in the house and feeling their titties."

Briefly, I try to imagine myself doing this.

"Wouldn't you, boy?"

"Er."

"Wouldn't you?"

Slowly, I start nodding along with him, as if his intimate knowledge of my brain and personality has unlocked a secret. Darth's on his fourth lager and obviously isn't going to let this go. I say, "Yeah."

"Eh?"

"Yeah."

"Course you would." He seems satisfied with this. "Right, I'll drive you back home to Mummy before I get paralytic."

116

He banters most of the way home: I nod, smile and laugh where appropriate, but I know I ought to be doing more talking. Being very quiet used to work fine for me, but since grammar school some people are starting to interpret my silence as aloofness or some kind of snooty judgement. That can't be right, I think: usually I just don't have anything to say. But it's worse around chatty, confident, quite pissed people like Dad. He's pointing out the houses that he wired when he worked as an electrician with his own father. Now we're passing woods or rivers where he used to shoot or fish. And this is how the village has changed, and this is how it will never change. "Some things will never change, boy."

Fuck off. I'm growing to hate all this village stuff. They're right. Half the time I *am* making snooty judgements. I *do* have ideas above my station. If for no other reason than "above my station" is where I might get some fucking air. Why wouldn't those kids shut the fuck up when I was trying to watch *Flashdance*? It's like they didn't *care* about the beautiful welder who wanted to become a famous ballerina! And how come it turns out that Dad used to take Mark and Andrew fishing? Why does he assume I wouldn't be interested in fishing? I might love fishing! OK, keep your bloody fish. This place crushes me. *He* crushes me.

"What do you want to be when you grow up then, boy?" he asks.

I do the usual. "Computers." It's the fastest way to close down this sensitive line of enquiry. Nobody over twenty has the faintest idea what a job involving computers could possibly mean, so it works well.

I don't tell him what I really want to do for a living. It's not that I don't know, it's that I'm trying to avoid knowing. There's an idea, just half a secret thought. It's so embarrassing it's almost frightening, like seeing yourself naked.

No one would believe me if I told them.

CHAPTER
FIVE

Boys Are Never Teacher's Pet

"If my father had hugged me even once I'd be an accountant right now."

Ray Romano (actor and comedian)

Zelda Linseed is pushing her luck. She's already in trouble for covering her English exercise book with a *Smash Hits* double-spread of Paul Young and writing "bumfluff" with an arrow pointing at Young's armpit hair.

Everyone was supposed to cover their exercise books to make them last longer. At home, my own method had been to find a roll of Anaglypta wallpaper in a cupboard and attack it with some very large scissors. The result made my schoolbooks look like they'd each grown an asymmetrical beige crust. You could stack them in a pile with all the ease of balancing ten clams. Surveying my efforts, Mum took pity and bought me some brown parcel paper.

But Zelda is a rebel. She's compounding her bumfluff transgression by chatting now at a high volume with Tiffany Rampling (still the younger sister of Tess Rampling) while our new form teacher is trying to speak. Our new form teacher is not the benign dictator of the Mrs Brockley style; this one will endure a certain level of background natter right up until the moment she won't. At which point, her own unique approach to class discipline kicks in.

Mrs Slater turns in the general direction of the noise and says, "Zelda, Tiffany, you appalling dogs, please be quiet. I'm trying to explain how you can make good on the crimes of your predecessors."

Zelda and Tiffany are cartoonishly open-mouthed at being addressed as "dogs". It seems to me that Slater is using the word like a pirate might — to mean "cur" or "wretch". That's already quite full-on, but what Zelda and Tiffany obviously heard was the teenage slang that boys use to describe girls who won't have sex with them: for example, "Madonna is a right dog".

We're in the library and it's a getting-to-know-you session not only for Mrs Slater and Form 1B (shortly, next year, to become Form 2S), but also our first close-up encounter with the Dewey Decimal Classification System. The "crimes" she refers to are the way some books have been sloppily returned to the wrong place. We're going to spend half the lesson sorting that out and the second half just . . . reading. On our own.

Much as I've grown fond of Miss Wain now that *The Endless Steppe* has finally ended, I can't imagine her describing the act of misplacing a library book as a crime. This new English teacher talks the way I suddenly decide all English teachers ought to talk: with an obvious delight in the abundance and ironic possibilities of English. She'll make jokes that no one

120

gets; she'll use vocabulary that no one understands; she'll talk to a class of twelve-year-olds in roughly the same way she talks to a class of eighteen-year-olds. It's like a teacher of Spanish conducting a lesson exclusively in Spanish — it's our job to keep up. This won't always make her popular. The fact that she obviously doesn't give a shit about that is another reason I immediately like her.

Having done some re-ordering, we get a few minutes to choose a book to read by ourselves and then borrow. I head straight for "D" in Fiction to find Terrance Dicks — my favourite *Doctor Who* author. I'm slightly ashamed of this because I know I ought to be looking for something more grown up like, I dunno, Agatha Christie or something. Dicks isn't a "proper" author in that sense — he's just good at adapting TV stories into books.

Amazingly there's one here and I haven't got it at home — *Doctor Who and the Horns of Nimon*, an old hardback from the Tom Baker days. I'm just reading the blurb on the back when suddenly Mrs Slater is at my side.

"Ah, a *Doctor Who* fan."

I nod sheepishly.

She frowns at the book. "I'm a bit of a sci-fi ignoramus, I'm afraid. You'll have to tell me what I'm missing."

I blink at her. "What, now?"

She half smiles and nods, still looking at the book.

"Well, erm, I like the stories."

"That's a start . . ." She says it to my elbow. I get the feeling I'm only going to be rewarded with eye-contact when I come out with something vaguely interesting.

"Well, I like it that you already know what the characters look like."

"Because you've seen them on the TV?"

"Erm, yeah. I s'ppose . . ." I feel like the world's stupidest wanker. "I've got quite a few of these at home."

She looks straight at me. "You're a collector?"

"Yes!"

"You're not going to pinch this, are you?"

"What? I mean, sorry?"

"You're not going to add this one to your collection?"

"Oh, Christ no!" Ooh. Am I allowed to say Christ? The panic makes her smile and then she takes a beat for herself, scanning the shelves.

"Pity," she says, "nobody steals from the library any more. It's a bad sign." She starts to move off and then, almost as an afterthought: "Smart chap — you know what you like. Enjoy it."

I'm relieved that the encounter is over, although I've no idea whether I've just been encouraged or ridiculed. On balance, I'm pleased. I look down at the blurb again. I see that the story was based on the Greek myth of the Labyrinth of Knossos. I wonder if that "K" is silent or if you're meant to pronounce it as in Willy Wonka's Vermicious Knids. It also says that "Nimon" is a play on "Minotaur". Damn, I wish I'd said that. "The point of science fiction, Mrs Slater," I should have said,

122

"is the same as the point of any other fiction. To take the world and re-imagine it. To refresh our understanding of human beings by imagining ourselves in a different place or time." But no, I mumbled about having a book collection. The fact that it was a collection that I spent time actually reading seemed to help for now, but it wasn't enough. I'm suddenly in a terrible hurry to impress Mrs Slater. But it'll have to be done quietly.

After the lesson, Pete Garvey catches up with me in the corridor. He'd been sitting opposite me and tucking into *Right Ho, Jeeves*. He won't exactly be shouting that from the rooftops either.

"Oi, Webb, what was Slater on at you about?" A few other boys are tagging along with him.

"Oh God, something about what book I was reading."

"She's a nosy fucker."

"Exactly. I told her it was none of her fucking business."

"Haha. Apparently her first name is Heather!"

"Oh God. Heather! What a massive . . . spastic!"

"I know! We're going outside after lunch for a bit of Ball Death."

Oh great, more Ball Death. The rules of Ball Death are easily explained. We take it in turns to be the Kicker. If you're not the Kicker, you're one of the Runners. The Runners line up on one side of the exterior brick wall of the Sports Hall and then, one at a time, run from one side of it to the other. As they do so, the Kicker kicks a football as hard as possible from close range at the vicinity of the Runner's testicles. If the Kicker's aim is not initially true, rebounds from the wall are allowed. If one is a Runner, it is illegal to protect one's balls. One must simply run with one's hands in the air whilst hysterically screaming "BALL DEATH!"

As the slowest runner and the worst kicker, I find the game to be of limited appeal.

I say to Garvey, "Cool! Count me in."

Jesus. It was better when we just watched the shit breakdancing. What do girls do with their time? They seem to just mill about, talking. We assume they're talking about how "immature" we are. That seems to be their main thing at the moment.

Of course, it's always possible that they're not talking about us at all.

Every family has a last family holiday, assuming there was ever a first one. It's the one that everyone enjoys so much they quietly agree never to do it again. I don't mean the odd break or visit. I mean the Full English tri-generational package piss-up in Spain. I was twelve in the summer of 1985 and this was my third and final experience of it. Of watching my beloved elders becoming maudlin and argumentative in a swimming pool context from Happy Hour till bedtime. It had never bothered me before, but it was much worse this year and with good reason. Nan had just died of cancer, aged sixty-four.

The phrase "It's what she would have wanted" really comes into its own when you've got a foreign holiday booked and then someone in the party dies. It was perfectly true of course — Nan was a lot of fun and would have been very cross at the idea of Dada, Trudy and Mum cancelling a holiday and wasting all that money just because they were grieving for their wife/sister/mother. So we're going anyway. We're being *tactful*.

Derek stayed at home because Derek didn't do holidays. Mark stayed at home because, while Mum was out of the country, he was secretly planning to buy a Ford Capri that he couldn't quite afford. Andrew came along and was nice to me for two weeks, which I found unnerving.

I wasn't invited to Nan's funeral. Bit weird? Twelve is plenty old enough for your grandmother's funeral, isn't it? I suppose we're not very "death-literate" in our family. Twelve is old enough to watch *Only Fools and Horses* in a small living room with four people smoking in it. And it's old enough to be constantly encouraged to climb trees and canoe off the end of Niagara Falls for the sake of some fresh air. But we protect twelve-year-olds from funerals. Or at least, I was protected from this one.

I was at John and Trudy's house on that Saturday morning for the arrivals. Everyone looked amazingly smart. We have extended family from Boston and Cambridge and the house became quite full. I sat on a chair, next to the door to the kitchen and my "uncles" (whether they were actual uncles, great-uncles, or just friends of my parents or grandparents) all did a strange thing when they walked past me.

To start with, they would be talking to each other and the various wives, looking serious and worried, like grown-ups. But on seeing me, the sad face would become a smile. And then, on their way to the kitchen, they would pretend to beat me up. One after another, for about half an hour, my male relations walked past me, smiling broadly and doing an "Ooh, I'm going to give you such a punch in the gob!" mime. The style varied from a fist patted against a flat palm with a nodding "you're going to get it", to a left hook millimetres from my nose. Uncle Alec did a fully committed, slow-motion head-butt. It took ages.

I sat there, sipping lemonade. They were being nice. God knows, I didn't want them to hug me, for aftershave reasons alone. But all the pretend thumping and crushing of the child on the day of his grandmother's funeral did strike me as a bit peculiar.

I had my tea at Roger's house. His mum, Sue, dished up the beans on toast and said, "I'm sorry about y'Nan, Robert. I didn't even know she was poorly." Roger was respectful of the moment. We played on his VIC-20 and then sat until it was dark in his dad's car, hailing for intelligent life through the CB radio. Roger's dad was a truck driver and Rog had picked up some of the gist. He set the channel to 14 and we took it in turns to invoke the CB mantra: "One-Four for a copy . . . One-Four for a copy . . ." Eventually, we got a copy.

126

"How many candles y'burnin'?" came the friendly question. Roger looked at me. I whispered, "He must mean birthday cakes. He's asking how old we are." Roger nodded and responded. "Copy that, amigo. Er, we're twelv — we're burnin' twelve candles . . . mate." Our CB amigo chatted with us for a couple of minutes and then signed off. It was a bit of an anti-climax, to be honest. I was mainly disappointed that the man had an accent as if he lived next door. We had both been hoping for some whacky American from *The Cannonball Run* or at least *B. J. and the Bear*. Anyway, it was good being with Roger on a night like this.

Roger caught the mood and turned on the overhead light. He took out his pocket penknife and offered to make a blood pact about staying friends for ever. I looked at the affectionately offered cutting implement and didn't fancy it. Instead, I told him earnestly that he was my best friend. He found that a bit embarrassing because obviously drawing blood would have been more fun, but cometh the hour, cometh the boy and he said: "You're m'best mate too, Rob. I'll not let you down."

He never did.

If you're determined to get to Costa Dorada but haven't really got enough money, then one solution is to go by coach. You just hop on at Lincoln and a simple nineteen hours later, you arrive at your Spanish beach resort refreshed and in the middle of the night — the second night.

To be fair, the first four hours were the worst. That got us to Dover. To lighten the load, one of the massively overweight drivers who didn't happen to be driving at the time put on a video.

He taps his mic. "Right then, ladies and gentlemen, boys and girls — it's time for our family film presentation. It's called *Who Dares Wins* and I hope you enjoy it!" He takes the VHS tape out of its box and then, as if the thought has occurred to him for the first time, says, "Obviously it's quite violent. And, to be fair, there's some pretty strong language." He looks for a bit longer at the back of the cassette box. "But I don't think there's much in the way of sex, as I recall . . . Although actually . . . yeah. Anyway, as I say there's some fairly strong language so . . . if . . . anyway it's bloody good."

The hero of *Who Dares Wins* is, of course, played by the actor Lewis Collins, who had made his name in *The Professionals* by driving through walls of empty cardboard boxes in a Ford Capri. On the occasions I was allowed to stay up and watch, I thought it was ace, fab and brill.

A digression. In a London pub in 1998, I'm describing how we played *The Professionals* at primary school. All join up for playing . . . The Professionals! NO GIRLS!

I say, "I was always Cowley. Roger Baxter and Matthew Tellis took it in turns to be Bodie or Doyle."

David Mitchell puts his pint down in surprise. "How come you always got to be Cowley?"

"Well, they — hang on, what do you mean, *got* to be Cowley. No one wanted to be Cowley."

"What are you talking about? Cowley was in charge. Cowley gave the orders."

"What, so at your school everyone wanted to be Cowley?"

"Yes."

"Seriously? You were all *queuing up* to be Cowley?"

"I don't remember a queue, but yes, essentially." He takes the drag on a cigarette I just gave him. "To be fair," he says, "we were quite weird, our little gang. It's probably more normal to want to be the macho men."

David will spend his twenties being the only example I've ever known of a successful social smoker. He bums a couple of fags in the pub (good luck with that, American readers) and then doesn't dream of having another the following morning. I don't mind this because every now and again he'll turn up with a pack of ten and hand them over as a contribution to an ongoing tobacco kitty where I keep the change. I mean the spare cigarettes, rather than the mutation of a cancer cell, although at some point I suppose I'll be keeping that change too.

We're fishing for ideas. We've just landed one of our first proper writing jobs, coming up with sketches for *Armstrong & Miller* on Channel 4. We go to the pub, get a couple of notebooks out and start talking. The aim isn't especially to make each other laugh because that would make us feel self-conscious. It's more that we just chat while keeping half an eye out for a funny idea creeping up on us. They always do — they wander in from the edges of sight. If you look straight at them, they disappear, like faint stars. You wait until they're in plain view before stealthily picking up a pen. Then you've got them.

Talking about TV is typical of us on these occasions, but talking about school is not — we're in our mid-twenties and too young to find children interesting.

On the coach, Lewis Collins has done his usual thing of carrying out a series of extra-judicial killings with varying degrees of regret. He's momentarily quite sad when his terrorist girlfriend gets mown down in a hail of SAS bullets, but quickly pulls himself together and shoots everyone else.

I'm still thinking about how exciting it all was when a boy approaches with a mini chessboard and asks if I want to play. Derek has taught me the rules and he even let me win our first game. So I might as well.

The boy, Gareth, sets up the tiny pieces and asks me to go first. I advance a middle Pawn two spaces as per the classic opening moves I've seen on *Play Chess* in the holiday mornings. Gareth responds by jumping his Queen into the space the Pawn just vacated. "Check," he announces.[1]

Right. I wonder if I should say something. His Queen is adjacent to mine so I take it. He frowns at this for a second but then advances one of his Pawns four spaces forwards and one to the left. "Check."

---

[1] If you're unfamiliar with the rules of chess, all you need to know is — so was Gareth.

I see. Shall I join in with the Chess Moves From Planet Git? Would that be fun or would it make the whole thing even more meaningless than it already is? I stick to the script and move a knight, correctly. Gareth is quick to object. "You can't do that, you're in check."

Christ, OK. I take his stupid Pawn with a madly illegal move of my Queen's Bishop. He doesn't seem to mind that. He just parachutes in another random piece next to my King. "Check."

This is making me so unhappy I want to cry. What am I supposed to do with this pillock? Talk to him? Engage with him? Teach him the rules?

It's out of the question.

I make a show of looking at the board very closely. "It's mate, I think. Yep, it's checkmate. Well done."

Gareth is concerned. "Are you sure? I mean, you could always . . ." His hand starts moving towards my King and he's clearly about to suggest something demented.

"Nope! That's checkmate all right. Well done."

"OK, shall we play again?"

"No. Well done." I can't think of anything to add to this, so I just repeat "no" and shake my head at him. He abruptly packs up his chess set and goes away.

I get the feeling I could have handled that better but don't know how.

Many years later I'll be talking to a friend (not David, but another comedy writer) who puzzlingly seems to have moved from one terraced house to an almost identical one in a slightly different part of Brixton. He tells me that, in the last place, the neighbours started using his bins for their overflowing rubbish. I ask him, "What did you say?"

"Oh God, I didn't say anything," he replies. "No, we decided it would be easier to move house."

This makes me laugh for about three minutes. I know he's joking, but mainly I'm enjoying the idea that I'm not the only grown man who will go to incredible lengths to avoid an awkward conversation. Especially with a rule-breaker. Yes, I'm looking at you, Gareth.

But I'm also looking at me. Getting rid of Gareth won't be the last time I resort to low cunning because I haven't got the social skills for anything better.

It's not quite the same thing as good manners. You have to improvise. You have to work out at lightning speed how best to respect the person with whom you're sharing this bit of space. There are no fixed rules to this game — let's call it Human Interaction — but you always sense when someone else is cheating. The grown-up thing to do is to address it. Like the centimetre of overhang on a standard two-ply loo roll that got itself out of sync — it's a situation that won't resolve itself.

But some of us don't want to resolve it. Some of us just tear the ragged bits of loo roll off and think, "Someone else will deal with Gareth." Even when other people don't cheat, there's always the option of walking away. People who do a lot of walking away from Human Interaction are called "unsociable" or sometimes "writers".

132

Girls, I think, are told from an early age that they need to be good at Human Interaction. Boys, less so. Those of us who catch up (and I'm the man who will always nod a friendly hello to fellow parents at the school gates before immediately getting my phone out: friendly hello = manners, phone = still shit at Human Interaction) only stand a chance of doing so with the addition of an ace card: confidence.

You might think I had a massive advantage when it came to acquiring confidence because, as a white boy in a rich, free western country, I was under the heavy impression that this was my world and I was the default human. But that's not confidence, that's just a wrong-headed sense of entitlement.

When it comes to the gaining of genuine confidence and genuine self-respect, even the supposed default humans need a surprising amount of encouragement. What they need, like everyone else, is a) one thing to be good at, and b) one person to notice.

With me, that starts at school.

It starts with Mrs Slater.

"Robert, I don't suppose you could be persuaded to step into the breach. It's about as close to a National Emergency as we're ever going to face."

It's 1986, the end of my second year at QEGS and I'm thirteen. Mrs Slater is being a bit twinkly, but the situation is serious.

One of QEGS' battier traditions is the Eisteddfod, where the three forms that make up the second year compete with each other in drama, music and gymnastics in front of an audience of parents.

For our form, Pete Garvey — he of the secret P. G. Wodehouse joy and the inventing of Ball Death — has written a ten-minute comic play set in the year 2000, in which we all meet for a class reunion. He has given himself the main part of narrator, who has also had huge material success: he arrives at the reunion in a Daimler driven by his chauffeur, Webb. Unfortunately for Garvey, and with far-reaching implications for Webb, Pete goes to hospital with appendicitis two days before the performance.[1]

Mrs Slater is looking at me, expectantly.

Jesus. What would Han Solo do? Screw that, what would Jesus do? The idea of stepping into the main part is absurd.

Up until now, the biggest part I've had to cope with was a one-liner in a Coningsby Junior School nativity. As King Herod's Captain of the Guard, I'd made an entrance by stepping on my own cloak, choking and then recovering just enough to say, "Someone threatens you, my lord?" I was on stage for about eighty seconds and hated every one of them. Acting was embarrassing. Which was a pity, because I would love to be an actor. Ideally I would be an actor without having to do any acting.

But something has happened while we've been rehearsing Pete's play during Mrs Slater's English lessons, something quite unexpected.

---

[1] Pete survived, in case you were worried.

I love it.

The character of Webb is a chauffeur, but also a kind of butler. Pete's encounter with *Right Ho, Jeeves* has made an impression and although most of my lines are either "Indeed, sir" or "No doubt, sir", I think I have a good idea about how to say them. It will be a few years until Stephen Fry gives his Jeeves masterclass on ITV, and I haven't seen any of the films. But I did borrow the book the moment Pete put it back on the shelf.

Some of it really makes me laugh. And I get the idea that Jeeves is the straight man. Like Tommy Cannon from Cannon and Ball. Probably a bit more posh. And clever. Something like that.

So in the rehearsals I play Jeeves like a posh Tommy Cannon and Form 2S starts to laugh. I stand with my arms forming a rigid V-shape, ending in folded hands in front of my balls — à la Cannon — and start to relish the moments when everyone expects me to say, "Indeed, sir." It becomes obvious that once you've got their attention, you can wait. And you can make them wait with you. In fact, the longer you make them wait for "Indeed, sir", the bigger the laugh will be when you say it. Confusingly, if you wait too long, they won't laugh at all. So I start to listen to the audience. I start to time it.

The timing depends on what I hear from them, but also what I hear from a little internal clock that I seem to have. It's always been there somehow, but it's only been useful around best friends. Roger, I suspect, likes me because I'm funny.

Now I'm being funny in front of people I've only known for a year. Presumably, on the night of the show, I'll have to be funny in front of people I've never met. That's quite a leap, but manageable as long as I only have to say, "Indeed, sir."

But the main part! That's massive! Mrs Slater doesn't look like she's about to offer it to anyone else. I think to myself that I'm being *told* to do it. Well, that's fine then because I didn't have a choice. If I'm a disaster it will be her fault.

I shrug and say, "Yeah, all right."

Form 2S win the Eisteddfod.

There's a dodgy moment in the gymnastics round because Zelda Linseed has athlete's foot so has to scale the climbing rope in trainers rather than the regulation bare feet. This means the judges can't tell if she's pointing her toes, although she swears indignantly that she is.

The drama round, though — we're a smash hit. Pete's narrator is surrounded by idiots and I play him as an exasperated Basil Fawlty. When I say "play him as" I mean "do an impression of". But the laughter comes in all the right places. Mum is standing at the back, smiling nervously and giving me a discreet thumbs-up.

There's some post-show milling around with coffee and people are looking at me in a way I've never seen before. It's weird enough that they're looking at me at all.

★　★　★

That night we're all in the living room watching the BBC sitcom *No Place Like Home* starring William Gaunt and a young Martin Clunes.

What would it take, I wonder, to be allowed to do that as your job? It really doesn't look that hard. Does it look easy because they're very good at it? Or is it just easy? They don't seem to be doing it as well as John Cleese does it. Do they know? Do they go to the pub afterwards and say, "Well, we can't all be John Cleese." Or is it because of the script? Would the young, tall one with the big ears be as funny as John Cleese if he had some funnier lines? Maybe he would. This is serious. I lean in and look hard for something that Mr Clunes is doing that I couldn't do just as well. Hmm, for a start he's a grown-up who looks like he ought to be on TV rather than a Lincolnshire schoolboy who obviously mustn't. And he's very clear and confident. And he talks with that accent from the south of England that so many funny people on TV have. He just looks like he belongs there. How did he do that?

Suddenly I have a name for that feeling I had in Dad's car on the way back from the *Flashdance* fireworks. That feeling, the one that made me blush, was an overwhelming desire to be famous.

Because that would help, wouldn't it? Dads don't hit famous children, right? They don't ignore them either. They take them fishing. You can be quiet when you're famous, but people can't ignore you. Not really. They look at you the way they did tonight after the Eisteddfod. It's a look I could get used to. When you're famous, people look at you like they're trying to figure something out.

And the other boys. Imagine doing something so wildly beyond the reach of the other boys. What would I care for their wasps and nettles and football and swimming and maths and fighting and science and shandy if I could do this one thing, this one thing that none of them could do?

So I'll be famous. And funny writing and acting is what I'll be famous for. That will help because famous people are safe. Famous people don't have problems. And they can probably have the radiator on as often as they like. And maybe girls like them.

That's decided, then. Unfortunately, almost the same week that I start to wonder if being funny can be used to impress girls, my body starts to make a chaotic, head-swivelling, nipple-swelling reply. Puberty rushes in like a pyrophobic arsonist, chucking petrol bombs in all directions while screaming "WHAT ARE YOU DOING ABOUT THE FUCKING FIRE!?"

The first girl I ever danced with was Cathy Shepherd. Her dad was landlord of a small local pub and he closed it one night for her thirteenth birthday party. Most of 2S were there. Cathy's older sister, Chrissy, was left to supervise.

Before the dancing came Spin the Bottle. I didn't think it was possible to be this bored and this embarrassed at the same time. There was no *The X Factor* in the twentieth century, so there was nothing in the culture to prepare me for this level of tedium and mortification.

Actually, I tell a lie. There was the night that my brother Mark's friend Larry was made to do some disco dancing in the bungalow kitchen on a Friday night. Larry had come round, ready to go out. Mark mentioned that Larry had just won an inter-county disco competition and encouraged him to do some disco dancing right there in the kitchen. It's not big, our kitchen. Larry tried to demur, but "no" is not a word for Fonzies and Mark was already at the record player, putting on "Stool Pigeon" by Kid Creole and the Coconuts. Mum was delighted, but just needed a moment and asked Larry to move aside so she could get to the washing machine and put some whites on. This accomplished, Mum sat down two feet away to enjoy the performance. So that's me, Mum, Mark, Andrew and Derek sitting around the table looking at Larry. Larry uncertainly retook his position in front of the slowly rotating laundry as Kid Creole's trumpets kicked in.

I see from a quick search that "Stool Pigeon" is three minutes and twenty-five seconds long. I think for Larry it lasted about a week. By Tuesday, Mark was supportively turning the volume up on the record player. On Wednesday Mum briefly tried clapping to the beat in case that might help. Towards the weekend, Larry said, not for the first or last time, that there wasn't really room to do a proper spin. On it went. Sometimes, you just have to see these things through. For Larry to give up, or for anyone to put Larry out of his obvious misery, would be like leaving the pub with an unfinished pint on the table. It could be a male thing, a working-class thing, a British thing or a human thing. But sometimes you're in the middle of a big mistake and you just keep going for the allotted time.

So: Spin the Bottle.

Almost everyone sits in a circle on the floor, watching the neck of the bottle go round like a roulette wheel in the Glum Casino of Enforced Snogging. It goes without saying that the snogging will be strictly heterosexual. Sure, you might have to kiss someone you don't want to kiss, but there are limits.

The only person I want to kiss, and to kiss her would make my decade, is Tiffany Rampling, friend of Zelda and the younger sister of my future dream-girl Tess Rampling. Yes, that's right. One day I will adore Tess and get nowhere. But only after two years of getting nowhere with her sister Tiffany.

Tiffany, of course, is not playing Spin the Bottle. She and Zelda are sitting aloof on bar stools, watching the game and shaking their heads in disgust.

I go to the bar to help myself to another Coke. Tiffany re-crosses her legs and says, "Why are you playing that immature game, Webb? Why don't you just get off with whoever you want to get off with?"

Tiffany, who would rather eat mud than kiss a boy her own age, is not making an offer here. I mumble something like "It's not that simple" and return to the game. Tiffany and Zelda exchange world-weary glancces.

Later, the supervising Chrissy puts on some music and says to me conspiratorially, "Cathy wants a smooch with you, Robert. Shall I say yes?" I look over to a corner where the birthday girl is sitting watching her sister's proposal with a mixture of hope and utter mortification. I do my Han Solo shrug and say, "Sure." Chrissy excitedly beckons Cathy, who now crosses the room literally dragging her feet and rolling her eyes at the ceiling so violently I think she's going to break her neck. "Sorry about my sister," she says, "she's always embarrassing me like this." She really is embarrassed, but she also looks like she's pleased this is happening — which is fine by me. I quite like Cathy. Although not as much as I like . . . I glance over to where Tiffany and Zelda were perched. They've disappeared somewhere.

"Now then," says Chrissy, who is having a great time with this. "Have either of you had a slow dance before?" We both shake our heads.

"Right. Well, Robert, you put your hands here," Chrissy efficiently puts my hands on Cathy's waist. "And Cathy, obviously you put your hands around Robert's neck." Cathy does a face like this is the stupidest idea she's ever heard and promptly does exactly as suggested.

I've never been in such close proximity to a girl. She smells lovely.

"And now you just sway to the music!" concludes Chrissy. There are a few other "couples" now and it doesn't feel so bad. Not bad at all, in fact.

The last track has just ended and we hear the introduction to "Feed the World" by Band Aid.

The trouble with "Feed the World" by Band Aid as a "smooch" track, however, is that even if you ignore the

141

romantically underperforming topic of starving children, you are nevertheless quickly into an anthemic knees-up while clinging on to a girl and solemnly rocking from side to side. Neither of us has the confidence to stop so we just do this for the whole song. At the end, we let go of each other with relief. I feel like I ought to bow or something, but instead, and with a novel rush of courage, I give her a kiss on the cheek. She looks around the room, nodding and smiling. "Yeah, thanks," she says.

Tiffany and Zelda burst back in and fall over, laughing hysterically. Oh, so that's where they were. They'd pinched a bottle of wine and got shit-faced in the car park.

One of the people I'd been glad to see before Nan's funeral was Auntie Dot. Nan and Trudy's sister, Dot was another great-aunt and a lively one. She lived on the outskirts of Cambridge and Tru would sometimes take me for a visit at half-term.

It's a council house on an estate just off Newmarket Road. On previous visits I had been with Dot and Tru to Bingo, where I would get chips and join in.

This time, I've decided that I'm too old to be hanging out in public with a pair of old ladies. Or at least, that's what I think I'm supposed to feel, so that's what I choose to do. Trudy asks if I'd like to come out to Bingo and, for the first time, I say that I'd rather stay in and read. It's bullshit — I'd *love* to go out with them to Bingo. I register the disappointment that flickers across Tru's face, but then she smiles. She's seen this all before. Still, I get the feeling that what happened to Mark and Andrew wasn't supposed to happen to Robert.

But what *did* happen to Mark and Andrew? For all I know, aged thirteen, either one of them would have enjoyed hanging out with the old ladies and would have been cool enough to say, "Nice one, Tru and Dot! I am a bit partial to a spot of Bingo!"

I like to think so. But anyway, I'm nowhere near that cool. I have to go with the flow. And the flow is: stop doing stuff you like when it becomes somehow inappropriate. It's not so much Act Your Age as Act Your Gender. The two rules are related — it's as if a "boy" can amateurishly muddle through, but a "teenage boy" has to turn pro.

To be fair, I'm perfectly happy staying home alone with my current *Doctor Who* book.

I'm in my bedroom, reading in bed. It's a pity that the Doctor's companion, Nyssa, has chosen to part company with the Doctor, staying behind to help with the space leper colony. But then, I think, as I remove the last of my clothing, that's Nyssa for you: beautiful and kind-hearted. I put the book to one side, and think about beautiful Nyssa and how, on the space leper colony, she wouldn't have anyone to help her if, for example, she somehow got a splinter in her vagina.

I'm not sure how often this happens, but I'm pretty sure that if Nyssa had a splinter in her vagina, I'd be a good person to call. I'd probably be one of an elite squadron of teen space-doctors who happened to be passing through.

Nyssa and I would probably get chatting in the TV lounge of the space leper colony and, relieved to be talking to someone who didn't have space-leprosy for a change, she would confide her embarrassing predicament. After I had reassured her about my discretion and experience, she would gratefully allow me to extract the splinter with infinite care and precision using my teeth. At that point, and recalling the diagrams I'd learnt at the Elite Teen-Doctor Space Academy, I'd probably provide the customary aftercare service of licking her clitoris with nerve-electrifying skill and artistry. And then Nyssa, what with being such a kind girl, would probably teach me how to wank properly the way other boys probably do and I would . . . HANG ON, SOMETHING VERY ALARMING BUT FANTASTIC IS HAPPENING! I SHOULD STOP THIS — IT'S MAKING ME GOING TO DO A WEE! NO! IT'S NOT A WEE, IT'S SOMETHING ELSE! IT'S . . . OH MY FUCKING LORD!

And thus it was that the would-be Doogie Howser MD of space cunnilingus had his first orgasm.

I dart to the bathroom and try to do a wee in case somehow that was just a wee gone wrong. But no, I don't need a wee. Anyway, what has just spurted out of the end of my cock is of a colour and consistency quite apart from any world of wee. Bloody hell. OK, well at least it all works. Is that how it's supposed to work? I mean, it was pretty fucking alarming. My penis is painfully sensitive now and I wonder if I've damaged it. No, that's probably how it's meant to happen. That was a wank.

144

There's a full-length mirror in the bathroom and I turn to see myself in it, still naked and more than a touch flushed. Was God watching? Was Nan watching? Holy crap! No, surely they've got better things to do. Should I feel ashamed? I do feel ashamed and don't want to see myself like this. I streak back to the bedroom and get dressed.

Still, that was amazing. That was bloody amazing. Who can I tell about this amazingness? Not Tiffany or Zelda, obviously. Certainly not my brothers. Not Pete Garvey, who's probably been doing it for years.

Oh yeah . . . Will, maybe. It's the kind of thing I could tell Will.

CHAPTER
SIX

Boys Don't Fall in Love
(with other boys)

"You're born naked and the rest is drag."

RuPaul

Roger and I fell out over Bros. That's the pop group, Bros. Younger readers may be interested to learn that you pronounce it "bross".

Childhood friendships often begin with convenience — the same classroom, the same street — but then, if you're lucky, the best of them evolve into something that feels an awful lot like love. I never had a crush on Roger — not compared to what was to follow — but if you held a gun to my head I would admit to the plain fact that I loved him. Obviously, it would take a gun to extract such an admission from either of us. Boys do Pals, we don't do Love. But the attachment was strong enough for the feelings of separation to be familiar to anyone who has ever caught a whiff of a love affair on the turn. In this case, there was no great betrayal, no grand and defining point of difference — just a gradual moving apart. Three years had gone by since Roger had suggested we become blood brothers, and here in 1988 it was a pair of actual brothers, those Goss twins, who provided a laser-like focus for the abundant truth, like the magnifying glass the two of us would use to burn holes in dock leaves. The sun was as bright as ever now we were fifteen years old, but the light was more complicated. There were more colours.

"'When Will I Be Famous' is a complete piece of shit," I announce one morning after Roger has joined me on the bus. There's already been some tension over the bus ride to school. Roger had started to resent that I always had my bag on the seat when he got on, forcing him to put his own on the floor. In fact, on PE or Games days, he would be sharing a seat with me and my *two* bags. He had stored up that bad feeling until the morning came when he had decided to Bloody Well Say Something. I saw that he had a point and kept my own bags on the floor from then on.

But clearly, he didn't see the bag issue as some quirk in an otherwise functioning bus ride. Ominously, it was *bloody typical*. And by the time things become *bloody typical* in a relationship, you either work hard to fix it or you accept it's time to move on. I didn't know how I was supposed to fix it with Roger and I wasn't sure I wanted to. He'd obviously concluded that I was a snooty bastard. My reaction was to get even snootier.

"They look like plastic Aryan dolls," I continue. "They can't sing, they think they're Michael Jackson but they can't dance because they're so fucking fat. The drummer looks like the other two keep him in their Aryan dungeon. They're dicks. Talentless, Nazi dicks."

There was a time when this sort of thing would have impressed Roger, but he'd had enough. As far as he was concerned, this was just Webb being a ponce again. He says evenly, "I just think it's a good, fun song. It's just a pop song."

"Pop songs don't have to be so bloody mindless."

"OK, so what do you like at the moment, then?"

"I dunno." This is an annoyingly reasonable question. I say, mainly because I have decided that I am Strongly Against Apartheid, "'Ideal World' by The Christians!"

Roger snorts. "Really!? You think 'Ideal World' is better than 'When Will I Be Famous'?"

"Yeah, I do!"

Roger starts doing a tunelessly sarcastic impression. "Ooh, in an Ideal World, everything would be fucking suuuuper . . . in an Ideal World, being black is fiiiine! Ooooh, why can't people just be niiiice? Let's all be niiiice!"

Roger was right. "Ideal World" has an agreeable melody, but if I wanted to show off my anti-racist credentials, by 1988 I could have picked half a dozen better songs. Notably, "Gimme Hope, Jo'anna", "Sun City" and, of course, "Freeeeeeeeeyeee Nelson Mandela'!" (I draw the line at "Biko" by Peter Gabriel because Peter Gabriel is very annoying.)

Anyway, although I am now happy to admit that "When Will I Be Famous" is a vital and compelling teen anthem, I had my reasons for loathing that song in particular and Bros in general. All the girls in my year wanted to shag Bros. And none of them showed the first sign of wanting to shag me. I was aware that they were not actually *allowed* to shag me: I just thought it would be nice if one or two of them indicated that this was a pity. It was basically acceptable to be a male virgin at fifteen, but I'd become aware of an impatient mental stopwatch and the ticking got louder by the month.

And, oh good, here come Bros on *Top of the Pops*, singing the equally infuriating "Drop the Boy".

"I'm a man, he says!" I almost yell at mum. "Only a boy would need to say so." It's a line I've been waiting to try out for days.

Mum shifts in her chair. I'm doing my GCSEs and I'm in Set One for English and — less explicably — Maths. She likes it that I now come near the top in all the school exams. In the last few years I've gone from confirmed "borderline" to confirmed "smartypants". I worry less about that now. There are certain times and places where I don't have to dissemble and apologise. Alone with Mum is where the silent seven-year-old yelled "Sailing" at the top of his voice, and it's where the fifteen-year-old shows off his new superpower of being able to deconstruct the lyrics of Bros while really overdoing it with the "air quotes". I apologise for what follows.

"Did he actually just say that if whoever it is — his unnamed oppressor — 'drops the boy', that he will literally be 'jumping for joy'? Did he say that?"

I don't wait for an answer.

"Because if he is indeed 'a man' as he keeps *insisting* ('yes I am'), then he'll be the first man I've ever seen who goes around jumping for joy. Do you see much of that? When was the last time Derek jumped for joy?"

The thought of Derek attempting any such thing makes Mum giggle. She says, looking at Matt Goss, "I think he's trying too hard. He looks like he needs a holiday."

This makes no sense to me. I was talking about something else. What? Holiday? What holiday? Any minute now she's going to start going on about how all music was better in the sixties.

"I mean, they're not exactly The Beatles, are they?" she says, cheerfully.

I scowl at the TV and say in a slow pantomime of controlled rage, "Not everyone . . . can be . . . the sodding . . . Beatles."

She chuckles to herself. "Soz, Rob," she teases.

I blink at her queenily and then do a reluctant grin.

Reader, be honest: you liked me better when I didn't say anything, didn't you? Teenagers can be awful. I know I had a big suitcase of awful and I was raring to share it out.

It is, of course, the kind of awful a mother can love. I wonder if getting on well with your mum would, in the opinion of Matt Goss, make me a boy or a man? Whatever his view, I would stridently claim the opposite. At this point, Matt Goss could sing about how manly it is to wear stone-washed jeans and I would immediately take mine off and throw them in a skip.

150

It was bad enough when I realised I had the same birthday as Matt and Luke Goss. But now I see we have something else in common. I want to be famous too. And I've just noticed that wanting to be famous just for the sake of becoming famous makes you look like a massive twat. I'll have to come up with a better reason. I'll have to start saying that fame is an unfortunate side effect of my, I dunno . . . art.

So what is it about this "Will"?

I just like his attitude. He's in my year at school. He's about the same height and build as me. His hair is darker and he can grow it longer. I've lost my angelic curls, thank God, but if I try to grow my hair long it just gets frizzy and big, like a blond Afro. Will can get his to just wavily flop either side of his thin-framed glasses. He's skinny like me but his collarbones travel just that little bit further before they reach his shoulders, his muscles are slightly more defined, his knees just a bit less knobbly, his legs . . . But let's not get ahead of ourselves. I was talking about his attitude, right? Not his body. It will be instructive that, when introducing you to my new Best Friend, the first thing I want to do is undress him. Probably because I would spend the next five years trying to do exactly that.

He's cool. Among his peers at school, he is the first to stop wearing a digital watch. He is also the first to grow his hair long and the first to cut it very short. The same goes for white socks, or liking U2: first in, first out. He isn't the first to need a shave, but he does make sideburns look good, and ditches Paco Rabanne for

151

Fahrenheit before the rest of us have found a paisley shirt that doesn't look too "gay". By which time his own paisley days will be long gone.

His clothes just *fit*. It's mesmerising. They cling and swing around him like adoring fans.

Still, as I say, I just like his attitude. Also, his legs.

Finally, in GCSE Media Studies, I'm sharing a classroom with Will. I chose this much-maligned subject partly because I believed the bad press: I thought it would be easy, or, in the Lincs teen parlance of the day, a massive doss.

It isn't — at least not to begin with. We write a series of dry essays about ownership and control, news values and BBC Charter renewal in the impossibly distant year of 1996.

But soon, it's time to start working on a practical project — making a documentary with a borrowed camera — and the massive "dossing about" begins in earnest. Will, Pete, Matt, Russell and I are going to make a twenty-minute video with the snappy title *Representation — the Damaging Effects of Stereotyping*. We tell Mrs Slater that we need to "rehearse" and then essentially disappear to fuck around for an hour — sneaking into town to buy chips; taking it in turns on Pete's motorbike; sometimes regressing entirely and playing tig[1] in the Sports Hall with the lights turned off.

---

[1] Also known as "tiggy", "tag" or "it". We called it "tig".

Pete Garvey will be the main presenter, leaving me free to star in what will essentially be a bunch of sketches about stereotyping on TV — parodies of sexist game shows, depictions of teenagers as thugs on the TV news, ads for soap powder featuring dads instead of mums etc. Oh yes.

I am now achingly right-on and loving it. Lincolnshire in the 1980s, apart from Lincoln itself, is about as true-blue as it gets and I have decided that I am Vehemently in Opposition to This. The influences aren't hard to make out. The SDP/Liberal Alliance poster in the window of Mr and Mrs Slater's Horncastle home in 1987 has not gone unnoticed. Neither has the fact that Mum is a Labour supporter or that almost everyone who makes me laugh on TV is some kind of leftie. Politics is suddenly an area where secret hopes (university, being a funny actor) neatly overlap with a general wish to side with Mum against the Men. The facts may be that the Parliamentary Labour Party is composed almost entirely of men and that Mrs Thatcher is a woman, but these facts are to be overlooked for the time being. Where Mum agrees with Mrs Slater and both agree with Stephen Fry and Victoria Wood . . . and where all four disagree with Derek, Dad, Norman Tebbit and Bernard Manning . . . well, let's just say it will be a long time before I feel the need to read a manifesto. I'm Labour. That's it.

I appoint myself writer and director of the documentary and nobody seems to argue. By now, I've written the sequel to Pete's "Class Reunion" and Form 3S has staged both in morning assemblies. In Form 4S,

I've put on three end-of-term revues (starting with a "sponsored sketch" for the first Comic Relief) and have recruited Will in the key straight-man parts. For example, Will does a pleasingly smarmy impression of Education Secretary Kenneth Baker (whom I devastatingly rename Kenneth Faker — oomph! Eat that, Tories!) and I play a contemptuous interviewer which owes a great deal to other people's impressions of Jeremy Paxman.

Sometimes when I make Will laugh, he throws his head back and I stare at the symmetry of his jaw. I like to think he doesn't notice.

I spend the hours between five and seven on my sixteenth birthday in the same way I usually would on a Thursday — stacking shelves at Gateway supermarket.

I'm hot. I'm a Gateway part-time superstar. I'm nearly as fast with a price gun as Tony, and he's been here for two years.[1]

I'm the youngest part-timer and like hanging out with the others, like Tony, who are doing their A levels. Not long from now, there will be a change of manager who starts recruiting exclusively from Gartree (the secondary modern school), and by the time I leave I'll be on my third manager and the other part-timers will call me the Professor because I've been caught reading

---

[1] A price gun was used to put little price stickers on goods, before the advent of checkout lasers. The idea that lasers would soon be in general use, but for something as dreary as grocery barcodes, would have upset me greatly at the time.

The Independent. But for now it's all friendly enough and I get £1.36 an hour. I like saving, but have splashed out on a Bush Midi System with a Vertical Loading CD Player from Mum's catalogue. So far, along with many cassettes, I have three CDs: *Revolutions* by Jean-Michel Jarre, *Kick* by INXS and *Lovesexy* by Prince. All read by a laser. Cool.

As a birthday present, a couple of the older grammar-school girls at Gateway give me a triple-pack of Mates condoms. "There you go, Robert," says Lucy, quite loudly as if complimenting a toddler on his first toilet-based crap, "now that you're sixteen, you'll be wanting these!" I muster what I imagine to be a knowing smirk, as if Han Solo is big enough to take another of Princess Leia's witty put-downs. The effect is probably undermined by the scarlet blush that I know has just filled every capillary of my scalp, face and penis. It's obviously the effect that Lucy was hoping for and she and her friend cackle delightedly and mince off with as much sass as an A-line overall will allow. I go back to pricing up Tate & Lyle with more than usual speed and diminishing accuracy.

The Han Solo thing is really not working for me any more. Lucy doesn't go out with Han Solo: she goes out with a spotty twenty-year-old called Dean who is often in fights and can play the bass line to "A Forest" by The Cure. Surely everyone but me can play the bass line to "A Forest" by The Cure.

Obviously, Will has a guitar and can play the bass line to "A Forest" by The Cure. He also has a girlfriend. It's 1989 and we're in our fifth year (year 11)

— she's in the year below. She's called Daisy and she's irresistibly bright, blonde, outgoing and fun. She respects her parents and Will is basically law-abiding — so I'm fairly sure they're going to wait until she's very nearly sixteen rather than definitely not quite sixteen, but I'm counting the hours with dread. Will is nothing if not frank, and I know that when he Does It With Daisy, I will be literally the third to know.

In fact, I'd quite like to be there. Not especially for the perv-value; more to experience the agony in real time and not have to hear the news from him. He's going to throw it away, like someone who just won the Pools but then immediately starts moaning that he can't get a sports car in exactly the right colour. How does he get to touch her at all? How does she get to touch him at all?

One morning before registration, he wanders round to Form 5S and announces that he's going to see Prince at Wembley. That is, he's going with Daisy, Daisy's dad and some of Daisy's friends. To London. To see Prince. Because he's going out with Daisy. I am not invited. Why would I be?

No wonder I yearn for a time long ago in a galaxy far away. This galaxy obviously hates me. I start writing poetry.

Reader, I suspect you think you want a piece of that, but trust me you don't. I've been as candid as my ego allows but I have to draw the line somewhere. No teenage poetry. Not even a Best Of. Not all bad art is entertaining: some of it is just upsetting. You might think, "I'll be the judge of that!" Respectfully, no you won't. You have literally paid me to be the judge of that. You were right to do so. We're agreed, then. Let's move on.

The other thing I was supposed to do on my sixteenth birthday, apart from knowing how to accept a box of condoms as a friendly gift instead of a sick taunt, was attend my audition for the TV talent show *Bob Says Opportunity Knocks*. It's a reboot of *Opportunity Knocks* in the same way that *Strictly Come Dancing* had its genesis in *Come Dancing* and Jeremy Kyle was originally conceived as a human being.

I post the *Radio Times* application form without the first idea of what I'm actually going to do. "Stand-up comedy," I vaguely announce to myself, having never written or performed a word of it in my life. Nobody does sketches on that show so, yes, I'd better just write a couple of minutes of stand-up comedy.

Erm, right. So, observational comedy. Things I've noticed. That's how it works, is it? You go around noticing things and then the audience go "Ah! Yes! We've noticed that too but didn't realise that we'd noticed. Good one! Good noticing!"

"OK, so . . . you know that thing when you're trying to get *Cresta Run* to load on a Spectrum and it doesn't work because you've set the volume on the tape too . . . No."

"OK, so . . . what's the point of GS? Who the hell needs GS? Sorry, GS stands for General Studies. It's, er, a subject that we . . . No."

"OK, so . . . you know that thing where you love and fancy your best friend so much that your heart aches like you've just slammed it in a door and you can't tell anyone and you want to tear up the sky? No? Just me, then."

Hmm, stand-up could be a problem. There are plenty that I like watching: Billy Connolly, Eddie Murphy, Victoria Wood, Robin Williams. But even then, I'd rather see Eddie Murphy in *Beverly Hills Cop* than doing stand-up. And I'd much rather watch Victoria Wood in *Acorn Antiques* with Julie Walters than out there all alone.

And none of it excites me the way sketches and sitcoms do. *Fawlty Towers*, *Rising Damp*, *The Young Ones*, *Blackadder*, *Brass*, *Absolutely*, *A Kick Up the Eighties*, *A Bit of Fry and Laurie*, *French and Saunders*, *Saturday Live*, anything involving Emma Thompson, Harry Enfield, John Cleese, Morwenna Banks, Ben Elton, Barry Humphries, Peter Cook, Clive James or Clive Anderson . . . just look at all those funny people being funny with each other! And where did they first meet, these funny people? I watch them being interviewed on *Wogan*, I scour the *Daily Mirror* at home and *The Listener* in the school library for clues. Well, quite a few of them met at university, it seems. And of those, a surprising number of them met at one university in particular. At some kind of comedy club called the Cambridge Footlights. So maybe . . .

But that's *nuts*. From our school, only the odd academic supernova like Tess Rampling goes to Cambridge. She's on for an A in A-level History, which everyone agrees is basically impossible, including her History teacher. The thought of applying to such a place makes me shudder. The imposture of it! Matron! Who the hell do I think I am!?

But the thought starts to turn in my head. Maybe I'll ask Mrs Slater about it — but only if no one else is listening.

And I don't go to the audition for *Opportunity Knocks*, whatever "Bob Says". I haven't got an act. Anyway it's in London: I might as well ask Mum to drive me to Greenland.

So stand-ups aren't my favourites. In fact, when it comes to solo performers, the person who most inspires me isn't even funny. He's called Michael Jackson.

Of course, it was not OK to like Michael Jackson. This was before the allegations of child abuse, you understand. At which point it was *really* not OK to like him. This is just when everyone thought he was a bit eccentric.

I think I was drawn to him partly because of his stolen childhood, which manifested as childishness. It turns out that some dads *do* hit famous children. This dad, Joe, was rehearsing The Jackson 5 with a belt in his hand. They didn't get to play, they only *played*. It turned them into consummate professionals with various forms of mental illness. With Michael, developing acne and having his voice gradually break in front of a global audience probably didn't help. And what he reminded me of in 1987, when he released *Bad*, was a painfully shy child playing at being tough. If you want to see a real-life Guy-Buy, have a look at that album cover. There he is with his silly costume and unlikely bravado. And that terrible fear very nearly hidden in make-believe.

There's a video hagiography of Jackson, modestly entitled *Michael Jackson: The Legend Continues*, which I watch at home now we have a VCR. Adoring fan that I've become, even I can see that 80 per cent of it is sectionable claptrap. Near-forgotten megastars like Sophia Loren pop up to say batty things like "Michael's like litmus paper — he always wants to learn." But the good thing about the video is the clip from the TV Special, *Motown 25*, where Jackson performs "Billie Jean" live on stage.

I've never seen a performance like it. I sit with a slack jaw, watching and rewinding, watching and rewinding. It's annoying because it's intercut with a choreographer telling you why you should love it and Katharine Hepburn informing you that Michael is good at dancing. But even this isn't enough to put me off. It's so beautiful. The way he moves around that stage, you'd have to be mad to take your eyes off him for an instant.

It's also a hell of a song, despite, or perhaps because of, the same weird boy/man disconnect — he's written a song about contested paternity when the last thing you can imagine Michael Jackson doing is having sex. I like it that he might be a virgin. I also have to admit that I like the way he's accidentally outperformed his older brothers and utterly eclipsed his violent father.

I freeze-frame the moonwalk. There's no advance-frame button on this machine, but I press Play and Pause as near to each other as I can. Ah! That's how he does it! The foot moving backwards has to be flat against the floor. He's taking his whole weight on the toe of the other foot. That must hurt. But maybe he's got the right shoes, with a hard toe and no grip on the sole, and he knows what kind of floor he's dancing on. Then he's swapping them over as smoothly as he can, which is very smoothly indeed.

And I find out something else too. Even though I think I've worked out how he does it, when I watch the whole thing again, it still looks like magic. Taking something to pieces doesn't spoil the whole when you put it back together. You can still love the effortlessness even when you've noticed the effort.

Not before time, I finally start reading books in the same way. Not just to enjoy what a writer did, but for the pleasure of figuring out how they did it. That and being able to come up with an essay about it are really the only things an English student does all day. Apart from the odd spliff. If you like it, then it doesn't feel like practice, and the more you practise the better you get. Eventually, what started as a general willingness, plus a load of work that didn't feel like work, acquires the name "talent".

Here it is then, the Golden Age of my teenage reading. Starting with the funny ones, of course — Wilde, Austen and Forster. And then Hardy, Lawrence, Conrad, George Eliot, Woolf and Orwell; the Romantic poets, especially Shelley; the war poets, especially Owen. The somehow wonderful misery of Philip Larkin. But hardly any plays except Shakespeare, which I read like crazy. Which I read (whisper it quietly) for fun.

I wonder if I could get good enough at English to help with the *Bob Says Opportunity Knocks* situation? So that I don't have to try the impossible shortcut, and instead try the impossible long way round. The Footlights way round.

I wait till no one else is in the Form room and ask Mrs Slater if it's ridiculous for me to think of Cambridge. "No, not ridiculous," she says quickly, and then, "We've certainly sent dimmer people than you there." This is encouraging. "Although," she adds thoughtfully, "not for quite a while."

Fine. I'll just have to read everything. That shouldn't be too hard. As long as there's nothing distracting going on.

CHAPTER
SEVEN

Boys Are Not Virgins

"You think you're sensitive, but you're not: your sensitivity only works for things that people do to you. Touchy and vain, yes, but not sensitive."
Dixon to Bertrand in Kingsley Amis, *Lucky Jim*

I have a baby sister.

Derek pops his head around my bedroom door while I'm energetically dancing to "Smooth Criminal". I turn it down, annoyed. His fag smoke is drifting into my room.

"Well, Robbie, y'know y'mum said y'might be getting a little brother or sister? Well, you are!"

I try to make my face look pleased. "Oh, good," I say, followed clumsily by "well done".

Derek nods, smiling, and disappears. I open a window and look at myself in the mirror to find out what I think. My face doesn't offer much encouragement.

So — not the youngest any more. Not the youngest. Mum will have a new priority. That's fine, I'm a teenager. I shouldn't mind. Why do I mind?

I do slightly mind. But Mum seems chuffed, especially when she finds out it's a girl. I spend her pregnancy trying to be nice. When she has to swap stretchy jogging bottoms for a full-blown maternity dress, she registers my ill-concealed alarm. "Mum's going to look a bit of a funny bugger for a while," she says to me. I try to wave it off with an awkward series of nods, grins and actual waves. She looks at me and I get that she gets it. Things are changing. She's out to reassure me and I'm out to reassure her. It gets done, more or less — we just can't quite do it with words.

It all happened when they got back home after her fortieth birthday party, she says.

Blimey. Show me a teenage boy who can contemplate such an event with equanimity and let's make him Prime Minister. I'm partly amazed because Mum and Derek spend so much time arguing. Mainly about the central heating. Warm as I think of her, she's always cold. Derek's big and doesn't feel it. And there's never enough money. So the arguments often centre on the boiler — they have done for years.

We knew people who were worse off and I never dreamt of questioning anything as normal as ice on the inside of windows. Where else was I going to practise my autograph? But Mum also had friends who were better off. And she *did* question it. She questioned it for England, especially on Sunday afternoons.

Sunday afternoons. Just . . . bloody hell.

I know I'm not the only one. In fact, saying that I dreaded Sunday afternoons as if this is interesting puts me in the same company as people who say "I just don't like hospitals".

Still, they sucked. When I was little, I spent every weekend at the Golf Club with all the plastic swords, Lego, *Tiswas* and sandwiches with the crusts cut off as I could handle. And Sunday teatime signalled the re-entry into the normal world: the smell of congealing gravy from a roast that Derek had complained about, and Mum in the middle of another outpouring of disappointment and gin. Derek would take his weekly ear-bashing like a man — in near total silence, occasionally mumbling passive-aggressive retorts over his shoulder as her voice pursued him from room to room. And there weren't many rooms.

"I don't know anyone else who has to put up with a twenty-year-old cooker," she would say. "I don't know anyone else who sits on a three-piece suite that's a thirty-year-old hand-me-down from her mum and dad. Other people have husbands who go out to work every day instead of sitting on their arse doing the bloody racing. Other people have husbands who don't mind turning on the bloody heating in the middle of bloody February, and who don't moan about my gravy every bloody day . . ." She could keep this up for a good hour. Everything she said was fair enough, but obviously I kept the hell out of the way.

Almost worse was the calm after the storm. He would retire to the living room to watch a Grand Prix; she would stay at the kitchen table, a hand nonchalantly supporting one side of her face, watching her cigarette smoke rise towards the yellowing ceiling and listening to Elkie Brooks singing songs about thwarted women. Jesus.

The stereotype of the Nagging Wife has proved very useful to those of us who are often the primary cause of all the nagging: the Useless Husband. Because these days, women who find their domestic situation deeply unsatisfactory won't just need to complain, they'll need to apologise for the complaining. Times change: the gin has given way to Pinot Grigio and nagging has gone post-modern.

When I was behaving like a useless arsehole of a husband and father, circa 2009–13, I would experience a temporary wave of guilt as, once again, I heard Abbie say something like, "I don't want to be some whining bitch but . . ." or "I don't want to go on like some fucking harpy but . . ." and I'd think to myself, "That's unlucky, that. It's really unfair that she has to negotiate the cliché as well as put up with me being next-to-shitfaced by 3p.m. most weekdays."[1]

Mum didn't complain every day, just every Sunday. I had a dim sense that the bungalow really did contain some kind of . . . injustice. I didn't try to help exactly because helping definitely wasn't my area. Should I ask how to use the washing machine? Fine for my own clothes, but then what? Should I go into Mark and Andrew's bedroom and pick up their underwear? Or

---

[1] You can safely assume we'll return to me as a domestic screw-up later.

166

Derek's? Or my mother's? Where would it end? I think not.

I wasn't asked to help and I didn't. But I made token gestures like always thanking her for tea, not dissing her controversial gravy and at least carrying my plate to the sink even if I had no intention of washing it up. For these minuscule concessions, Derek would tease me for being a "goody two-shoes". These days the term would be "virtue-signaller".

But someone did help the situation and that was Anna-Beth Limb.

Suddenly there's a purpose and cheerfulness about Mum and Derek that's long been missing. My baby sister is gorgeous — I love her instantly and for all time. I've never been a big brother before but I hope to grow into it. Mark and Andrew finished school at sixteen and both have jobs — Mark left home a while ago and Andrew now follows. So now we are four, Me, Mum, Derek and little A-B. The pack has been shuffled. We are, for the time being, a happy little unit.

My penis, on the other hand, is a less-than-happy little unit. I distract myself from mooning over Will and Daisy by developing the world's most urgent obsession with one Tessa Rampling. I've given up fancying her younger sister, Tiffany. It's obvious that Tiffany will never go out with me. So, naturally, the thing to do is to Fall In Love with her older sister in the Upper Sixth Form because, as we know, if there's one thing more likely to happen to a teenage boy than a beautiful girl his own age wanting to get off with him, it's a beautiful girl two years his senior wanting to get off with him. A better-conceived plan is hard to imagine.

Maybe the best way to get to Tess is through Tiffany. Since Tiffany made her lack of sexual regard for me abundantly clear about a hundred years ago, the tension has eased and we've somehow become quite good friends. How to describe Tiffany? She's a sort of adolescent Louise Mensch, but then so is Louise Mensch so that doesn't get us very far. Tiffany is like Mensch but with a good excuse. Tiffany is sixteen.

I find her capricious and difficult and massive fun. Her rebel alliance with Zelda Linseed is still intact and she's a middle-class girl on the war path. She's beginning to despise her hippy, liberal parents and soon she and I will have huge rows about politics: "Socialism!? Ugh, let me tell you, Rob, on my French exchange they were all socialists and they were eating their dessert on the same plate as their main course. It was *disgusting*." For now, Tiffany seems to have identified me as interesting. It will have to do.

There's no point fancying her anyway because she's going out with an older guy called Gary who she met in a pub. She loves his earthiness, his authenticity and that he has a car. I've seen Gary around at parties. Gary is, in my view, a thug and a moron. On a good night, Gary's brain can just about coordinate a blink. Mainly, he just stares. But Gary is eighteen and treats girls appallingly and is obviously therefore *something of a catch*.

One lunchtime, at the end of our fifth year, Tiffany confides that she recently had dreadful sex with Gary. She also shares the information that Gary didn't like it

168

when Tiffany put on "When 2 R in Love" for the occasion, didn't appreciate her joss sticks and didn't remove his socks, trainers or jeans. In fact, the only thing that Gary wasn't wearing which he should have been wearing was a condom.

I nod through this, thinking about what a spectacular lay I would probably be compared to Gary. It's always possible that this would be a good time to say some nice things to Tiffany, who is relating the kind of encounter a jury would have to call "consensual" but which was in every other way an obviously horrible experience. But mainly, hero that I am, I'm thinking about how I could have both warned her and saved her. All she had to do was put her hand down the front of my pants at some point over the last two years and all of this unpleasantness could have been avoided.

Now Tiffany's telling me she's worried she might be pregnant. You can tell how shit Gary is in bed by watching him dance, I think to myself, as Tiffany dries her eyes with a hanky she's found. Yes, the bloke is just fundamentally ungenerous.

Tiffany's just saying how she daren't confide in her mum.

I mean, "When 2 R in Love" isn't my favourite track on that album, but if a girl wanted me to have sex with her and that song was playing in the background, I would actually keep the beat. I'd probably ejaculate "on the two". What is it with these Garys and Deans and Jasons, with their socks and monkey eyebrows and no johnnies? They're all wankers! What's wrong with ME?! WHAT IS THE FUCKING PROBLEM HERE? *My* red and grey ski jacket is as good as anyone else's ski jacket! *My* jeans with pleats in are short enough to show my white socks! *My* white leather tie works with my lemon V-necked jumper obviously! For fuck's sake!

"So, what do you think I should do, Rob?" Tiffany is suddenly asking.

"Er. Dump him."

Tiffany puts her hanky away and blinks at me. "I've just told you I've dumped him already."

"Yes," I say, recovering, "but does he know he's dumped? You should make it clear. Probably write him a letter or something."

She sighs and looks away. I try again. "I see the problem, though. He can't actually read, can he?"

Tiffany stares back at me. She's either going to laugh, slap me or just walk off. It seems for a second like she might do all three. It's very much up to her and I feel what is now the usual rush of adrenaline. Never a dull moment with our Tiffany. She covers her face with her hands and her shoulders start to vibrate. Then she pulls her hands away and the silent laugh turns into a full-throated howl. Christ, it wasn't that funny. Maybe she's got her period. Oh no, she's anxiously waiting for her period, that was the whole point, wasn't it? Crikey. Girls.

"You make a bloody fair point, Rob. Bloody fair. He's a fucking Orc, isn't he?"

"He really might be, as you say, a fucking Orc."

She laughs and the emotion almost visibly disappears as she blows her nose again. I remain on high alert. This could still go anywhere.

170

She contemplates her snotty handkerchief and seems to come to a decision. She's going to do one of her turns on a sixpence. She quickly mutters, "Probably not preggers anyway and Mum can fuck off," and then suddenly, "NOW THEN! What about you, young Mr Bobs, how's *your* love life? I hear you're on the shark for my sister, n'est-ce pas?"

I shrug. God, this is exciting.

"You know she's going out with Eric?"

Eric? Who the fuck is Eric? "Yeah, I know," I say.

"And she goes round to his flat and bonks him senseless whenever she feels like it, the old slag."

I nod a "yeah" quietly. He's got a flat? Oh, terrific. Game over.

"But she does like you, young Webbington — she likes the revues and assemblies and all your other artistic conundrums."

I don't mind being called "young" by someone six months my junior and I certainly don't care what the hell she means by conundrums. The news is: Tess *has* seen the revues and she likes them! Even my savage take-down of Rick Astley, probably! This is massive.

"Well, never mind all that," I say, giving Tiffany an awkward rub on the shoulder, "as long as you're all right."

She looks at the hand on her arm and then to my face and starts laughing again. "God, Rob, you're such a stupid bastard!"

Eric. There he is in the Angel. Pete Garvey and I are by the jukebox and I get a good look at Eric across the

171

room. In fact, I've seen him in here quite a few times — I just didn't realise he was called Eric or that such a person could get within ten square miles of Tess Rampling. What's he doing in here, anyway? This pub is for hard-drinking children — that's been the rule for generations. He should be in Old Nick's Tavern with all the other geriatrics.

I'm sixteen and I have a name for my pain: Eric. This is no time to be reasonable.

He's about twenty-three, tall and scrawny. He doesn't drink snakebite and black, obviously — why would he? — he's got his own flat. Guinness. He sips Guinness and gets the foam on his ferrety little beard. He has a personal style that we might call proto-grunge, which is to say that he's ahead of his time in looking like he doesn't wash. He plays pool like it's snooker, plodding around the table, lining up safety shots and chalking his cue interminably. I listen to him. He thinks Neil Kinnock has betrayed the Labour movement. He gets into arguments and says "infer" like it's a posh word for "imply". He points his pool cue at people who disagree with him and says in his reedy voice things like "Walk a mile in my shoes, friend. Walk a mile in my shoes." He wears tiny little Trotsky glasses. He sucks up to the landlord at closing time, having made sexist wisecracks to the female bar staff all night. He's taken the fall of the Berlin Wall personally. He's always in shorts and sandals. His fingernails are such a disgrace I daren't look at his toes. His whole personality seems to comprise an uninterrupted series of failed gestures and stupid remarks.

172

He's a *cunt*. A more open-and-shut case of a cunt I could barely imagine.

"All right, Eric?" says Will, returning from the bar with a glass of brandy.

Of course.

Eric is pondering an especially difficult choice of pool shot, one quite distinct from the traditional *getting the balls in the fucking holes* approach. "All right, Will," he says distractedly.

Of course Will knows him and is friendly with him. Perfect. Will joins us at the jukebox to inspect what we've chosen. "Michael Jackson?! Whose idea was that?"

"It's fine, it's from *Off the Wall*," I say quickly. "So you know him, do you?"

"It is *not* fine! The minute bloody 'Rock With You' comes on, I'm disowning you both and going to Old Nick's."

"You won't get served. You know him, then."

"Know who?"

"Fucking . . . Eric."

Will glances at the pool table. "Course I know him, he's a good chap. What's the matter?"

Pete Garvey is grinning to himself. "I think p'haps our Bobby's a bit perturbed that Eric's going out with his *darling* Tess."

"Pete, shut up and eat your crisps," I say. Pete crams a large handful of Walkers Cheese and Onion in his mouth and eyeballs me with amusement.

Will puts 50p in the jukebox. "Bobs, at some point you're going to have to face the fact that you're about

173

as likely to have sex with Tess Rampling as I am with bloody . . . Trevor McDonald."

"I didn't realise you fancied Trevor McDonald."

"I'm saying it's unlikely."

I turn to Pete. "Did you know he fancied Trevor McDonald?" Pete nods.

"I'm saying it's unlikely," Will repeats, sipping his brandy and keeping his eyes on the jukebox. He runs a careless hand through his hair in a way that makes me want to jump him right here and right now and says, "Although, it'll probably be Daisy first."

"Have you fingered her yet, then?" enquires Pete through another gobful of crisps.

"Honestly, Peter, don't be so crude," Will replies, putting his brandy down and producing a soft-pack of Lucky Strike out of his black 501s. "Of course I've fingered her. She's lovely."

I'm trying to level myself with this news when Tess Rampling walks in.

She's with her friend Susan, who goes to the bar. Tess moves slowly through the room in a khaki-green poncho with oversize jeans and heavy boots. It's August. She ought to look ridiculous. She does not. Anyway, you don't look at her clothes, you look at her face.

Somehow she doesn't need to change expression all that often because literally nothing could surprise her. Her default attitude is faintly amused and ironic. You get the feeling that she can't take anything seriously because she alone understands how sad the world really is. Tiffany says the Tiananmen Square massacre made her cry — I marvel at the way she genuinely gives a shit about things on the news. She has fierce brown eyes and clean, scruffy brown hair that just about covers her ears. She is, to me, easily the most beautiful woman the universe will ever dare to create.

She reaches Eric and kisses the pubic hairs growing out of his chin. I hear her cut-glass contralto say, "I'm going to help Suze with the drinks. D'you want another Guinness?" Eric is just contemplating a safety shot on a ball I could pot with one arm. "Yeah, all right, doll," he says.

I mean, for fuck's sake. All right *what*? I wait for him to put his hand in his pocket and offer some money. He does not. He's got a flat and a full-time job involving some kind of van but he's going to let his girlfriend get the drinks in.

I struggle with this for about eight seconds. My brain is hosting one of the first contests in what will become a regular fixture — Feminism versus the Patriarchy Where Feminism is at a Disadvantage Because the Referee is My Erection.

It goes like this. Obviously, Tess has every right to buy him a drink. Girls (correction, young women) are allowed to buy drinks and it would be wrong to criticise Eric out of some ancient and reactionary sense of gallantry. Tess has a summer job and her own money. Of course she should do what she likes with it and of course she should go out with whomever she chooses. It's charming that she wants to buy her boyfriend a Guinness. No, not charming, natural. Completely normal. Of course it is.

175

On the other hand, Eric is a shit and I hate him. Eric gets to sleep with Tess and should therefore be lashed to a cruise missile and fired into the sun. End of argument.

At home I listen to "Slow Love" by Prince and think of Tess. I listen to "I'm Not in Love" by 10cc and think of Will. It's difficult to know which one to have a hopeless wank about first. I try to look on the bright side — at least the way I feel about Tess proves that I'm not gay. Rationally, I can see that being gay is fine, but it looks like gay men have to put up with a whole world of stupid nonsense that straighties with a one-off fixation get to ignore. And, if I'm honest, the way I lust after Will feels not only dangerous and exciting but also shameful and wrong. The Sovereign Importance of Early Homophobia has done its work. It's like I'm left with a closet homophobia — a Farage in the garage. Or, as I would have pronounced it at the time, a Farridge in the garridge.

It could be worse. At least Will and Tess are not going out with each other.

"Is there any romance greater than the one a teenage boy has with his own loneliness?"

That, I'm afraid, is the kind of thing that starts cropping up in the diary I begin to keep after my seventeenth birthday. The author is clearly quite pleased with the question and decides not to spoil it by offering an answer. He also doesn't seem to notice that "loneliness" is itself quite a romantic way to describe

176

what is really just a combination of jealousy, insecurity and, above all (or rather, beneath all), massive, head-swivelling, ball-bulging sexual frustration.

By the beginning of the sixth form, my virginity weighs me down as if I'm walking around in a pair of lead knickers with matching iron stilettos and a concrete tiara. It's emasculating. Teenage boys are supposed to be *at it*. If you're not at it, then you're not really a boy, never mind a man. "Men think about sex every seven seconds" is a meme knocking around at the time. We didn't call them "memes" obviously; we called them "old wives' tales". This, I suppose, is progress of a sort.

I think — really? Every seven seconds? But then, what do I know? Maybe other blokes really do think about it every seven seconds . . . maybe I'm still a virgin because I just don't think about sex often enough! I mean, Jesus, it feels like I think about it QUITE A LOT but . . . seriously? It takes me seven seconds to tie my shoelaces. Did I think about sex while I was tying my shoelaces? I doubt it. But maybe I should have.[1]

I was certainly thinking about sex quite a lot while writing in the diary. Reader, I spared you the poetry because it was bad without being entertainingly bad. A bit like when someone retweets something by Piers Morgan and I think, "Oh great, he's going to say

---

[1] The seven-second myth is, of course, mythical. Nobody knows where it came from, but it's often attributed to the 1948 Kinsey Report: *Sexual Behavior in the Human Male*. Alfred C. Kinsey and his co-authors make no such claim.

something enjoyably shit." And then he says the shit thing but it turns out to be shit in a way that's not fun at all and just shit. And everything's the same except now you've got this bit of shit in your head. It's disappointing.

But the diary, I hope you'll agree, is badly done in a way that's informatively, if not amusingly, bad. So in October 1989 (I've just started the sixth form), I have this to say. Apart from [square brackets for clarity], I promise I haven't edited to make this any better or worse. Here we go then.

> I rang Will and we decided to go to the flicks. It was *Young Einstein* which was FUCKING CRAP. Yahoo who calls himself Serious. The lady doth protest too much methinks. I [am] definitely becoming more critical of comedy, although maybe it was just objectively bad, n'est-ce pas? Anyway, him, me and Clive walked out halfway through and then he [Will] hit me with it. He started talking about how he's shagged Daisy on Friday night while watching a video of *Krull*. Of course it was a deliberate wind-up but of course it hurt me very badly. Surely he knows that repeatedly underlining his success and my failure is an act of breathtaking insensitivity surely.

Yes, surely. The next five closely written foolscap pages are about fancying a girl at Gateway called Jill — then finding out she has a boyfriend, asking her out to a

178

party, getting very excited that she said yes, not getting off with her at the party and getting told that she "just wants to be friends".

> I walked her back to Craig's house and waited for her mum to collect her. There was no question of a goodnight kiss. That was so clear from the start. As for the future, I don't know. Jill might fancy me a bit: it's so hard to say. The next step will be the Gateway staff party on Jan 6th.

While I'm waiting for the Gateway staff party and its next step, there's a Christmas concert featuring local school bands Communion (lead singer, Daisy) and Underpants (bass guitar, Paddy, Tiffany's new boyfriend who plays the bass line to "A Forest" by The Cure). Isabel is a lovely girl, also in the Lower Sixth. Marina is another lovely girl, but in the fifth year. I fancy Marina more than Isabel but not as much as Jill. Jill isn't there.

> Isabel said hello and we started getting on really well, e.g. I made her laugh like a spaz. And then after a Bacardi or two, we sort of started getting off with each other. After that, we were sort of "together" all evening, you know, holding hands and stuff. It was all a bit mushy for my liking especially since I hardly fancy her. Well, later in the evening I nearly fell over when I saw Marina getting off with RUSSELL MACALLEN! CAN YOU FUCKING BELIEVE IT? I was so fucked

off. How can a nice girl like her get off with a social incompetent like him? Plus, he was totally fucking sloshed after about 2 vodkas. UNBE — fucking — LIEVABLE. Obviously I was manically depressed and so totally ignored Isabel for the rest of the evening.

The sensitive young man finds time to make a macho comment about Russell's alcohol tolerance (just as I despised Eric's caution at the pool table) and takes it out on Isabel. Which is nothing compared to how he will take it out on Marina. This is where it gets a bit dark. There follows a ten-page narrative in which it turns out that Marina — who recently turned fifteen — does fancy me after all (I have it *directly* from her older sister! "Chloe said Marina was crying afterwards because she thought she'd upset me. She didn't want to snog Russell but was too polite to say no."), but her mother has reasonable concerns. On 19 February 1990, Little Lord Hard-On is highly vexed.

I always suspected her mum would be a problem but didn't imagine she'd be such a stupid bitch. Every weekend since 7-1-90 I've asked Marina round and she's said, "I'll see what my mum says" and mummy dear invariably says FUCK RIGHT OFF DEAR. Everyone knows how Chloe has turned out, right? You'd think that Mrs Kay had got the message about telling her daughters "no you can't". But apparently not. What a fuckhead. Now it turns out she's telling

180

her "he's too old for you" and "you're not to have a serious relationship till you're 16". We all know what she means by "serious", right? If Marina actually liked me enough, you'd think she'd put up more of a fight but apparently not. So that's it. It fucks up again. It always fucks up. It always will fuck up.

Aside from Mrs Kay's outrageous desire for her child not to break the law, I love that brief lecture about Chloe's promiscuity. The big sister is damned for having sex, the younger one damned for not having sex, the mother damned for exercising a fairly run-of-the-mill duty of care. But despite the three-sentence burial hymn at the end, our hero won't take no for an answer until he hears the magic words.

If I thought I was depressed on Thursday, that's nothing compared to when the events of last night sink in. After an hour in the Angel, we went to the Town Hall. I knew Marina would be there and Russell was on the shark for Nancy Tanner although God knows why. Well, Marina was there, obviously drunk, obviously having a good time with her friends and obviously ignoring me. And then she pulled her master card. [I think this is either meant to be "ace card" or "master stroke" — at no point did Marina try to get rid of me by waving a Mastercard.] I mean what's the worst and I mean the WORST thing she could possibly have said? That's right. After about ten minutes, short Sally, her friend who's always fucking around with her hair, came up and said "Marina says she just wants to be friends". The words pierced me like a javelin. Anything, anything would have been better than "let's be friends". It stinks of patronising indifference which, let's face it, is how she has always regarded me. Obviously I just walked out.

Obviously. And somehow negotiating the doorway despite being pierced by a javelin. The author then hits on a particularly terrible idea.

My natural reaction is to write her a fucking acidic letter. She's hurt me and she ought to bloody well know about it. But I remember how much I regretted doing that with Louise. Generally it's just a rather spiteful and childish thing to do.

Phew! Yes, let's not write the letter. Louise had been a girl in the year above who actually let me feel her breasts before suggesting that we might be "just friends". I wrote her a letter detailing how offensive this was of her. She never spoke to me again. So, good thing we won't write the letter. But not so fast because —

I'd love to. I still might.

Nooooooo! Sweet Mother of Jesus, let's see if I can even type this.

182

Of course it would put any chance of us getting together next year beyond question and I have enough doors slammed in my face without closing them myself. But the time I wasted on her; her total absence of contribution; her arrogance in the way she finished it; her lack of vision, and her obvious and total incomprehension of any of my feelings make me simmer with something close to hatred.

DUDE, WE HAVE A SAYING IN THE TWENTY-FIRST CENTURY — "SHE'S JUST NOT THAT INTO YOU". YOU'RE OUT OF YOUR MIND AND YOU MUST NOT WRITE THAT LETTER!

3-4-90. Well, I sent the letter. It wasn't half as bad as it could have been. She belatedly sent it back with a reply. I spoke to her sister and she said Marina read the letter on Saturday and spent all morning crying. This was quite a shock — I certainly didn't mean to upset her.

You idiot.

There was a quiet dignity in her reply which I found rather impressive.

You patronising idiot.

I wonder if I really am guilty of the charge of "selfishness?"

183

Hmm, good one. Let's think.

> I really can't bring myself to admit that. I know the letter was vindictive but I was hurt and I had to hit out at someone.

I give up on this dick. Or rather, I would if I didn't know that something else was going on.

Early in March, a couple of weeks before the blameless Marina said "let's be friends", I'd written this:

> My concern for Mum deepens. I'm quite ashamed to realise that this is the first reference in this diary to worrying about anyone but myself. Mum has been in hospital since last Friday with what was supposed to be a chest infection. In fact she has a few cancerous cells on her lung. She might have to have chemotherapy. Jesus Christ I'm so worried — I love her so much. I must resolve to be less selfish, to talk to her about things more often. Life without her is unthinkable. Literally unthinkable.

And then, at the end of the same entry where I talk about Marina's reply to the spiteful letter —

> Found out for sure, the week before last, on Wednesday March 21st, that Mum definitely isn't going to recover. She has about four months. I don't want to talk about it. Even to you.

184

I found out that Mum had cancer in early March, and three weeks later, I found out that she wasn't going to survive it. And it was after that I sent Marina the letter because, "I was hurt and I had to hit out at someone".

In other words, the girl picked up the bill when the boy turned fear and grief into anger.

And that Wednesday teatime conversation — the one where I found out that the best person in my life was about to vanish — all the seventeen-year-old can find to describe it is those four words: "found out for sure". For once, I don't blame him. It is not a boy's job to write about such things.

That day, I arrived home from school and felt a sudden tightness in my chest. Dad's van was parked neatly outside the bungalow.

CHAPTER
EIGHT

Boys Don't Cry

"For we all of us, grave or light, get our thoughts entangled in metaphors, and act fatally on the strength of them."

George Eliot, *Middlemarch*

Mum is home, asleep in bed. She's obviously very ill, but nobody has said anything about exactly how ill, and I haven't asked. I walk into the kitchen and put my school bag down carefully.

"Now, boy! Come and have a word!"

Dad is around the kitchen table with Derek, which is a novel sight and not a welcome one. I sit down with them. Dad's eyes are bloodshot. He's got something on his mind, Something That Needs To Be Said. And he seems to have decided that he's the one who's going to have to say it, because other people lack his common-sense ability to face facts. He's actually angry. He starts talking and the world ends.

"Y'mum's poorly, boy. It's terminal."

You can get quite a lot of juice out of that word "terminal", if you speak with a Lincolnshire accent and are quite drunk. The way he says it, the "er" sound is dug from the very depths of his diaphragm. I look across at Derek, who is leaning an elbow on the table with a hand covering his mouth. He nods a tiny confirmation. Incredibly, somewhere in the room, Dad is still talking.

"It's 'orrible, boy, but that's it. That's life. Now, I don't know if you want to come and live with me or . . .", he looks around the kitchen, "I mean, you're probably going to need a cleaner, Derek, because . . . well, it's hard, int' it? It's hard keeping a place clean." Derek nods. It is indeed hard keeping a place clean. This is what we are now talking about. Dad warms to the theme. "I mean, she's probably too busy but Josie, who cleans my house, she could probably come and do a couple of hours a week. It's all you need really, a couple of hours."

Derek says, "Well, this is it. Is she not Woodhall, then?"

"She is Woodhall, mate, but I know she does a couple of Coningsby properties on a Thursday."

"What does she tend to charge, like?"

"Well, I give her a fiver, mate, but I don't know if she might be wanting a bit more for petrol, coming out here."

Derek is alarmed by the prospect of paying Woodhall Josie £5 plus petrol money and he's about to haggle, but stops because he's noticed I'm crying.

"I know, boy," Dad says, "it's 'orrible."

Here I am then, with Mum about to vanish, stuck here in the kitchen with the Dickhead Brothers talking about Dad's fucking cleaner.

Dad takes me outside and gives me an awkward hug. My sobbing has drained some of his anger and he's on the verge of tears himself.

So he leaves. Having discharged his duty and given everyone a firm lesson in how to face up to reality, he gets in his van and fucks off back to the pub. It's quite a new van, actually. On the side is painted the name of his business, which today looks less like an advertisement than like a rare flash of self-awareness: "Paul Webb, Ltd".

"Fred's a bloody nuisance, he always has been." I'm next to her on her bed, later that day. With effort, Mum draws herself up on her stack of pillows. "I'm sorry, darling, that wasn't a very nice way to find out. I should have told you myself."

I make an ineffectual gesture to help with the pillows but I'm scared of getting in her way. She's got *Dallas* on the portable telly with the sound turned low. Bobby Ewing is having a long meeting with assorted oil barons.

"Don't worry about me," I say. Her skin is a yellow-grey now and at the top of each breath there's a distant gurgle which gets closer by the week. All the signs that I chose not to see suddenly reveal themselves with pathetic eloquence. She's obviously dying.

She says, "Now then, is there anything you want to ask me? Or is there anything you want to say to me?" I feel a thousand future selves lean in to listen with interest. I rack my brain: there is no question up to the task and no statement either, apart from "I love you",

188

but I don't trust myself to say that without losing it. I don't want to do that; I'm her son and I want to be strong. So I say the thing that bothers me most about being seventeen and me.

"I suppose . . . I mean, this isn't important."

"Go on . . ."

"I suppose, well, people talk like I'm having sex all the time and I've sort of gone along with it. But actually I'm a virgin."

She starts to smile, but doesn't want to look like she's taking the piss. Also, smiling takes effort and she's working hard to talk. She says, "I won't say I'm surprised; I won't say I'm not surprised. But you'll catch up."

"All my mates have got girlfriends."

"You'll overtake them. In everything."

This emboldens me, so I try a promise. "I'm going to get three As and go to Cambridge, Mum."

She's ready for this one. "I know you'll be happy wherever you end up, Rob. I'm proud of you already, so don't worry."

We watch *Dallas*. It looks like JR has gone round to Cliff Barnes's office to do some gloating. We both love the show and have watched about a dozen versions of this scene. But tonight it looks like they're just going through the motions. It used to be fun — when Bobby would throw JR into the swimming pool, the annual punch-up at the Oil Barons' Ball . . . when no one had grey hair, when my brothers were still at school, when Mum used to tuck me in every night after reading a story.

— Goodnight, God-bless and see you in the morning.

— I 'ope so!

She says, "I know your father said something about moving in with him. You do as you think best. But as far as I'm concerned, this is your home."

I nod at this, wondering if there's something she's asking me to do. "I'll try and spend more time with Anna-Beth."

"No, darling, she's got her own father. She won't remember me, but she's got a father. You do your own thing. I'm saying you don't have to live with Fred if you don't want to. He's a bloody liability."

And then, suddenly, she adds, "You came along soon after Martin died and I think that's why we've always been close."

I look at the children's illustrated Bible that appeared next to her bed a few days ago. The one that I know has "To Martin John" inscribed in her handwriting on the inside page. My atheism still has a few weeks to run — it will disappear when she does, because I won't accept that she has disappeared. It takes all my remaining courage to say: "Maybe you'll see him again."

She turns to me and says, "I 'ope so."

I beam at her but she senses that I can't keep it together much longer and neither can she. "Now, be a good lad and go and make us a cup of tea." I do as I'm told with relief.

Derek falls ill under the strain for a couple days and Mum's friend and boss from the Dower House, Carole, steps in and quietly takes charge. Over the next few weeks she demonstrates what could be fairly described as the point and meaning of friendship. She all but drops her hotel, she brings casseroles and lasagnes, she coordinates the Marie Curie nurses, she maintains and regulates Mum's medication when the nurse isn't around, she doesn't flap, she doesn't showboat, she talks and listens to Mum, cushioning her pain and hiding her own, even eliciting the odd laugh. She is a model of practical good sense. When I grow up, I think to myself, I want to be Carole.

In contrast, and in the middle of all this, here they come: the well-wishers, the payers of respect, the pains in the arse. We entertain a procession of half-forgotten friends and the kind of intimate family members who ring up to ask for directions. They've just popped in to say — wait for it — "hello". Mum insists on getting herself upright in a wheelchair and it's obvious that this ritual parade of visitors is just another part of her endurance. One of the oddest things about being terminally ill is that you get a new job — host. Essentially, she is looking after them — telling Derek where to find another vase for the flowers, nodding through the strained banter, the mirthless gags, the bullshit about "when you're back on your feet" etc. One friend that she's never much liked even weeps on her — cheers. If dying is a test of character, so is being that person's friend. Mum and Carole get top scores. Some fail completely. Most of us muddle through.

The whole place smells like a medicine cabinet. I'm listening to *Violator* by Depeche Mode, which seems about right. I keep the volume low.

April 17th
Derek was ill this morning. Mum's condition
deteriorates. I felt so alone, so pathetic today.
She's dying. I'm not ready for any of this.

April 23rd
Dr Campbell says 24 hours at the most. Christ, I
want it to be all over. Is that wrong of me? The
drugs ensure that she's in no pain but mean that
she is only ever semi-conscious. I miss her.

April 24th
Mum dies at 2.45 p.m.
I love you.
Sometimes it snows in April.

I was in my bedroom, supposedly writing an essay for
Economics, but actually just staring out of the window.

Carole knocks lightly on the door and puts her head
round. "I think you'd better come into the bedroom,
dear."

I get up from my little desk and go into Mum and
Derek's room — a room which now scares me.

Mark is there. "She's gone, mate," he says, "she's gone."

I look to the bed. Mum is there but not there,
seemingly asleep as she has been for days. But now the
long-distance breathing has stopped. Whatever is in that
bed is something new. It's not unfamiliar, but then
neither is it Mum.

Mainly, I just don't believe it — the endness of the
ending. I mean, this has all been very unpleasant, but

she wasn't going to just *stop*, right? She wasn't going to just *disappear and never come back, right?* It's not like I was never going to hear her voice again, or look in her eyes again, or feel her embrace or smell her smell again, right? That stuff can go away for a while, but it's not going to go away *for the rest of my life*, is it? Right? That's impossible.

Mark leads me out into the back garden.

"Oh, Robbie Robbie Robbie." We hug tightly. I've never seen Mark cry and he's trying not to, probably for me. I'm trying not to as well, for him. What strange creatures we are. We stand apart then, looking out on the land where Derek keeps the effects of his business — "the yard" — a wilderness of brambles from which rusting tractors poke their heads, like relics in a neglected theme park. I suddenly say, "John and Trudy!"

"I know, mate, I know. They must be wondering what they did to the world to deserve this." I try to look for a consolation.

"At least we're young," I say.

"We're young. You're right, Rob. It'll be easier for us." Mark tests what he's just said against the situation and the result is a bleak joke. "Although it doesn't much bloody feel like it." I give him a smile as clenched as our hug. Every muscle in my body has contracted. It's hard to breathe.

Andrew is home not long after. His hair is madly ruffled like he's been rolling his hands tightly around his whole head. I say, "Are you all right?"

He replies, "Are *you* all right?" We don't answer each other's questions because we are plainly both not all right.

Nan Webb, Dad's mother, arrives too late to see Mum. She takes the news and sits quietly in the living room. Anna-Beth, aged three, wanders in and asks, "Where's Mummy?"

OK, that's it. Stop the world. That's enough. We've all had our fun with the impossible disaster but this is getting silly.

Nan Webb doesn't miss a beat: "With Jesus!" She says it with serious eyes and a cheerful voice. The disconnect is startling — the eyes have seen it all; the voice is there for the child — the children, counting me. Another actor in the family and you need a lot of conviction to get away with a line like this.

"Mummy's gone to live with Jesus."

I want it, I *will* it to be true. I stretch for the truth of it like reaching for Narnia through the back of the wardrobe. You'll feel the cold air if you just *concentrate*. If you just try harder. At this point, anything is better than nothing.

Anna-Beth is sceptical — she suspects the old lady has made a joke and gives her a slow grin. I take A-B in my arms for a cuddle and for some reason start to think about bicycles.

A welcome digression about bicycles.

The Grifter had always been temperamental. One day at the Golf Club, I was standing up to pedal when the chain slipped, bringing my eleven-year-old crotch

194

into violent contact with the crossbar. My granddad John happened to be nearby. "Ooh, you poor thing!" he said. "Y'poor old goolies, mate!" But then, "Yeah, don't cry then, mate. Don't let Nana or Trudy see you cry." It seemed a perverse thing to say since I couldn't care less about Nan or Tru seeing me cry — the shame was in letting John see it.

And then in the front room, I'm thinking of the bicycle that came next. A racing bike that was a Christmas present from Mum. And I'm thinking about my one and only road accident.

I'm riding my new racer through Coningsby, on my way to work at Gateway. There's a turning on my left but I'm heading straight ahead. Coming towards me is a car, signalling to turn right. I assume he's going to pause and wait for me to pass as per — what's it called? — the law. I assume wrong. He makes the right turn directly in front of me and the racer and I concertina into his passenger door at about fifteen miles an hour.

The driver — posh, tinted glasses, RAF officer — gets out and addresses the crumpled heap of boy and bicycle with considerable self-importance. "Now that . . . that was *entirely* my fault!"

I pick myself up and he helps me get the bike to the pavement, where he gives it a brief inspection. "Should be fine," he says, turning the obviously buckled front wheel back and forth in his driving gloves. "Yup, that was lucky." And then off he goes.

And it *was* lucky. I had a slightly bruised knee, a graze on one hand . . . and that was it. But the moment I'm thinking about as I cuddle Anna-Beth in the front room of the bungalow is the one just before that collision.

I'm remembering its implacable *seriousness*. The way the danger, the terror was unswervable, non-negotiable — this was going to hurt and there was nothing to be done and nowhere to hide.

That is what bereavement feels like to me. A wide-eyed rush towards a painful impact.

The good thing about being three years old, I think, stroking A-B's hair, is that she might be vaguely aware of the impacts happening all around her, but she herself has not crashed. She's little enough to slip through the gaps in the wreckage. There will be consequences, but the consequences will form her idea of what's normal, just as it was normal for me to be scared of my father and wake up shivering on those winter mornings.

And the good thing about being a teenager, I further reflect, is that we bounce. We bounce for Britain.

A-B and me, three and seventeen — wow, this could have been worse. Six and ten? Seven and twelve? Bless them and no thanks.

And although this is a reasonable thought, it provides a springboard for a less reasonable thought, and this is where the bouncing goes wrong. A romantic narrative, a story, starts to take shape. The reality is too much to bear, so it has to be turned into a story. It has to be given meaning. The dreadful news has to be balanced by good news, the clouds demand a silver lining, the suffering hero must find a purpose. Death, I believe from the example of Martin, has to give way to new life. My life. And this "outspoken" woman who just fell silent has to be given a voice. The voice of someone with a childhood Messiah complex who used to have twelve imaginary bodyguards. Someone younger, stronger, better educated, male. Someone like her, but with unfair advantages that she didn't get in this unfair world. Her youngest son.

I'm the good news. I'm the silver lining. I don't need a meaning: I *am* the meaning. Me. She'll sing through me.

It's an exciting idea and almost completely insane. It would be bad enough if this big-screen self-image had come from a healthy imagination. As it is, it's a desperate parting shot from emotions that are otherwise busily trying to shut down. Something in my heart just turned to ice. That's a reasonable self-protective measure in the short term, but will cause a lot of trouble later. Believing that I'm about to conquer the world on someone else's behalf — someone I think beyond reproach — will cause even more trouble.

I set Anna-Beth down and go back to my room. I'll finish the essay, I think. I'll show them. Whoever "they" might be. I sit at my desk, pick up my pen and look out of the window. I'm fascinated by the idea of what a hero I'm going to be.

I do nothing.

Mark drives me directly to school from the funeral. The QEGS sixth-form blazer and tie are both black and so, this morning, I had an off-the-peg funeral costume so long as I unpicked the gold badge from the blazer.

I had the badge in my back pocket during the funeral. I sew it back on in the car, quickly and about as well as you'd expect for someone who would normally have asked his mum to do it.

There's a Lower Sixth Form trip to Nottingham, to a university fair. It's a sort of open day where many university admissions officers will be gathered in a big hall to hand out prospectuses and have a chat. I don't want to miss it. If Mark is starting to think I've gone a bit strange — his little brother madly sewing away in the seat next to him — he doesn't show it. The badge on my blazer is now at a slightly jaunty angle which I decide to like.

If I'd left last year, to do A levels at Lincoln or Boston College, as some did, I wouldn't have this uniform, or any uniform. I could have been one of those guys who waited a month before making a special trip into school in their ripped jeans and new piercings to tell the rest of us how they "couldn't believe" that we "just haven't moved on". They pissed me off at the time. Now I have the Dead-Mother-Load of "moving on". Now, doing my running stitch, trying to compensate for the bends between Woodhall and Horncastle, I long to talk to one of those boys. I'd let him go on for a while about how cool college is, about how he's grown, how he can't actually believe we're still here with a "uniform" and a "headmaster". And I'd listen. And wait for the perfect moment. And then quietly, modestly, drop my dreadful news on his arrogant, know-nothing haircut. And then just sit back with a benign shrug and watch the fucker squirm.

Grief turned to anger.

We should really start a *How Not To Be a Boy* drinking game where you take a sip of a tough guy's drink like Bacardi and Coke every time you notice a male turning a negative emotion into anger. But without me pointing it out. I'm going to stop pointing it out. I predict that top students will be arseholed before Chapter 12. Non-drinking students are allowed herbal tea. You just have to count trips to the loo.

The head of sixth form, Mr Edwards, a friendly Welsh man who normally teaches RE, is giving a briefing about the Nottingham trip to the whole Lower Sixth — about seventy people. They're gathered in the common room and he has his back to me when I open the door.

He turns. "Join us, Robert, join us."

It feels like every one of them knows where I've just come from. I quickly spot Tiffany and Will sitting together and they simultaneously shuffle apart to make a space. Will is frowning with a pursed grin and looks almost sick with sympathy; Tiffany smiles broadly and gives the space they've made for me a playful pat. Oh, thank God. Thank God for friends.

I walk towards them as Mr Edwards resumes. And I'm aware of something else, as I feel seventy pairs of eyes on me. I'm slightly enjoying this.

Not the attention exactly, but the way I get to shrug the attention off. Not the Impossible Disaster, but the way I'm humbly and bravely coping with it. They are all wondering how they might react if their mum died and I'm going to show them. Considering that this morning I tossed a rose into her grave, and had to listen to a eulogy delivered by one of those unlucky vicars who clearly doesn't know who the fuck he's talking about, this is easily the most fun I've had all day.

In Nottingham, the university reps are seated behind desks around the sides of a huge hall to talk to A-level students from far and wide. The longest queues are to see the guys from Nottingham or Leicester Polytechnics (they become universities a year later), followed by a medium number for big civic universities like Leeds and Manchester, a shy smattering for Bristol and Durham and then . . . I peer into the far corner — ah yes. A grey-haired lady with a Cambridge sign on her desk is sitting completely alone. She's reading but occasionally glances up to give passers-by an encouraging smile, trying, it seems, to radiate approachability.

I start walking towards her, wondering who the hell I think I am.

I hover awkwardly next to the empty seat across from her. She looks up suddenly and says "Please!", gesturing to the chair and whipping off her reading glasses. "You'll have to forgive me, catching up on a spot of work."

I take the seat, saying, "No, I . . . I just thought I'd . . . say hello."

"I'm glad you did. Tremendously bad form for me to be reading at all. Most forbidding." She gives me a conspiratorial smile and waits. I don't have a thought in my head. She's tall in her chair, slim and in her late fifties, her long grey hair pulled loosely into a ponytail. Her voice is beautifully modulated, which reminds me of Tess Rampling. None of this helps.

"Well, I'm doing my A levels . . ." Oh, you dick. Every fucker in the room is doing their A levels. ". . . and erm . . ." I go completely dry.

"And you have an interest in applying to Cambridge," she offers.

"Yes!" I almost shout with relief and embarrassment. I'm actually blushing. This was a terrible idea. Just keep talking. "I'm only at a grammar school . . ."

"Which one?"

"Er, it's in a market town in Lincolnshire. I mean, it's only . . ."

"Queen Elizabeth's. In Horncastle."

I stare at her. "Yeah. You've heard of us, then."

"We've heard of everyone."

Oh my God. She's going to recruit me as a spy! Do I want to be a spy?! No, not really! I'm still looking at her, dumbfounded.

"And is there a particular subject you're interested in studying at Cambridge?"

I wish she would stop saying Cambridge. People will hear. "English."

"My own subject. And a particular college?"

"King's."

"My own college! Well, now!" If this were a first date, it would be going quite well. But I know that the moment will come when I accidentally let slip that I'm a pathological liar with halitosis and a criminal record. Best if I get that out of the way now, so she can tell me to get lost and we can forget the whole thing. Then I can go back to Derek and the morphine bungalow.

"The thing is . . . I only got four As and four Bs for my GCSEs. So, y'know, nothing to write home about."

She gives a little chuckle. "But nothing to be ashamed of. I assume one of your As was in English?"

"Yes."

"And you're doing English at A level."

"Yes."

"And you expect to get an A in that."

". . . Yeah, I do actually."

"And you could manage one more A grade? Another A and a B, possibly?"

My confidence evaporates and suddenly this is ridiculous. AAB? I haven't finished an essay in five weeks.

"Well, that might be . . . it's been a bit tricky lately."

She leans forward with her chin in her hands, looking down at the desk. "If it's any consolation, many of my students tell me that they found A-level study and preparation more pressured than the degrees they are taking now and I quite believe them. It's not easy, as you know. It's not really supposed to be easy."

I feel like calling it a day, but luckily that last comment has made me slightly cross. I say, "I know it's not supposed to be easy and I don't mind doing it while I'm doing it. It's just sometimes hard to get started, what with . . . I mean, like this morning, it's not as if . . ." I can hear my voice start to wobble.

She's frowning in concern and puts her palms flat on the table. "What was it about this morning? Sometimes if we can identify a particular barrier to . . ."

"Well, this morning doesn't really count because it was my mum's funeral. But generally, I've just found it . . ."

"I'm sorry, did you say that this morning was your mother's funeral?"

"Yeah."

"This morning?"

"That's right. So it's all gone a bit . . . I feel stupid for even thinking about . . . your . . . university." She's looking at me with a level of compassion that makes me want to tell her to cheer the fuck up. I blink at the wall behind her, feeling dizzy, and put a hand on my edge of the table to steady myself, even though I'm sitting down.

She says, "I'm very sorry to hear that news. May I at least offer you some reassurance, erm . . . ?"

"Robert."

"Let me at least say this, Robert. I'm Catherine, by the way. You're sitting in the right chair, talking to the right person. It's not stupid in the slightest for you to think of us."

Catherine talks briefly about open days and how I ought to come and have a look around at least two colleges. Then she reaches across and gives my hand a quick squeeze. "Good luck."

I take a prospectus — a little booklet with pictures and information about all the different colleges — and quickly drop it into my bag. Well, I suppose that could have gone worse, I think, ambling unsteadily back to my friends. Although why she had to make such a fuss about the funeral, I don't know.

May 6th 1990
Some good news! Well, Isabel and me have been getting on really well recently. She finished with hairy Edmund. I'd been flirting a bit and to my delight she seemed to be doing the same — quite blatantly in fact! Well, today we were talking all lunchtime and well, we seem to be "going out" with each other. I like and fancy her loads. How many times have I written "this is it" or "could she be the one" or some other such crap? I don't know but something is different this time. Something is different.

Well spotted. This one actually fancies you.

May 9th 1990
Saw Isabel on Sunday. We met at 2 o'clock, went for a walk. Nice chat, no tension. Then we went to hers where her parents were doing a barbeque. So then, well yes, we went upstairs. I'm not sure if I should include EVERYTHING in this diary, just in case one day I'm ever dumb enough to show it to someone. But yes, we massively got off with each other. Then we came back here. By that time it was dark and the moon was shining really prettily through the blinds of the bedroom window. Maybe even my body looked OK in that

light. Hers bloody well did. It was amazing. I am amazed. Condoms are quite crap, though, aren't they?

Given the song and dance, or rather the five-act tragedy, that I'd turned my virginity into recently, you might find this diary entry a touch underpowered. I think I was just being discreet. After all, when it came to the diary, I had every intention of being, one day, exactly "dumb enough to show it to someone". More Fame Than Sense — that's pretty much what I was aiming for.

Still, I'm going to follow 17's admirable restraint. When it comes to sex — as opposed to imaginary encounters with Nyssa — we're suddenly talking about someone else's sexual experience as well as mine. I can't track down this quotation but maybe you know it: "Sex is vital to the novel. Fucking is not." Not for the first time, what's good for a novel will do nicely here too. There's going to be plenty of sex from now on (hooray!). Just no fucking (boo!).

Isabel came along just in time and obviously my next move was to start treating her like crap. After about two golden weeks following Super Sunday, I find out what kind of boyfriend I am.

I ignore her at school. I tell her in some detail why I don't like her friends and refuse to go to the pub they prefer. I only laugh at her jokes when they're funny, which would be fine given a funny person but rude in this particular case. I don't ask her a single question about what it's like to be Isabel. She's quite "artsy", doing A-level Art, and one day in the common room I notice that she's embroidered pretty ribbons on her bag. "If I loved her," I think, "I'd love those ribbons." I think the ribbons look weird.

Like me, she's nobody's fool until she runs into someone who's willing to make a fool of her. She writes me a letter which is full of loving details and saucy compliments, but which includes, dropped casually into a middle paragraph, "Do you see our relationship as anything more than a regular three-hour shag session every Sunday afternoon? Just wondering."

If I was capable of an honest answer, it would have been: "I haven't given it much thought. The three-hour shag session is certainly a highlight. Given that one of us is in love and the other one is enthusiastically making up for what he perceives to be lost sex-hours, Sunday afternoons are definitely more fun than they used to be. Does our 'relationship' add up to more than that? Erm. Ask me an easier one." What I do instead is write back with a torrent of false emotion and bad poetry. Incredibly, that seems to work.

That and the fact that, compared to most of her ex-lovers (her tally is impressive, but I don't care as long as she likes me best), she thinks I'm kind. You can get away with some amazingly bad behaviour, it turns out, as long as your predecessors were complete shits. And no matter how bad the poetry is, she now has a boyfriend who writes her love poems, and becomes silly when drunk instead of physically threatening. The bar on teenage boyfriends is so astoundingly low, she puts

206

up with my version of boyfriend bullshit for six months. It's only when I don't turn up to her eighteenth birthday party that I finally manage to get myself dumped.

Actually doing the dumping myself, you understand, is completely out of the question. That would require all kinds of things that I haven't got to spare — tact, courage and a willingness to go back to Sunday afternoons with no sex. Sunday was best because Anna-Beth would be at John and Trudy's house and Derek would be in the living room preoccupied with *Bullseye*.

The locks on all the internal doors of the bungalow are identical, but there's only a couple of keys. One day I notice that Derek has discreetly transferred the key in his door to mine. It's a touching gesture but I wasn't expecting to receive some kind of sex-baton from Derek of all people, and to be honest it makes me a bit queasy.

Why did I want to get dumped? Because she was too much trouble. She was some kind of actual human being with actual needs of her own. That was fine when they coincided with mine, but not fine when they didn't. What are we going to do about that? "Discuss it"? "Talk it through"? Did you ever see Michael Knight "really try and thrash this stuff out"? Does Dick Turpin "have an honest but non-judgemental discussion"? No.

Also, I wasn't in love with her, something I found difficult to forgive. I found it frankly rather thoughtless and selfish of her. She was a friend. She was *fine*.

I held her, according to one of the tortured Isabel-justifying diary passages, ". . . in really quite high esteem. No, it's better than that: I'm really very, very fond of her indeed." Christ.

Compared to the mad-cat-on-a-wall-of-death infatuations with Tiffany, Jill, Tess, Will, Marina and about three other girls and a boy that I haven't troubled you with, Isabel was someone to whom I could sing "I'm Not in Love" without irony and to her face. I just about managed not to do that.

Her mistake was to be real and reality wasn't my thing. I could try to invent a story for her — "She Rescued Me From Loneliness" or "She Is Important To My Important and Ongoing Important Growth" — but that didn't really wash when she was trying to get me to go out to the Community Centre on a Friday night, a place literally five minutes' walk from the bungalow but twat-packed with her ex-idiots: the Deans, Darrens and Jasons. Real men, proper boys, "those others". They scared the hell out of me, so I chose to be aloof. Essentially, I wanted a girlfriend but I couldn't be bothered to deserve one.

To be fair to myself, I was really very unhappy.

I registered Mum's absence from the bungalow as a daily assault. I would dream of her all night and wake up to a punch in the face. The absence was more like a presence — about as small, harmless and unnoticeable as your average black hole. She was everywhere I looked. She was also dead.

The sound of Derek trying to bring up a three-year-old on his own, with zero previous experience, was also deeply unrelaxing. The poor bloke didn't have a clue and neither did I. And then the pressure of A levels and internal exams, always real but now with a self-imposed fantasy of Big Screen Escape welded to them — that was distinctly problematic. Eventually I just got ill.

Derek had his hands full, but one of the things we might have expected him to do was dispose of the Tupperware box of Mum's medication that was still next to the toaster in the kitchen seven weeks after she'd died. You know, the box containing the kind of painkillers you give to people with stage-four cancer. That box. It was safely out of Anna-Beth's reach, but not out of mine.

I should have got rid of it myself but I didn't think that was my job. And anyway, people in this kind of danger don't always tend to notice that they're in danger at all.

I know some people think "trigger warnings" are silly, but it seems only polite to mention that there follows a diary entry of someone trying to talk himself into suicide. So look, if you're having a particularly rough time and you feel like skipping this next bit, go ahead. You won't be missing much that you don't already know about. Suffice it to say that you're not alone.

The entry goes on for three pages, with the handwriting getting wilder by the line. I'll give you the first bit.

June 12th 1990
It's 11.33 pm. I've got an English exam in the
morning, History on Thursday and Economics
on Friday. I don't know any of it. None. I've
been ill for the last 3 weeks and I'm so tired and
so fucking sick of it. I'm never going to see her
again and everything is pressure. I suddenly
thought I could make it all stop and I cried for
about an hour and wrote the note. I looked at
the box and then I came back and looked at the
box and then brought it in here with a pint of
water. It's all just a painful march towards death
so why prolong it and all that stopped me was
what it would do to everyone else. Tru and Dada
and all of them. So I'm still here but I don't
want to be I don't want to be I don't want to be
leave me alone God just let me drift forever
where no one can touch or reach me I think
"this is it, just fucking do it" but there's no
escape and I can't do that to them and just
someone give her back to me and let me be her
little boy that she's proud of . . .

All right then, mate, that'll do.

But then you remember what I said about young
people and bouncing, right? The next morning:

June 13th 1990
Christ, what was all that about? I'm off to school
to fuck up an Economics exam — who gives a
fuck? I'm trying not to regret being honest last

night but feel like scribbling all that shit out. I'm ashamed of the hand that wrote it. I'll leave it for now, in case it's useful one day but God knows why. The note's in the bin in a million pieces. It's a fucking disgrace. Get a grip, boy. Get a fucking grip.

Boiiingg! Yes, there's a self-dramatising element to both entries which won't come as much of a surprise to anyone who's ever met a teenager or an actor. But the impulse was real enough. It was a peek over the cliff edge and it wouldn't be the last. And obviously, you don't have to be a teenager or an actor. Three-quarters of the people who kill themselves in the UK are men.

Anyway, I was alive, which is always a good start if you want to get better.

And I had friends.

Two seventeen-year-old boys are holding hands in bed. One of them is Will; the other one has just stopped crying.

Will is wondering how long this is going to take. It was likely that being best mates with someone whose mum has just died was going to involve some kind of emotional doobly-woobly, but he wasn't expecting it here and now, at 5a.m. in a double bed in a rented holiday house in Torquay. There again, there's never a good time for this sort of thing. I feel an urge to get up and put some clothes on. But then — not so fast — because Will is holding my hand. He never holds my hand.

"I thought," he ventures, "I wondered when it was gonna . . . hit you. Y'know, when it was going to sink in." In the dark, my breathing has returned to desultory after-gulps and I can half smile at this. "Sink in" is a sporting metaphor, as in: "Gary Lineker, you just shat yourself in front of a World Cup TV audience of 700 million people. Has it sunk in?"

We listen to the hiss of the cassette player as the tape reaches the end of its side. It's a mix-tape and the last track was a song by Prince called "Sometimes It Snows in April". That's what triggered this particular bit of sinking-in. It's August.

Lamely, I say, "I suppose I've had plenty of time to get used to it." This is the best I can do given that I'm now talking to him long-distance from the Land of the Recently Bereaved. I'm in a new state. We do things differently here — we know things that people in the old country, the Land of Everything Is Still Normal, do not know. It's already obvious to me that Mum's death is not going to Sink In and neither will I ever be Over It. The best I can do is coexist with it. Grief has to talk to normality, normality has to talk to grief, and they both have to listen. It's an ongoing peace deal, a two-state solution.

I'm not thinking about this in bed. Instead, I'm thinking the thing that I usually think in the company of Will — "I wonder what Will is thinking?"

He shifts his weight slightly. "I didn't hear Ralph come in. D'you think he's sleeping on the beach again?"

Oh, OK — that's that then. Gently, I let go of Will's hand.

Ralph is one of the five other school friends we're sharing the house and the holiday with. Yesterday he wouldn't shut up about how amazing it was to sleep on the flat, warm rocks, and the day before that he wouldn't shut up about his distaste for under-arm deodorant because, "I don't like putting chemicals on my body."

I say, "I don't care as long as he has a bloody shower when he gets back." This gets a bigger chuckle than it deserves and Will's relief makes me glad. Still, the emotional temperature is only just returning to normal and he leaves what he imagines to be a tactful pause before checking his watch with his now free hand. This is the kind of thing that makes me want to found a minor religion in his honour.

It's a hot summer and neither of us can be bothered any more with that extra bit of admin to do with special night clothes. Practical enough — and I guess there must be plenty of other male friends who would be happy to share a double bed naked. I just don't know any. Something is clearly going on, although neither of us could quite say what. Will patrols his heterosexuality like a prison guard who has recently lost faith in the penal system. Or maybe one who favours reform of the penile system (thanks and sorry . . .). It's unthinkable that Will is secretly gay or even secretly bisexual, but his curiosity — maybe his sympathy — allow him to be secretly something-or-other with me. And as for me, I don't know what I am, but I know what I like, and what

I like is Will. What happens exactly? I touch him; he doesn't mind; I'm grateful. And repeat. It's not exactly Torvill and Dean. A few years later, he touches me. I'm even more grateful. Frankly, the sex is pathetic.

But the love . . . my goodness me. You don't choose your first love. I was lucky with Will.

Whatever's going on, it's only the eye-catching headline of the real-life story of everyday teenagers titting around. We drive to Boston and walk into River Island, hearing En Vogue's "Hold On" playing through the speakers and suddenly notice we're striding down parallel aisles to the beat. We get to the end of the shop, turn round and stride straight out again, like idiotic dudes.

And all the rest — the hysterical argument about whether Oliver Reed was in *Castaway* or *The Blue Lagoon*, the underage piss-ups in fields before barn-dances, the joint love for all things Prince, Robin Williams, and Fry and Laurie, the competitive impressions of friends and teachers, the pound-a-pint games of pool, my attempts to teach him the moonwalk, his attempts to teach me the chords of A and D, the many splendid parties and the fun, the honest-to-God fun of it. And there he is, holding my hand in the dark because he's friend enough and man enough.

The friendship will last. But soon, he'll have a girlfriend, one he'll be crazy about. The sense that he's crossed the boundaries of his masculinity will catch up with him and he'll become colder towards me for a while. And he'll remember that he should care, as he

214

currently does not care — now, in August 1990 — as he gets out of bed and saunters from the room towards the loo, that I am watching the lean, easy movement of his body in the breaking dawn light.

As things are, he looks straight back at me with a tarty smirk as he goes through the door. In the window the closed drapes have begun to glow with the last day of the holiday. Gentle beams of light pierce the cracks and tears in the fabric as if a benign alien power were probing the room for signs of intelligent life. I notice the moment, and because I am seventeen, I notice myself noticing. I marvel that something so present will soon become real only in memory. This moment, a happy one, will vanish. But it will be there to be recreated another time, any time — just as I daily reconstruct the sound of my mother's voice.

Another friend.

I'm sitting outside Room 9 at school with Mrs Slater. It's a sunny day and she's opened the fire exit which gives onto a patch of grass. We've got two chairs and two copies of Wordsworth's "Tintern Abbey".

I'd been off with glandular fever but that had subsided by the time I finally hauled my ass to the doctor's. "Tintern Abbey" wasn't on the syllabus and this wasn't an English lesson. Heather Slater just collared me during a free period and sat me down outside. Ostensibly, we were looking at it to catch up on practical criticism.

"I was talking about you with Bob Edwards," she says, "and he said something which might be useful. 'He needs to be a friend to himself.'"

"Right. Thanks," I say.

Ah, so all these years Mr Edwards was a Bob. Fancy that. Absurdly, I want to giggle — I'm still holding on to the childish notion that teachers shouldn't really have first names; it only humanises them and we can't have that. I read the poem aloud and for the first time; slowly and without much interest at first, but then something starts to happen. By the time I get to this passage, it's as if I can feel my soul being stitched back together.

> For I have learned
> To look on nature, not as in the hour
> Of thoughtless youth; but hearing oftentimes
> The still sad music of humanity,
> Nor harsh nor grating, though of ample power
> To chasten and subdue. — And I have felt
> A presence that disturbs me with the joy
> Of elevated thoughts; a sense sublime
> Of something far more deeply interfused,
> Whose dwelling is the light of setting suns,

. . . and on it goes, the writer reflecting on his youth, his memories flickering backwards and forwards across the present, the love for his sister all the more powerful because it already contains grief, his simple acceptance that one of them will one day lose the other, but that the memory of this present joy is a future consolation. And the Abbey, never referred to directly, standing for a subtle spirituality located in nature — Wordsworth's own rhododendron bush, his leafy cathedral.

216

"Just take plenty of fluids," was what the doctor ordered.

What the teacher ordered was Wordsworth. I'd known Mrs Slater's first name for years, and saw now I would have to start using it, what with her being my friend.

I lower the book and squint at the barley fields beyond the edges of the school, just managing to say in her general direction, "Thank you, Heather."

"The One and Only" must be on everybody's list of top ten favourite songs by Chesney Hawkes. But this defiant memorial to the recent downfall of Margaret Thatcher (I assume that's what it's about) was actually written by Nik Kershaw who, here in 1991, already seems like a wizened survivor from a lost world of pop.

I mention Chesney because I borrowed his name for my first car. Four seasons (with the length of four short decades) have gone by since Heather Slater provided a break in the clouds via "Tintern Abbey". All told, that included: the rest of that horrible summer, a melancholy autumn, a pitilessly Mum-free Christmas, and a spring where every diary entry begins with something like: "I shouldn't be writing this, I ought to be doing some revision. I haven't done any revision." I have a timetable for A-level revision which itself becomes much revised, a fixed amount of work slowly corrugating under the pressure of time . . .

But never mind because I've bought a car! It's a second-hand Nissan Cherry — "Chesney". Mum's "estate", such as it is, has gone to Derek and

Anna-Beth, but she had a life insurance policy which is split three ways between the boys. This gives me a windfall of £615 and I blow £500 of it on Chesney. It's a sporty-looking two-tone blue coupé with a curvy back windscreen and a five-speed gearbox which belies its tiny engine. It beeps when you put it in reverse. I love it.

Despite this, when it comes to important visits or interviews, I don't trust myself to navigate the two-hour hop down the A1 to Cambridge, and, if I'm honest, I don't quite trust Chesney to make it there and back either. That car proves itself to be a two-tone rock of dependability unless it happens to be raining. If it's raining, Chesney won't start. Derek shows me how to spray WD-40 under the distributor cap, but that doesn't always work. One day soon, as with my beloved Grifter, Chesney's chain will slip in the most spectacular way.

Carole, my mum's top friend and increasingly one of my own, steps in with the offer of a lift, which becomes the offer of three lifts. We visit King's College, then Robinson College and then finally she drives me to my interview — at Robinson College.

Although colleges weren't formally allowed to discriminate on any basis except academic merit, I looked around at the students at Robinson and was encouraged to see eighteen- to twenty-three-year-olds who didn't necessarily scare the daylights out of me. They were all quite badly dressed and normal-looking. Outside, a couple of male undergraduates were dicking about with water-pistols and some female students

218

walked by and told them to grow the fuck up. All very familiar — I could almost imagine a game of Ball Death.

I didn't think the interview went well, but it didn't feel like a disaster. I'd been expecting a certain amount of the fabled Oxbridge Don Bullshit — you know, an old man who looks like J. R. R. Tolkien staring at you in silence and then shouting "Surprise me!" And then you're supposed to set fire to his beard or something — to show independence of thought or whatnot.

What I actually got was a couple of lightning-fast teachers asking me straightforward questions about books. Since Heather Slater herself was no slouch, this, like Ball Death, was familiar enough.

Carole drops me off back at the bungalow. I thank her and then, as I'm unclicking my seatbelt, she says, "I know you'd rather your mother had taken you, Robert — I hope you don't think I'm overly interfering."

The idea that such a close friend of Mum's and such a proper grown-up is now slightly fishing for reassurance from the likes of me is in itself a compliment, albeit an alarming one. But then, I think, it's her friendship with Mum that's doing this. Carole doesn't have any children and she's genuinely wondering if Pat would approve of this help. She's wondering if she shouldn't just have said, "Get on the bloody train, Robert."

My instinct is to say, "Noo, noo, Carole — you went to the LSE and worked in the City! Only you could help me in this academic way!" But while those facts would be true, the sentiment would be quite false. Of course I wished I was doing this with Mum. I wanted Cambridge to turn her head the way it turned mine. But then, if Mum had been healthy and alive, I'd have probably insisted on taking the train. What I partly miss about having a mum is the teenager's God-given right to refuse her help.

I say, truthfully, "Well, if it can't be her, there's no one I'd rather it was than you."

The woman who kept it together while nursing her great friend keeps it together still. But for once, she blinks away a couple of tears. She squeezes my hand. People keep squeezing my hand and I like it.

"Thank you, dear."

Robinson sends me an offer of a place if I get AAB. My second choice, Leeds, offers ABC. It ought to be amazing news. I ought to find it inspirational.

I almost completely seize up. I love English and I'm good at it, so I do the very least work that I can get away with. In History and Economics, I'm nowhere near so diligent. At forty-three, I still dream about those History and Economics exams. Unlike the bike crash, they were so completely swervable if I'd done some work. Here come the essay questions on the exam papers, one after another: "No, I can't do that one. No, I can't quite do that one. No, I definitely can't do that one at all. That one I could at least . . . no, I can't do that one."

My results, when I drive into school to collect them one morning in August, shouldn't have come as any surprise, but they take my head off anyway. In the common room, we all form a silent gaggle around Bob Edwards, who hands us pieces of folded paper.

Tiffany is there and notices my expression. She's got what she needs for Durham and I'm pleased for her. She does her best when I hand her my own piece of paper.

"Wow, an A in English, you brainy bastard! And . . . yeah . . ." She looks again at the other results, crinkling the paper between her turquoise fingernails, ". . . two Cs. Oh, fuck. Probably enough for Leeds, though!?"

"No."

"Or a poly?"

"Didn't apply."

"Right," she mutters quickly, "neither did I. Or . . . Clearing? Or you can retake?"

"Yeah. Something like that."

She gives me a hug. We were going our separate ways anyway, but this is much worse. She is instantly, before my very eyes, a university undergraduate. I am confirmed as a geriatric Lincolnshire schoolboy. Unlike the guys from Boston and Lincoln College, she won't need to pop back to tell us she's cool. She was always going to disappear without giving the rest of us a backwards glance.

That had been my plan too. In my head I'd become a ruthless bastard. I'd just forgotten the bit where ruthless bastards actually put the hours in.

The next morning, a letter arrives from the Senior Tutor at Robinson. I read as far as "I regret to inform you . . ." before screwing it up. I make a half-hearted attempt to ring around some admissions departments, but English is massively oversubscribed and ACC isn't going to do it for anyone. Anyway, Derek is appalled by the implications for the phone bill, which is a good excuse to stop. The bill is quarterly and I can't wait till he finds out I called Aberystwyth.

I numbly fill in a clearing form in the certain knowledge that if I get an offer from De Montfort University (last year's Leicester Polytechnic) I'm going to turn it down. The Leicester Footlights? The De Montfort Players? It's intellectual snobbery as well as comedy snobbery. Probably some normal snobbery in the mix there too. I liked a couple of the people in the year above who went to Leicester, but generally the place seems to be a Dean-magnet and Darren-trap. They come home in the holidays and laugh about it being "pointless" and "a total doss". In my head, and no doubt unfairly, poly equals Gartree. It's a boys' place. Little Lord Reject won't be having that.

Resits then, in November.

But that's impossible. How do you turn two Cs into As when you're living with Derek?

My step-dad was a gentle chap and kind in many ways. Mindful of Anna-Beth, if I were the sort of writer who puts Post-it notes around the edges of his computer screen, I'd now be looking at a really big one that said, "Try not to be too much of an arsehole about Derek in 1991." The diary is surprisingly fair, up to a point. I acknowledge that this is my very own balls-up.

Yes, there's an emotional context to the exam bike-crash. But I also get that I could have done much better and I take ownership of most of the failure.

But wait a second, because when I start contemplating resits — doing it all over again — I can't help thinking of the other context: the bungalow.

Many years later, when she was about sixteen, Anna-Beth came to stay with me for a couple of days in the flat I was renting in Kilburn. One night she asked, simply enough, "Why did you leave?" I'm not sure I did a very good job of explaining. I think 31 said something groovy like, "I just needed a change of scene."

Mm-hmm. Let me take another swing at that.

The bungalow was a slow-motion nightmare of almost total dysfunction. Frankly, it's amazing nobody else died. Two men in grief, two men who can't cook and don't know how to work the washing machine, two men who don't know how to talk to each other and who haven't got the first clue about bringing up a child. One man who is still a boy, who thinks his exams are the most important thing in the universe, but who can't or won't do any work. One man who left school at fifteen, but goes along with the idea of education while finding it faintly ridiculous.

If this were a heart-warming TV drama, the characters of Rob and Derek would find a way to communicate about their shared loss and form some kind of madcap team. A younger Martin Freeman and an older, larger Craig Cash would invent a crazy system for doing the washing-up and drying the dishes in an upbeat montage to a soundtrack by Right Said Fred.

But no, it was even shitter than that. Which is saying REALLY QUITE A LOT about how shit it was. There was no team and no system.

The *Robert and Derek Do Emotional Articulacy Summertime Special* gets off to a cracking start when he gives me the bill for my eighteenth birthday party. I'd hired the Community Centre. It was £20, which represents two nights and a full Saturday at Gateway. He hands it over.

"Oh, right. Are you not going to pay this, then?" I ask.

"Well, y'mum would've paid it and she gave some of her money to you."

I see. I wonder if he's going to invoice me for the flowers and the hearse. Clearly, having someone else pay for my eighteenth birthday party is the kind of *outrageous treat* that I can now expect a lot less of around here.

One evening he puts his head around my bedroom door while I'm revising for an exam and asks me, not for the first time, to "nip down the shops on your bike and get a pint of milk". It's a twenty-minute round trip and, for once, I refuse. Derek protests, "But I do everything!"

It's true — he does do everything, which is a tough beat for a man who previously did nothing. I continue to do nothing while he does everything . . . badly.

★   ★   ★

And then there was Chesney's chain-slipping finest hour. When I have morning exams, I try and cram at home and then drive to school, instead of doing the sensible thing and taking the school bus. On the morning of my first English paper, I don't notice that it's been raining all night. You already know how Chesney feels about rain.

"Des, mate, the car won't start and I've got an exam. Can you drive me to school?"

My index finger is bleeding from Chesney's crappy little ignition key digging into it as I tried to get the stupid fucker to start. It's a Monday and Anna-Beth is still at John and Trudy's house. There's nothing to stop Derek giving me a lift, except his habits. He's always been a creature of habit, a monster of habit. He looks at me like I've just asked him to go pearl-diving off the coast of Antigua.

"But I've not had me Mellow Birds, n'nothing!"

"Yeah, but I've got an exam. I've got an exam!"

"But I'm not even dressed and I've not had me coffee!"

I run the half mile to John and Trudy's house. John, who is also in his pyjamas, and who also left school at fifteen, gives me his car keys in a heartbeat, despite the fact that I'm half hysterical and fully uninsured.

But the really tough stuff was with Anna-Beth. She ruled Derek with a rod of iron. She was, of course, only doing what small children do when they don't know the rules — mainly because they're being raised by a parent who keeps asking them what the rules might be.

"D'you think it might be time for bed, ducky?"

"No."

"Right. I mean, it's half past ten now, so it might . . ."

"No."

"Shall I get y'milk? Eh? I'll get y'milk, shall I?"

"NO, I DON'T WANT M'MILK YET!"

"Right."

One night, she was climbing onto a kitchen chair and obviously about to fall off. I asked her to get down and she wouldn't. So I lifted her down. She grabbed a tea-towel and threw it at me with that ineffectual toddler fury that makes them even more furious. I'm sorry to say that I shouted at her: "You DON'T throw things at people!" She stood there, bamboozled for a moment because this wasn't like Robert, in fact it wasn't like anything she'd ever heard. And then her face crumpled and she ran from the kitchen.

She had to run to the main bedroom, of course. Great. She went round Mum's side of the bed, buried her face in the carpet and howled. Maybe she chose that room at random, but my teenage, storytelling mind wouldn't hear of it. No, she ran to Mummy to protect her from the scary man, just as I did. And now I was the scary man, and there was no Mummy to run to. It's just us. I lifted her up and cuddled her and said, "Sorry, I'm so sorry." Presently, she made a funny face and tried to dry my eyes with the sleeve of her cardigan.

It was too much, far too much for me. I had to resit those exams, but not from here. The thought of staying in the bungalow with the same unbearable absence hanging around the place . . . the black hole present in every room, every smell, every sound, from the squeak of the sofa to the hum of the fridge . . . this place was a tomb and not even a quiet one.

Forgive me, little A-B. I can't look after you; maybe in the future I can look out for you. First, though, I need to be stronger. Much stronger than this. I'm sorry, my love, I have to run away.

It's not just the exams. In his romantic, grief-stricken brain, something is calling to Luke Skywalker — some unfinished business. Somebody must be to blame for all this. Somebody's going to get this in the neck and it's not Uncle Owen. Not the surrogate dad who thwarts our hero's quest for adventure. The other one, the hidden dad, the Dark Lord of the Carling Black Label.

Where does a Mummy's Boy go when he's got no Mummy? Where do you turn when you've run out of space?

You turn around. You run at the thing you've been running from.

He was waiting for me.

ACT TWO

CHAPTER
NINE

Men Are Organised

"You live and learn. At any rate, you live."
Douglas Adams

He's chewing gum, which is odd because it's the kind of thing which, in others, he would describe as "a bit yobbish if you ask me, but anyway". He sees my surprise.

"You'll have to excuse the gum, boy, I'm trying to stop smoking."

"Righto."

He's grinning at me through the chewing. A few seconds ago I said, "Dad, can we have a quick word?" This is the first time I've actually asked to talk to him about anything. We're outside the kitchen of the Dower House where Carole has given me a job washing dishes and painting window frames. He'd stopped by to deliver some chillies which he grows and sells to local businesses — one of his various hobbies and sidelines.

"Erm, you know you said that I could come and live with you if . . ."

"Yes?!"

"Well, if the offer's still open, I think I'd like —"

"Oh, YES mate! Good old boy! You don't need to ask, bo — Rob. It's your home, Rob. Good!"

"It's just I've got to retake these exams and . . ."

"You can have your old room, mate. Now, it's mucky as hell at the minute because I'm propagating marigolds in it, but I know exactly where to put them. I can soon get that sorted, no problem. When are you thinking of moving in, so to speak?"

"Well, I need to tell Derek. It's really only for a few months, what with these exams and . . ."

"Derek been driving you up the bloody wall. Poor old boy, he'll never change. And little Anna-Beth, bless 'er. It's not what you NEED, is it, boy? You need some bloody PEACE, mate. For your exams!"

"Well, this is it . . . mate."

"I'm right, aren't I?"

"Yeah."

"I'm right, aren't I?"

"You are, yep."

"I know I am, mate. Now my lady-friend Delia comes to stay with us a few days a week, but we won't mind her. You remember Delia, boy?" Ah yes, Delilah.

"Yep."

"She'll not bother you, mate, you do your own thing." He takes his gum out and looks around, but can't see a bin so puts it back in his mouth. He's frowning with concentration now — there's a lot to think about.

"I'm not saying the place is spotless, but it's *clean*, boy, that's the main thing. I have this woman come on a Thursday and she . . ."

232

"Josie?"

"That's right! Oh, d'you know Josie?"

"You must have mentioned her."

"Bloody good cleaner, boy, bloody good. Hard worker. Real grafter." There's a brief lull while we both stand there nodding and considering Josie and her tireless dedication. I say, "So I'll tell Derek tonight and p'haps move in at the weekend."

"Righto, boy. Poor old Derek. He'll never change."

I break the news to Derek that night over tea and he makes it easier for me by saying all the wrong things. "Well, y'poor old mum wanted you to stay here with us."

This is how he's been referring to Mum for the last sixteen months — "y'poor old mum". I suppose it's meant with love, but the condescension of it drives me nuts. In my memory, she's alive and well, not poor and old. Any year now, I might have to say something. Actually no, easier just to move house.

What I do say, as calmly as possible, is: "Well, she didn't quite say that, did she? She said I didn't have to live with Fred if I didn't want to. But now I sort of want to. And she didn't know I was going to have to retake my exams, did she?"

"Anna-Beth's gonna miss yer."

I take another breath. In 1991 the phrase "guilt-trip" isn't yet in common usage, but somebody needs to invent it and quickly. I feel terrible about A-B. It doesn't occur to me that when he says she's going to miss me, he's actually saying that *he's* going to miss

233

me. If he liked me that much, why had he been so bloody annoying? In fact, why was he still being so bloody annoying now?

The priority now in the masculine mind of the boy who claims he doesn't like masculinity is to become angry with Derek. Obviously I'm still heartbroken about Mum, so I'm angry with Derek. I feel guilty about abandoning Anna-Beth, so I'm angry with Derek. I feel sorry for Derek, so I'm angry with Derek. I'm anxious about what it's going to be like living with Dad and scared of screwing my exams up again, so I'm already angry with Dad but equally angry with Derek. There again, even if I noticed any of this, I wouldn't share it with Derek because I'm obviously afraid of upsetting Derek, which itself makes me angry with Derek.

Now that I am a Man, I have graduated to an advanced level of blaming other people for unwanted feelings. Luckily I'm handling this brilliantly. It's not as if I'm going to nurse that grievance about the bill for my birthday party into my mid-forties, is it? No, I'll just pretend that all I need is a change of scene.

Derek says, with touching innocence, "It's nothing that I've done wrong, is it?"

I give an involuntary yelp of laughter, but try to turn it into a "the very idea!" kind of chuckle. He smiles along with me. "No, Des, it's nothing like that."

"Oh . . . good."

"I just need a change of scene."

"Yeah . . ." I can see that he doesn't really buy it, but I haven't given him a choice. It turns out I am a ruthless bastard after all.

234

Except, that's not how it feels when I've finished packing the car the next day and say goodbye. I tell him I'll see him on Sunday, which is true enough, and with Tru and John around I'll see plenty of them all. But there's no point pretending that this isn't a big deal. The bungalow was home for fourteen years. Then Mum died; then I moved out. I'm closing the front door when I hear his voice calling from the kitchen. "We'll miss yer!"

I hear the catch in my throat as I call back, truthfully, "I'll miss you too."

I close the door as gently as I can.

He's at pains to avoid calling them "rules"; instead, he mentions "just a few guidelines, so to speak, so we don't drive each other crackers". This is very welcome — I'm extremely keen not to annoy Dad. Really very keen indeed. Obviously, if I think too hard about how he used to treat Mum, there's always the chance I might kill him. Otherwise I'm just scared of him. It's the perfect domestic arrangement.

The deal is that he cooks and I do the washing-up, including the milk bottles. They need to be thoroughly clean so that the milkman doesn't get milky fingers when he picks them up from the porch outside. Dad seems very confident that the milkman's preferred technique when he picks up a pair of empty milk bottles is to insert his fingers into the bottle necks. I can hear the contempt in Dad's voice for those other, thoughtless wankers who don't wash their milk bottles. Not only would the milkman get all milky, but the milk would make the bottles slippery and they might get dropped and smashed. And that, as Dad points out, "is the last fucking thing we need". I privately wonder what might be the second-to-last fucking thing we need and I suspect the list thereafter is quite long. But this is the honeymoon period and I try to admire his consideration for a fellow working man.

There again, I had no idea that in the last fourteen years he had grown so fastidious. I note with alarm that the items on the table in the front room — telephone, pens, notepad, place mats, wallet — are all arranged at perfect right-angles to each other.

He tells me that he understands that teenagers find it a bit of a struggle to get up in the morning, but he would appreciate it if my bedroom curtains were open by 8a.m. — even if I subsequently go back to bed — so that the neighbours opposite don't think I'm a sloven and a layabout. I'm about to say that I don't really mind what they think of me when I realise it's not my reputation that's at stake here, it's his. He won't have it whispered darkly that his son is a layabout or, indeed, that he's the sort of man who could possibly tolerate living with one. So . . . what I now do reflects directly on him. A feeling of unease begins to take hold.

Could I *please* park my car exactly here? It's not much to ask, is it? There's a public track running past the side of Slieve Moyne which splinters off to curl around the back of the house. At that point it becomes private and what we might grandly call a driveway. There's plenty of room but, merely as a guideline, it's worth showing me to the nearest square inch where

236

Chesney's front right tyre will need to land before it "starts to make the place look untidy".

It's 10.30a.m. and he's got a can of Carling on the go as he takes me through all this. That's quite a departure from Derek, but I figure it's a Sunday and what the hell. Still, he's now boring himself and so speeds up.

"D'you know how to work a washing machine, boy?"

"Well . . ."

"Didn't think so. Here." He puts his can down and shows me the washing powder under the sink. "Powder. Expensive. Goes in 'ere." He yanks open the powder drawer on the washing machine. He then teaches me very badly about what the various dials do. I'm nodding along in my best impression of taking in complicated information with surprising ease. At the same time I rack my brain for a memory of Woodhall Spa ever having a launderette. Like the one in the Levi's advert with the soundtrack of "I Heard It Through the Grapevine" and that beautiful model taking his clothes off. No, don't think about the model. Anyway, to use a launderette in Woodhall would surely invite censure and ridicule, as if you're letting the side down. I've still got a hundred pounds of my inheritance left, plus what I earn at Gateway — maybe I could just carry on buying underwear until I move out? I now regret turning down the offer of a lager.

"I think that's it, boy. Obviously use the loo brush properly and don't leave any crap round the pan, especially when Delia stays. You know what women are like."

"Yeah," I say, trying to communicate a worldly tolerance of these fussy women and their quirky aversion to human shit. He rattles his empty can and thrusts it in the kitchen bin before moving to the fridge. "You sure you won't have a beer, boy?"

"I will actually, mate, yes please."

It'll be fine.

As long as he doesn't know I'm still thinking about Nick Kamen in his boxer shorts, it'll be fine.

There's another interview at Cambridge and another offer. My headmaster, Thomas Beaker, tells me that a second offer is extremely rare and that "You've got a good chance now." I have to turn the two Cs into two As. The resits are in November, so I've got two clear months and a quiet house to revise in. Great.

You'd think I'd do some work at this point, wouldn't you? You'd think I'd want to get this A-level stuff out of the way, if for no better reason than to avoid boring the patient readers of my future memoir. Sadly, some of us really are slow learners.

I do the washing-up at home; I do the washing-up at the Dower House; I hang out with Will, mending and spraying over bits of rust on our cars. I go out most nights, without much enthusiasm. I give meticulous attention to my revision timetable, using different coloured pens to outline exactly when in the future I'm going to open a book. I open a book and look at diagrams of Supply and Demand. I think of the bungalow. I close the book. I quit Gateway, saying I need to concentrate on my studies and then ask the manager for my job back the following week. It occurs to me while listlessly taking in the teatime repeat of *Neighbours* that I'd already watched four hours earlier, that something is up. But then, self-awareness is not the same thing as wisdom, nor wisdom the same thing as action.

I spend September imagining how hard I'm going to work in October. I spend October wishing I'd done some work in September.

By November, I speculate with almost out-of-body detachment that it's quite likely I'm about to turn my Cs into Ds, Es, or just "We're sorry you spent all that money on pens."

It's four days until my first exam. I've done nothing.

The moment calls for a decisive gesture — I give up. Or rather, I attempt what "Stormin' Norman" Schwarzkopf — much in the news earlier that year — might call the "Mother of All Tactical Deadline Adjustments". I drive Chesney slowly into school and ask to see Mr Beaker. He enquires how my revision is going and whether I'm excited about the upcoming "simple task". I tell him about *Neighbours* and ask if I can return to school, sit in the classes of the year below and retake the exams next summer.

It's always difficult to tell with a man with a beard, but I'm pretty sure I've just ruined his week. The look on his face as he calibrates his answer is increasingly familiar. It's that "I knew we were going to have to cut this guy some slack but this is ridiculous" look.

He agrees to take me back but concludes that this sends a terrible message to Cambridge and it's probably "curtains" as far as they are concerned. He doesn't put it in exactly these terms, but it's quite clear that I've royally bollocksed everything to arse.

I go home to tell Dad that I'm going to be living with him for another seven months. I'll do my "straight-talking" — short, concise sentences, fairly loud. He appreciates that.

I wait till after tea. Half an enormous marrow each (from the garden), stuffed with mince and onion. With potatoes, carrots and broad beans — also from the garden — and bacon and Lincolnshire sausages on the side. Also beer. He does something like this most days. We live like kings. Or, at least, Hobbits of the Shire.

"Dad, I haven't been very honest with you about the amount of work I've been doing."

"Righto, boy."

"I've actually done fuck-all."

"OK."

"I've found it really hard to concentrate. I don't know why — maybe I . . ."

"Y'mum just died, mate."

He says it like it's the most obvious reason in the world, which it suddenly is. So much for my straight-talking. I wasn't expecting this.

I say, quietly, "Yeah, but that was over a year ago."

"It was yesterday, boy. Might as well have been yesterday." He lights a cigarette and looks down at his knackered hands. His comment was a flash of brilliance

240

and I think for a second that we're going to stay in its warmth, but he's already embarrassed by it and looking for some shade. He's still grieving too. I had no idea.

"It's 'ard, Rob, what you're doing. I couldn't bloody do it. I was a dead loss at school. Apart from gymnastics. I enjoyed gymnastics — old Gerry Leighton used to teach me."

"He's still there."

"Is he still there?"

"I think I told you before."

"Is he really?"

"Yes."

"Fancy that. Anyway, I'm sure you're doing your best, boy, in your own way, bless your old heart."

He seems pleased that we've had this frank discussion, but now, rubbing what's left of one chain-sawed thumb over the other, he's visibly cheering himself up by reliving his achievements on the trampoline or parallel bars or whatever it was. I'm tempted to leave him there, but want yet more reassurance and I know how to get it. Sorry, Headmaster.

"Beaker says it's curtains for Cambridge."

He looks up. "Cunt! What does he know?"

"Well . . . he knows quite a lot, but . . . we'll see."

"We will bloody see, boy. We will. 'Curtains,' he says. Bugger Beaker."

So then, *Back to Skool*. I put on my sixth-form uniform in the bedroom that used to have Rupert the Bear wallpaper and a poster of Steve Austin. Everything

241

is too small. It's wrong to sleep in this bed now that I've got armpit hair. It's also wrong to put a school tie on when all your friends are taking a degree. I feel like a giant — overdeveloped and stupid, walking into doorframes, clumsily doing up his buttons.

I keep thinking of what John said when I was trying to help him in the Golf Club garden: "Yeh — you're getting in your own way, mate."

I really have got spectacularly in my own way this time. At least the curtain people have gone — the ones who used to organise the bad dreams. My dreams are fine now. Whatever I failed to do over the last three months, there's one thing I did manage by accident — I had a rest. "He needs to be a friend to himself," said Mr Edwards. I'm not sure that this — what is euphemistically known as a Third-Year Sixth — is quite the self-care he had in mind.

One Sunday in the pub, Andrew asks me if Dad makes me a packed lunch for school and gives me a kiss as he waves me off. I tell him that's exactly what happens and I also tell him to fuck off. I'm just relieved that the situation merits a joke. It's when the jokes dry up that you know you're in trouble.

I'm sharing the sixth form with people that Pete, Will and I used to refer to as "winkles". The little kids. They're not so little any more — they're my History and Economics A-level co-winkies. Pete has got himself a job and so has Will, although the latter is bound for a two-year course in Preston that he's obviously going to hate. Accountancy, for crying out loud. To me, Will is

242

destined to be an accountant the way Jay Gatsby was always going to end up selling pet insurance. But I suppose the way I see Will isn't the way he sees himself, so I try to look encouraging.

Tiffany writes to me from Durham and has given me her incomprehensible History notes. Ex-girlfriend Isabel is doing an Art course in Lincoln.

My only available tactic for coping with this level of self-inflicted humiliation is to get the jokes in first. Otherwise, I roam the corridors quietly. My edges are being planed off with a power tool. I'm gagging on humble pie. I tread softly like one who has just performed an eighteen-month tap dance on his own dreams.

The present Upper Sixth treat me with a sort of fascinated horror, but also a weird respect. I am, after all, the school superstar, the one who does all the funny plays and sketches. Most of them also know my mum died and that I'm here because I'm hell-bent on Cambridge — all rather glamorous, intentionally or not. It's the glances I get from younger pupils that give me the fear. I'm a cautionary tale. I'm the scary story you tell your children to get them to do their homework — "Once upon a time, there was a nineteen-year-old man in a school blazer . . ."

It's not like I don't know anyone. Daisy, Will's ex-girlfriend, is as friendly as ever. I even forgive her for shagging Will, though not out loud. And, incredibly, Marina seems to have forgiven *me*. She's in the Lower Sixth, but crosses the invisible border in the common room to say hi.

243

I notice that there are rumours about me and Will which I do nothing to discourage. In fact, I start to cultivate a deliberate sexual ambiguity. In a common-room chat about *Thelma & Louise*, I casually mention that Brad Pitt is "obviously some beautiful model they've given a few lines to" and my co-winkies seem to appreciate my bullshit insights into Hollywood while going a bit quiet at that use of the word "beautiful". It doesn't take much.

Similarly, when our Economics teacher describes (bisexual) John Maynard Keynes as "certainly very confused about his sexuality", I ask him what could possibly be confusing about it. At this point, there are posters of key economic graphs and diagrams that suddenly fall to the floor all around us because I've created a level of embarrassment in that classroom that melts Blu-Tack. To his credit, the teacher good-naturedly corrects himself, but I seem to be on a kind of mission.

Some of this is a demand for attention just to liven things up around here. Mainly, it's a growing exasperation with Dad and the peculiar opinions he shares with me every evening. For example, there's an amiable couple of middle-aged men, Tim and Frank, who run a local fish and chip shop. Dad admires their fish and chips. He says one night, "The thing about shirt-lifters, they've always got something extra. It's true, isn't it? I know you like your Stephen Fry, boy, and he's clever, in't he? I can't be doing with Boy George, the dirty bastard, but you can see he knows his business. Same with Tim and Frank. Bloody good chips. *And* fish. They've always got *something*. Not just Tim and Frank — I mean arse-bandits in the round."

I briefly promise myself to one day write a play called *Arse-Bandits in the Round*, but otherwise nod quietly through this, tucking in to my massive mixed grill with cheesy mash.

I get lazy in my observance of Dad's "guidelines" and he occasionally throws a wobbly. His technique is to store up about a fortnight's worth of tiny resentments and then let them all flood out in a noisy mini-bollocking.

"You do the washing-up IN THE MORNING, boy! Not when you feel like it. D'YOU 'EAR? And don't think I haven't noticed that you never bother on a Thursday so you can leave it to Josie — because I have."

"Right, well, sorry about that but . . ."

"There's no need to be sorry! This is your home! And another thing — you need to wash the bath out after you've been in it."

"I do!"

"Not yesterday you didn't."

"OK, well, that is embarrassing because I thought . . ."

"It's not embarrassing! You live here. Mark was just the same when he first came here and by the time he left he knew how to live with someone without being a twat."

I start to walk upstairs.

"Where you going?"

"I'm a twat, apparently. So I won't keep you."

Walking away is the only reply that actually gets to him. I hear him swearing and banging a few doors downstairs for a couple of minutes and then he pulls himself together. He calls up, "I'm only hard on people I care about, boy!"

I don't answer. He goes to the pub.

The diary becomes a storage vessel of angry denunciations along the "who the hell gave him permission to talk to me like that?" lines. On paper, I'm a fearless warrior. In the house, I hardly speak. For obvious reasons, I particularly hate it when he loses his temper. I start to dread teatime when he'll put on *Channel 4 News* to have an excited rant at whatever queer, leftie, bleeding-heart or woman is currently failing to support the status quo. His only area of self-censorship is in the matter of race: I never hear him use the n-word, for example, but this level of self-restraint costs him dearly and everyone else will pick up the tab. He reserves particular contempt for Jon Snow, whose blue eyes and brightly coloured socks and ties present Dad with some kind of primal challenge. "Who's a pretty boy, then!?" he yells at the television one night when Snow is giving some Anglican bishop an averagely hard time.

He rightly suspects that I disagree with him about basically everything and is always keen for us to have a lively debate and a frank exchange of views. So obviously I give him nothing. I go for whichever tack will close the conversation down fastest: I shrug, mumble, dissemble, falsely agree with him, allow him to think I find his views unworthy of my important consideration — whatever it takes.

I do this a) because I'm a lousy debater and hate arguments; b) because there's no arguing with him anyway so what's the point; and c) because I'm still scared of him.

I start to pray. Earnestly and properly, every night, on my knees by the side of the bed. I recite the Lord's Prayer as a sort of gateway prayer. Then I chat to Mum for a while, telling her about my day and complaining about Dad, trying for her to make it funny. Finally I try to barter with God or Jesus, or whoever — I don't know how it's supposed to work — and promise him that I'll lead a decent and useful life if he just gives me this one thing. If he just lets me go to Cambridge, I swear I'll be a kind man and a good servant. Just this one thing, Lord. Just get me the fuck out of here. Sorry about the swearing, Lord. Hope you don't mind.

By the spring of 1992 I'm so sick of Lincolnshire I'm almost struck dumb. I can't say anything in the staffroom at Gateway without someone two years younger than me going, "Ooh! Someone's swallowed a dictionary!" So I don't say anything. At school, the novelty value of having me around has worn off and the sixth form seem to have concluded that I'm a freak and a weirdo. I keep out of their way. With Mark and Andrew, the family dynamic takes hold and I have no confidence in their boisterous company. And I certainly say as little as possible at home. All my friends have gone, apart from Will and he's utterly wrapped up in

247

his new girlfriend. Everyone I fancy isn't interested because I'm too old or too strange.

From April, the diary goes quiet. I stop writing about how I need to do some work and actually do some work. I still pray for two As but also start to try and make them happen. One Saturday, a few days before the exams, Dad invites me into the garden, where he and Delia are having a beer and a barbeque. I say no thanks. He can scarcely believe such incredible willpower. I've won his highest praise — I am now officially "a grafter". It's now or never. Prince Hal is either going to leap onto his horse in a single bound or carry on getting pissed with Falstaff. Luke is either going to leave Tatooine forever, or go to work as a rent boy in the Mos Eisley cantina.

Delia kindly makes me a cooked breakfast on exam mornings, which I manage to find traumatic because that's what Mum used to do for my GCSEs. It feels like I've sold her out.

On the morning of the results, Will picks me up to drive me to school. He laughs and gives me a hug when he sees the sick-looking bastard that greets him at the door. On the way, he swerves the car around to try and cheer me up, which makes me want to strangle him. Mr Edwards is there in the sixth-form common room, standing exactly where he did a year ago, with the same poker face, giving me another carefully folded piece of paper. I take it to a far corner and sit down. Oh well, fuck 'em if they can't take a joke. I open it.

| History | A (a) |
| Economics | A (a) |

Well now, would you look at that? Me, I can't take my eyes off it. Uncomplicated joy doesn't get much less complicated or much more joyful. There again, these days even the best news comes fully loaded. Daisy approaches, concerned. "Bloody hell, Rob, are you OK?"

"Yeah, Daisy, yeah. Very OK, thanks. This is good crying. Very good crying."

That evening, if the sun had known of the pub-crawl to follow, it would have set with a shudder.

I'm sitting at the top of the stairs when Dad comes home. "Boy? Rob?" he shouts as soon as he gets through the door. I come down the stairs, shakily and being careful not to trip. These bloody stairs.

"How d'you get on, son?!" he shouts.

I smile at him, wishing I was cool enough to pause. I'm nowhere near that cool.

"I've got three As and I'm going to Cambridge University."

He throws a fist in the air and says, at the very, very top of his voice, which is quite a loud place, "YEEEEEAAAAAHHH!!!" He then comes at me with frightening speed and gives me a hug that I think might snap me in half. He seems pleased.

We start at the outskirts of the village and steadily work our way in. At every pub, he starts chatting to me or to the people he knows and then suddenly remembers what just happened and randomly gives another full-volume victory-roar. Much as we've had a tough year, I'm inordinately proud to have made him so happy. He takes special pleasure in the fact that his friend Neil's two privately educated sons didn't (for whatever reason) apply to Oxford or Cambridge. He translates that into my having more, or larger, "balls". Well, whatever — let him enjoy it in his own way, I think, magnanimously. Of course, I'm also secretly fucking delighted that I was the first in my family to go anywhere and that I did it from a state school. The fact that I took three years over it will be, in the future, a detail which I tend to glide over.

Never mind. Here are six pubs.

I'm already asleep when he wanders into my room by accident and falls on his face. "Dad, mate. I think you've got the wrong bedroom."

"Righto, boy," he says, getting up. "Comfy!" He wobbles out and I hear him collapse into his own bed. "YEEEAAAHHH!"

I wake up the next morning with the kind of headache only a nineteen-year-old should seriously be expected to deal with. But instead of sawing my own head off, I check the post. Robinson College's Senior Tutor has sent me another letter. "It is with great pleasure . . ." This time, I read the whole thing — but only about thirty times over.

Two months later, Dad is driving his Vauxhall Cavalier with Mark in the passenger seat. I'm crammed in the back, along with the massive suitcase John gave me and a new but artfully battered rucksack. Normal service has been resumed: Dad completely lost it trying to take the front wheel off my bike before stuffing both parts into the boot. Anyway, he doesn't call me lazy any more. He sees the stack of books I've bought from Robinson's English reading list and stops mentioning the 8a.m. curtains. He knows I read all night.

It's drizzling on the A1 and Dad offers an ongoing commentary about how the interval — when his windscreen wipers are on "interval wipe" — is either too short to merit the wipe or too long for him to see where he's going. Mark is not enjoying the ride. If it was him, he'd be driving at twice the speed with four times the competence, so he distracts himself by asking me questions.

"What do you think the bird situation will be like at Cambridge then, Bobs?"

It's not as if I'm indifferent to the bird situation, although I'm fairly sure I won't be calling them birds. I expect the female undergraduates to be exactly like all the other girls and women I've ever met, except that these birds will surely want to fuck me. What with me being so clever and imaginative and everything.

I reply, "Yeah . . ."

Luckily, I've never called them birds out loud, so I won't have to adjust that bit of vocabulary. I've been practising for years talking the way I think a Cambridge student talks, but only to a selected audience — Isabel, Carole, Heather Slater and a couple of other teachers. I'm currently under the impression that it's all to do with irony and detachment. I think that whatever they say, clever people don't mean it. I expect in the next

251

hour to be in the exclusive company of people who would never *dream* of calling a spade a spade. The very idea! Surely, it's all going to be rather camp. And by the time we pass Huntingdon, my accent is finally in line with the geography of England. It was a good four years ago that I started to say "carstle" instead of "caastle" and "ahp" instead of "oop". All the affectations are coming home, I think. To the place where they won't be affectations any more. No more pretending.

We find my room at Robinson and Mark and Dad nearly piss themselves when they see a note on the bed, reading "YOUR BEDMAKER'S NAME IS ALISON". Finally, Little Lord Fauntleroy has staff.

I walk them back to the car. Mark now has business cards and he gives one to me. On the back, he's written, "Whatever the time, day or night, if you need me, give me a call." It occurs to me for the very first time that he's worried about me being here on my own in this new place where he can't keep an eye out for me. I thank him, even though the guilty truth is that I've been at Robinson for ten minutes and haven't felt safer or more at home since Mum died.

"Right then, boy," Dad says. "See you at Christmas. Try not to get VD. Good luck with it all, me old beauty." He's looking emotional too, but mainly he's already annoyed about the drive home, as is poor Mark. We shake hands. They get in the Cavalier and I wave them off until the car is out of sight.

It's a pity I'm wearing trainers because I have no heel to turn on. I turn anyway, put my hands in my pockets and saunter up the brick walkway of the main college gate. I didn't give Darth much of a battle. This will be different. I can stop worrying about how to be a boy. I can stop showing off about how not to be a boy. I'll just be myself.

That shouldn't be too difficult, should it?

CHAPTER
TEN

Men Don't Take Themselves Too Seriously

"So we are a boy, we are a girl."
"Moving" by Suede

"Music is very important to me," says Phil quietly. We all nod at the simple truth of this and watch Phil gently readjust his glasses and take a sip of his peppermint tea. I'm beginning to hate Phil.

There are six of us sitting around the floor of his room and he's just put on a Nina Simone album. Not a Best Of . . . a proper one. It's the second night of Freshers' Week and we've been going round each other's rooms, playing our *very favourite music* to each other. After Phil's room, it's my turn next and I can feel the panic taking hold. I drain the can of Foster's that I've been carrying around. This is the first time I've heard Nina Simone and I'm instantly ashamed that I've never heard that amazing voice before. Everyone else is talking about "Nina" like she's an old mate. So far I've learnt that every one of their parents is a teacher, academic or writer. All ten parents are seemingly all still married.

I've just turned twenty. With my September birthday and my unmissable third-year sixth form, it feels like I'm two years late to the party and also two years under-prepared.

What the hell am I going to play them? Michael Jackson? At least he's . . . y'know, OK, he isn't really "black" any more but . . . oh, why haven't I got any Jackson 5? At least I could say, "Of course he's a joke now, but I quite like his early stuff." But no, that's no good because his early stuff sold millions of records. He did his early stuff when he was tiny — he could dance like James Brown before he could read. No one else seems to think this is cool. No, I won't be inviting them to my room to give them a recital of *Thriller*.

Phil and I are the only boys — there's a tiny, just a subtle feeling of competition. Of course, that's not coming from Phil. Phil isn't like that. Phil has travelled extensively in Thailand and has already offered to cook everyone a Thai meal next week just as soon as he can find a shop around here that could sell him "a decent wok". I ask, genuinely, "What, you mean a non-stick one?" and Phil gives me a look of infinite patience and says, "No."

We get to my room and everyone finds somewhere to sit.

Julie, a calm presence with watchful and watchable brown eyes, notes the giant Laurel and Hardy poster. "My dad likes Laurel and Hardy."

That wasn't quite the effect I was hoping for, but at least she's being nice. The poster isn't intended for a group anyway. It's there for someone like Julie on her own with me. It's supposed to say "Hey, look, Julie. I don't take myself too seriously. This is a friendly room so relax. I'm no trouble. So if that's all cool, you could probably take your clothes off?" That, at least, is the idea.

Phil is giving the poster his own brand of critical attention. "They're great, aren't they?" he says. "Although I much prefer Buster Keaton."

Of course. Of course you do, Phil. Of course you prefer Buster Keaton. All wankers prefer Buster Keaton. They don't for a second find him funnier than Laurel and Hardy, but they prefer him. They prefer his *work*.

But Phil isn't finished. "When was the shot taken?"

"The what, sorry?"

"The shot," he explains as if to a child, "the photograph they made the poster from?"

It suddenly occurs to me that I don't have to play by Phil's rules. "Fuck knows, Phil. From a film? The one with the piano? Most of the films are about them moving a piano, aren't they?"

I like the general chuckle. But something is wrong. I've taken off my jumper to reveal what was once a grey T-shirt but which last summer I cut into the shape of a grey vest. My longish hair has grown much faster at the back, so I look less like a foppish public schoolboy and more like a mullet-wielding footballer. The gold stud in my left ear that was daringly effeminate in Woodhall Spa now feels weirdly aggressive, as do my Doc Martens boots and the box of condoms visible from within the bedside cupboard, left artfully ajar. The

256

summer spent painting all ninety-four of the Dower House window frames has, for the first time, given me some muscle definition in my arms and shoulders but ... did I have to wear a vest? And why, next to the Laurel and Hardy poster, is there a page of A4 on which I've written "Je suis une Communiste" in chunky hip hop writing? Why, within hours of arriving at Cambridge, did I make a sign that said "Je suis une Communiste" in chunky hip hop writing and put it up on the wall?

More urgently, why am I about to play them INXS? The new can of Foster's is already light in my hand as I scan the song list on the back of the CD. In a crowded field I find the most tuneless and bombastic: "Guns in the Sky". I place it carefully in the vertically loading CD player. Julie, Fay, Suki and Collette all do versions of an indulgent smile when they hear Michael Hutchence shouting along to the introduction: "Ooh! Uh! OOH, A-ha-ha HAAA!"

I take a seat next to a speaker and cross one skinny leg over the other, leaving a sixteen-hole boot quite close to Phil's face. So I re-cross my legs while unobtrusively lighting a cigarette with the Zippo that Will gave me as a going-away present. I'm not the only smoker here, but I'm the only smoker not making a roll-up. To listen to Fay talk about manufactured fags you'd think rolling tobacco was some kind of health food.

There's some desultory chat during which Phil stares at a section of carpet in front of him, looking quite

257

upset. It's like Michael Hutchence is actually hurting him.

Everyone notices but Julie takes a cheerful interest. "You all right, Phil? You look a bit glum."

Glum. I'm starting to really like Julie.

Phil says, "It's silly. I'm being silly . . ."

We all exchange glances the way we've seen grown-ups exchange glances in films. Phil waits for some encouragement.

"What's up?" says Julie. "It's OK, we're all complete strangers and will probably never speak to each other again for the next three years."

I like this and join in. "Yes, you can tell us, Phil, we've all forgotten your name already."

Phil gives this a brave little nod. And then: "It's really dumb, it's just . . . this band, the singer, Michael Hutchence . . . it's just our family pet, our cat, passed away a few months ago and I haven't really got over it."

"Was it in a band?" I ask.

"He was called Michael," Phil replies evenly.

My upper and lower lips disappear into my closed mouth and I hold them there, trying to find somewhere in the room where it might be safe to look. The ceiling is as good a place as any. I sense Phil defiantly searching everyone's face for signs of mirth or satire, but I'm damned if he's getting it from me. I think maybe if I frown as well as keep my mouth like this, it will look like contrition or sympathy, rather than what it really is — a thin disguise for an overwhelming urge to laugh my guts up.

"I know it's just a cat," continues Phil, "but it was also losing a member of the family."

I get up quite suddenly and start stepping over people in the direction of the bathroom. Julie catches the look on my face. Somebody else has asked how Michael died and as I leave the room, I hear Phil say, "Just old age really, the vet said cancer . . ."

In the bathroom, my abdomen contracts and bends me double, but not with laughter. I straighten up and blow my nose, look in the mirror and try to reason this out. It's not Phil's fault. Phil is annoying but he's only eighteen and middle-class. Don't bully him, he doesn't know. None of them know. This would be the wrong time to tell them because it would look bitter. Bitter about Phil's reaction to the demise of a cat. Don't do it. They're in your room. They're guests. Keep it together. Be a man.

By the time I get back, the conversation has moved up a gear and now they're talking about how tough it is to lose a grandmother.

I think I'm doing pretty well, not saying anything.

There again, there might be something about the way I light my next cigarette, with a violent flip of the Zippo, that suggests a change in mood. And maybe I didn't need to stab the "Stop" button on the CD player quite so abruptly. And maybe I should stop looking at my watch. And maybe, despite how brilliantly I'm handling this situation, people are starting to look uncomfortable. It's quite late and they should probably make a move. That's what they start to say, anyway, and I agree with a mumbled "yeah" while I start to unlace

259

my boots. They see themselves out and I hear Julie whisper something to the others at the door. She's still on the inside when it closes. She comes over.

"Right then, you . . ." She sits in front of me and takes her time, looking from my earring to my hair to my shoulders and then into my eyes.

Finally she says, "With you, it wasn't a cat, was it?"

After college, Julie took a job in marketing which she didn't much enjoy. So she was more than happy to give it up and become a full-time mum to the three children she had with her devoted husband, Phil.

Her relationship with me was less of a big deal, lasting as it did that gentle night and the night after.

For one of the less formal colleges, Robinson sure knew how to give me the willies (the willies: *noun*, sensation of fear located in genitals. See also "the fannies" or "the vulva-tumbles"). On the first day there was a matriculation photograph and ceremony. This involved wearing an undergraduate gown over my one and only suit. The suit was a hand-me-down from Dad's dad, Ron, and at least it fitted me quite well even if it was from the 1960s and pale blue. If that sounds rather dapper, it wasn't — not in 1992. Stripy flared lapels from the 1970s, yes; square-cut, powder-blue polyester, no.

I begin to feel like I'm the unwilling star of a *Comic Strip Presents* film called *The Boy Who Thought He Was a Ponce but Turned out to Be a Yob*. I follow the others into the main hall, where I'm immediately hijacked by the choice of sweet or dry sherry. I've never

260

even tried sherry before and go for the dry one as I assume that's the sophisticated choice. Then, having swallowed a mouthful of paraffin, I start to try and make friends with the other freshers. Moving around the hall, and having found a cup of tea instead, I glance out of the window and check that the clouds are still clouds and the trees are still trees. Yes. This is still recognisably Britain. I have a cup of tea now. I like tea. Everything's fine.

"Hello there! So, where do you hail from?"

I've attached myself to a group of freshers. The wrong group. The question comes from a tall boy with chalky white skin and bright red cheeks. He sounds like he was at Eton and looks like he's driven directly from there with his head out of the window.

"From Lincolnshire," I say, "a couple of little villages in Lincolnshire."

"Lincolnshire . . ." the posh youth replies, rolling the word around his massive mouth like it's an novelty wine-gum. "Tremendously *flat*, Lincolnshire. Isn't that so?"

"That is s — that's right," I manage, "although Lincoln itself is quite hilly." Oh God.

"Fascinating. Lincoln itself is quite hilly. Fascinating."

Actually he isn't taking the piss. He's just doing his best with what I've given him. I hear myself saying, "I mean, it's the flatness that makes it good for arable farming, as well as the quality of the soil, although we also have quite a lot of sheep."

Why don't I just kill myself? Why didn't I kill myself in the bungalow when I had the chance?

The tall boy says, with a naughty grin, "You don't *roger* the sheep, do you?"

"Only on Thursdays."

He gives me a startled look and then lets out the kind of laugh that would embarrass Brian Blessed. "ONLY ON THURSDAYS, HE SAYS! Oh, you're a *tonic*. I'm Noel, what's your name?"

"Robert, er, Rob."

"Which do you prefer, Rob?"

"Rob."

"Well, Rob it is then! And what an extraordinary suit, Rob." Intrusively, Noel slightly parts my gown to get a better look at the polyester sex-dream.

"It's my dad's. Actually, it was *his* dad's, but . . ."

"And who is your dad, Rob?"

"Sorry?"

"Who is your father?"

"*Who* is he? Erm . . . he's called Paul . . ."

"Paul . . . ?"

"Er . . . Paul Webb."

Noel casts his eyes to the ceiling in concentration. "Paul Webb . . . no, sorry." There's a moment where I wonder if I'm supposed to accept his apology for never having heard of my father. "And what does he do? Does he have an occupation, Rob?" Fucking hell, can I go now?

"Yes, well, he used to be a woodsman, but now he's a gang-master."

"He was a . . . he's a *what*?"

"He hires and organises groups of labourers to pick fruit and vegetables from farms. From fields in farms. From farm fields, essentially."

Noel is looking at me as if I'm the most exotic creature he's ever encountered. I take advantage of his moment of helplessness. "Well, anyway, I'd better move on and . . . and wow some more people with my knowledge of Lincolnshire's tockological, toplodocklic —"

"Topology."

"Right, topology, thanks." I start to move off and Noel shakes my hand.

"Excellent meeting you, Rob. Stay in touch." He's visibly creating a file in his memory, most likely under the category heading: Full Maintenance Grant.

My first encounter with the diamond-hard courtesy and cheery humourlessness of the English upper middle class has left me drained. I circle the hall for a while longer, miserably contemplating going back to my room to open the complete works of Chaucer (that will need doing, sooner or later) or, more likely, to moan to the diary about how coming here was a mistake. There's another gaggle of first-years: it includes a boy with his head shaved at the sides and the rest of his hair dyed red and pulled back into a ponytail. Also a short, beautiful girl in full Goth make-up. They are both, nevertheless, wearing formal clothes and gowns. They look like they're hating this. OK, maybe worth one more go.

I hang around the edges of the group. Plum-hair and Goth-girl don't notice but someone else does.

"Hello! I'm Patrick."

"Hello. Rob."

Like Noel, like a lot of the men around here, Patrick is about six foot two. What have these boys been eating? I suppose their mums didn't smoke. Mum was scrupulous about giving up the booze when pregnant, but not so much the other thing. I reckon she owes me an inch or two as well as thirty years of company. I make a mental note to pick that bone with her the next time we have a pan-celestial chat.

Patrick says, with the others listening, "We've all been having exciting conversations about what A levels we did and what we did on our gap years."

The group quietly hums with a sense of irony and self-consciousness. Oh yes, this is more like it.

"I can get that over with quite quickly," I say. "English, History and Economics. I had a bit of unfortunateness and went back to school for a year. I'm from Lincolnshire and, yes, I do fuck the sheep."

"Rams or ewes?"

"That's a bit personal, Patrick."

"Sorry."

"Rams, mainly."

Plum-hair, whose name is Joe, adds helpfully, "The horns. The horns give you something to hang on to."

"Ah, a connoisseur," I say.

Joe giggles.

I'm sorry to tell you that this bestiality banter goes on for about another minute. The rest of the group divide neatly between those who think this is weird but funny and those who think it's just weird. As for

Patrick, Joe and me — it's perfectly obvious that we will attend each other's funerals. This is how my brain currently interprets good news about new friendships.

Patrick is the first to sense that we're being insufferable and tries to include everyone else. "So Rob, this is Joe, Lily, Phil, Julie, Dan . . ." He could do the whole thing in one breath but realises it's starting to look like he's showing off his social skills; not showing off your social skills being, of course, an important social skill. "Er . . . Glynn? Tara? And Dorothea. I probably got that all wrong." Everyone mumbles happily that he got it all right, like he's just tickled them on the tummy.

Phil, the one standing quite close to Julie, who looks as if he'd much rather be in his room with an earful of WOMAD, has been thinking. "You went back to school for a year?"

"Yeah. I thought about Thailand but realised I just hadn't had enough good old ruddy sixth form."

Phil isn't satisfied. "What was 'the unfortunateness'?"

Nope. Not here, not now.

I hesitate for just a second. Julie sees it, so does Patrick. The latter good-naturedly explains to Phil, "He'd tell you, but he'd have to kill you."

"Exactly," I say, locking eyes with Phil through his expensive glasses, "probably by clubbing you to death with a dead sheep."

Ooh, that was a bit much. Phil snorts lightly and looks around for somewhere else to be. The funny half of the group is amused, but I feel I've let Patrick down.

That's the thing about kind people: I can never live up to them.

Of all the things I currently want these Cambridge people to think I am — witty, clever, sophisticated, ambiguous, sexy, ironic, exciting, artistic, self-possessed, self-aware — it doesn't occur to me that "kind" should be at the top of the list. Nor "brave" or "honest" or even "reliable". I think, at this time, that these virtues are too obvious, too boring and too typical of some kind of normal man.

No, as long as you're very serious about not being like your dad, you don't really need to be "good" at all. What is "good" anyway? This is the method by which I give myself permission to start acting like a liar and a sleazebag.

It's about this time that I give up reading. That's to say, at the beginning of my English degree. So, naturally, this is also where the lying has to start in earnest. As an English student, reading books and writing essays about books should really be quite high up there in a time and motion study of how I spend my day. The trouble is, much as novels, plays and poems have previously been a solace and an inspiration, reading them is now my *job*. I used to be practically the only boy who loved reading: now I'm surrounded by them. Therefore: screw reading.

Yes, I could open that copy of *Sir Gawain and the Green Knight*, but first I should probably get myself a coffee and a KitKat from the machine next to the junior common room and then go in there to browse the newspapers for an hour. Then I should probably start that critical evaluation of a sonnet by Philip Sidney, but not before sauntering towards the discount shop in town to buy a tight-fitting scoop-neck top like Brett Anderson wears. Then I'll dive right into *Troilus and Cressida* once I've written a long and amusing letter to Will, Tiffany or Isabel; or a short, cheerful one to Auntie Trudy. At that point, I'm absolutely desperate to start learning Anglo-Saxon, but there again I could audition for those five plays or try to write something funny that might get me into Footlights.

And now . . . oh look, the bar's open.

All this requires a lot of lying. Frankly, it's hard work. I put so much creativity into my excuses for doing nothing that it sometimes occurs to me that it might have been easier just to read the sodding book or write the sodding essay in the first place. I become a sort of Method Actor in reverse — I spend so much time pretending to be ill that I actually feel quite ill.

My Director of Studies (chief teacher) is Dr Judy Weiss, an infinitely patient and brilliant tutor who interviewed me twice and took a chance. God knows, she must have seen this kind of thing before, but her policy is either to believe my excuses or at least do a very sound impression of believing them. The lies begin as evil saplings but by the end of the year are fully grown triffids.

"Sorry, Dr Weiss, I didn't write an essay this week because I had glandular fever . . . I couldn't come to this week's supervision because I was in a bike accident . . . Please accept this work in note-form because I have to attend a funeral in Lincolnshire . . . Unfortunately, I'm suffering from an unspecified mental condition but isn't it wonderful that the sun's out today?"

I was clearing the road for myself while leaving ever-more conspicuous piles of horseshit for everyone else to try and ignore. By the end of that year, I'd killed at least two members of my extended family and was considering a kidnapping.

At this point, Dr Weiss gave me a one-to-one ticking off so gentle it had the effect of encouraging me to do even less. "Robert, it's possible that you could secure a 2:1 with native intelligence alone, but unlikely. And certainly not a First."

Oh Judy mate, that's FINE! That's BRILLIANT NEWS! Who needs a First? I'm going to be a wealthy TV star! (This is also how I privately justify the tax-payer's money I'm currently pissing up the wall. I glibly assume I'll be in a position to pay it back through tax.)

I nod at her and look contrite, while wondering what I have to do around here to get thrown out. The answer will come next year in the language I have completely neglected to learn. On the shelf in my room, there's a copy of *Beowulf* ticking like some kind of Anglo-Saxon book-bomb.

Sexually, if not quite romantically, Little Tart Fauntleroy is having the time of his life. The diary becomes littered with what Twitter users now describe as a #humblebrag.

268

God, this thing is starting to read like Confessions of a Sex Maniac! It's awful I know, but I'm just recounting the facts.

Let's be clear, poppet, you don't think it's awful in the slightest. You're having a ball and good for you. Pity about all the lying, though, dearest. Pity about the "facts".

I immediately get myself into a relationship with a third-year called Mags. She's charismatic and slightly mad, but interesting company and, crucially, a Third-Year. I am literally dating an older woman! Sadly, the sex is consistently underwhelming, partly because we're going out with each other for the wrong reasons, but also because she has an overdeveloped critical faculty and won't shut the hell up. As a more mature lover (say, next week), I won't mind when women tell me exactly what they want. It's just that this is a bit new to me. And Mags has a particular style of running commentary.

"No, no, yes . . . all right then, yes. That is indeed my clitoris. Top marks. '*Well done you*' Et cetera. That — actually no, you've got lost again, haven't you? Oh dear. No, higher, my sweet. Gentler. No, not that gentle, I'm falling asleep. Ooh! Well, all right, if you say so."

And then, a few minutes later —

"Oh dear, it's not really your night, is it? Classic erection fiasco. Ho hum. And there we were, trying to avoid the cliché. Anyway, not to worry. Let me stroke your bruised male ego. Poor you . . ."

I carry on going out with Mags even though I'm now pretty sure that I don't like her. She says something about how nice it is to be in an exclusive relationship for a change. I hear it and agree. I, too, am a big fan of monogamy. Just not with her.

One Saturday, she goes home to London and I go to a sweaty "bop" (a dance, a disco, whatever — a room crammed with a hundred young people getting down) in what Robinson touchingly calls its Party Room. I seem to be on some kind of promise from a fun first-year called Bianca. We flirt and dance, then she disappears. But that's OK because here comes Collette, another fun first-year. The flirting and dancing resumes. We leave the party early and go back to my room.

Things are just getting a bit fantastic in the dark when there's a knock at the door. The room has a tiny corridor — you can close the bedroom door before you open the one outside.

It's Bianca: sweaty, smiling but quizzical.

"You left the party."

"Yeah, just tired."

"You left the party with Collette."

"Yeah, exactly. She needed to talk."

"Talk?"

"Yeah. It's her brother." I'm not going to say this, am I? Yup, apparently I am. "He's a heroin addict."

"What?"

"He's really struggling. And she wanted to talk."

"To you?"

"Apparently, yes."

270

Bianca has clearly been lied to before, by better liars and even worse men than me. She's now enjoying life.

"And she's in there right now, is she?"

"Er, yeah, actually."

"Discussing her brother's heroin addiction with you."

"I know it sounds mental, but yes."

"It does sound *fairly* mental, Rob." Bianca is quite gleeful as well as fairly drunk. She casts the odd glance at the white cotton top I'm wearing, with its see-through sweatiness and unevenly fastened buttons.

"So, I'll see you back at the party, yeah?"

"Er, yup."

She kisses me on the mouth. She smells fucking great. "Don't be long, then." She goes off, softly cackling to herself.

Right. OK. I go back into the room and turn on a lamp. Forgive me, reader. I don't know why you should, but forgive me anyway.

"So anyway, shall we go back to the party?"

"*What?*"

"I just thought we maybe left a bit early."

"Was that Bianca out there?"

I'm all out of ideas.

"Bianca . . . Yep!"

Collette starts indignantly pulling on her knickers. "I have never been treated so shabbily in my entire fucking life."

I slightly turn away while she finishes dressing. You know, because I'm such a gentleman.

She heads out of the door and never speaks to me again.

A couple of hours later, I'm in the same room with Bianca. We're both shit-faced. And, aah, here are two more lovely breasts and, aah, here is another soft, beautiful triangle in the dark. And, aah, she's just fallen asleep.

Okey-cokey. I tell her not to snore. She slurs, "You not snore neither, mister," and giggles at how that came out. I pull the duvet over her shoulders and give her a kiss on the cheek. Wow, I think. I just cheated on Mags with two women. Or at least I would have done if one hadn't stormed out and the other hadn't fallen asleep. But it's the thought that counts. Hope she doesn't find out.

A few days later, more in sorrow than in anger, Mags calmly destroys me. We're in my room again — H1, Robinson College. There should really be a blue plaque, commemorating the night when the author of *How Not To Be a Boy* had his testicles quietly removed and then pushed slowly and firmly up his nostrils.

"I think we're both aware that your behaviour has been deplorable," she states, neutrally. It's 5 November, and I've just got back from a fireworks display. After twenty minutes of wandering around with Patrick, Joe, Dora, Lily-the-Goth, Bianca and a few other first-years, I withdrew into a terrible sadness and then just gave them the slip. Partly it was the fireworks, conjuring memories of Mum and Derek in the bungalow garden.

272

And I missed my brothers and my Lincolnshire friends. Where were Will and Tiffany on a night like this? These new guys didn't know me at all.

It was in this frame of mind that I walked into the Robinson bar, bought four cans of lager and took them back to H1. Mags had witnessed this and then followed a few minutes later.

"Drinking alone, oh dear me. We *are* feeling sorry for ourselves, aren't we? I'll just sit down, shall I?"

She sits opposite me, cross-legged and scarily focused. "So what's the problem?"

I don't know whether to trust her, but I tell her anyway. What it adds up to is . . . I'm lonely. She listens, occasionally sighing with apparent sympathy, sometimes rolling her eyes at the ceiling with theatrical impatience. Troublingly, she isn't interrupting or even replying. I get the distinct impression I'm being given enough rope to hang myself. After about a minute, I stop talking and she starts.

"It must be hard being as important as you, Rob. I mean, all these feelings of sadness and loneliness — the rest of us never have to deal with those, do we? You don't think it's possible that Patrick or Joe miss their friends from school, for example? Because it doesn't sound like that actually crossed your mind. I think it's quite likely that they also feel confused and lonely. But somehow they don't go into a sulk and then fuck off without saying goodbye . . . and then sit around with a beer saying 'everything means nothing and it's all just "why . . .?"'. Do they? They didn't name their car after

273

a man whose only song was called 'The One and Only'."

She sighs and lights a cigarette. "Obviously I know all about Bianca and Collette. That was pathetic and I'm quite hurt, but it's beside the point, frankly. I think we can both agree that your behaviour has been deplorable and it goes without saying that I don't want to go out with you any more. If you want us to remain friends, then I think you need to get used to the idea that other people are real."

Well, that's me told.

She says, "What do you think?"

I say, "I think you should stop talking and go away."

She gives a mild snort of disappointment and does just that.

It feels like I've let someone under my skin and she just trashed the place from the inside. Mags, by the way, is young, hurt, and has just spent all night in the bar. But she hasn't said anything untrue or even unfair. I feel a vague sense of indignation — familiar from Dad's domestic bollockings — at the spectacle of anyone who isn't Mum presuming to tell me off. But the thought of Mum makes matters worse because, without quite saying it, Mags has left me with the heavy impression that my mother is ashamed of me.

The idea burrows slowly into my brain like a malign worm. I look distractedly around the wet, unfocused room for a Tupperware box — but then remember why I couldn't do it last time, so there's no point thinking about it this time either.

★   ★   ★

To be well enough to reject suicidal thoughts is not the same thing as being well enough not to have them in the first place. We are not responsible for our thoughts, of course. We're responsible only for our words and actions. There are no "bad thoughts", only bad deeds.

But obviously there are some lines of thought that are unhealthy to pursue, two extreme examples being: "How exactly am I going to murder this person who just barged onto the train when people were trying to get off?" or "How exactly am I going to murder myself?" We all have wayward thoughts. We don't choose them, but we can choose not to follow them.

With feelings, there is no choice at all. Zero choice. How are you feeling right now?

Right. Whose idea was that? I don't mean to be rude but I doubt that you had much to do with it. Not because of what you're reading now, so much as what you had for breakfast and that annoying thing your friend said to you last Tuesday night. We are not the same thing as our emotions. With practice, you just get to watch them bubbling up and simmering down again.

And you can sometimes tilt the playing field in your own favour. You don't discreetly lift the surface of a game of table football (or foosball) unless you're an outrageous cheat. It's acceptable to do so, however, if your opponent is the one in your mind who keeps saying "stop being alive". Going for a brisk walk or having a cup of tea are a couple of harmless ways to change the chemistry of your body enough, maybe, to change your frame of mind. At least, it works for some of the people some of the time. If your opponent wants you dead, tilt the table. Tea, exercise, talking therapy, meditation, prescribed anti-depressants . . . different things tilt different tables. Whatever works for you.

My problem in my twenties — a continuing but much diminished problem as I type now — was that I tended to miss out the teas and the walks and reached straight for a lager. Oh, I can change the chemistry, all right. It's just a pity that my chemistry-changer of choice is, among other things, a known depressant that gives you liver failure and a fat gut.

So, on that particular night (and I'm tempted to put the negative emotions in **bold** here, but I wouldn't do that to you), I was afraid that I was in the wrong place, afraid of losing my old friends, anxious that my new ones didn't love me and, as usual, in grief. On top of that, someone just correctly pointed out that I'd behaved in a selfish and self-indulgent way, so we can add shame and challenged pride to this bountiful platter of Reasons to Get Drunk.

If you're thinking right now that this catalogue of mishandled feelings is, in itself, all a little bit self-indulgent, then I suppose my reply is this: for men of about my age and older — those whose fathers had fought in a war, or those who were raised by the sons of such fathers — there can be few more powerful accusations than the one of self-indulgence. Paul got it from Ron, and I got it from Paul. This is the voice I hear all the time:

Be a man. Man up. Act like a man. Get a grip. Get real. Get over yourself. Pull yourself together. Sort yourself out. Stop moaning. Stop feeling sorry for yourself. You don't know you're born. BE A MAN. MAN UP. ACT LIKE A MAN . . .

It's no coincidence that this is the language frequently used by men who believe that we live in a "feminised" society where men (particularly white men like themselves) have become the victims of discrimination.

Men's rights activists tend to make a series of valid observations from which they proceed to a single, 180-degree-wrong conclusion. They are correct to point out that, worldwide, suicide is the most common form of death for men under fifty. It's also true that men are more likely than women to have serious problems with alcohol, that men die younger, that the prison population is 95 per cent male and that the lack of support for our returning frontline soldiers is a national disgrace. So far, so regrettably true.

They are incorrect, however, to lay any this at the door of "feminism", a term which they use almost interchangeably with "women". In my experience of reading the comments and replies to articles I've written on gender-related subjects, these are invariably the guys telling me to Get a Grip and Act Like a Man.

No, sir. No, lads. No, Daddy. That won't help us and it won't help anyone else. Men in trouble are often in trouble *precisely because* they are trying to Get a Grip and Act Like a Man. We are at risk of suicide because the alternative is to ask for help, something we have been repeatedly told is unmanly. We are in prison because the traditional breadwinning expectations of

277

manhood can't be met, or the pressure to conform is too great, or the option of violence has been frowned upon but implicitly sanctioned since we were children. We are dependent on booze when we try to tilt the table, try to change the chemistry in a way that is harmful, counterproductive and, of course, widely accepted as tough and manly, irrespective of whether the impulse comes from conformity or rebellion, from John Wayne or James Dean.

We die younger than women because, for one thing, we don't go to the doctor. We don't take ourselves too seriously. We don't want to be thought self-indulgent. The mark of a real man is being able to tolerate a chest infection for three months before laying off the smokes or asking for medicine.

Once in a long-term relationship, men are worse than women at maintaining same-sex friendships. I don't mean talking bollocks with Gary in the pub, enjoyable as it is. I mean being able to tell Gary you've got cancer and expecting Gary to be able to listen. I'm not saying none of us have that kind of friend in our lives, but women seem to have about four each. That's fine as long as your wife doesn't die or divorce you. If she does, men are left higher and drier not only because they relied on just one person for emotional support but because they tend to be less plugged into the local community. If we do less of the school run, less of the shopping, less sitting in dentists' waiting rooms with our kids, we aren't going to meet and get to know as many people, especially younger people. Loneliness is a man-killer.

Then there's work. Whether it's enjoyable, danger-ous, repetitive, well paid, badly paid, fulfilling or soul-destroying, work-related stress is our problem, thank you. You women, please, hello there, please stop banging on the door and smacking your heads against glass ceilings in the attempt to compete or support. Shhhhhh. We've got this. Ow, shit, my ulcer! My tumour! The ulcer on my tumour!

At least we have a job. When we don't have a job . . . fuck! I don't have a job! I'm not a man! My tumour! My ulcer!

Feminists didn't create these circumstances. Neither am I saying that men have gone along with this stuff like a bunch of passive idiots. I'm saying it's difficult to resist because it hides in plain sight. It's everywhere: a system of thought and a set of invented and discriminatory practices in our laws, culture and economy that feminists call the patriarchy. Feminists are not out to get us. They're out to get the patriarchy. They don't hate men, they hate The Man. They're our mates. The patriarchy was created for the convenience of men, but it comes at a heavy cost to ourselves and to everyone else.

To put it childishly, if you want a vision of masculinity, imagine Dr Frankenstein being constantly bum-raped by his own monster while shouting, "I'm fine, everyone! I'm absolutely fine!"

"I'm fine," I think to myself. The message that I get from Mags is that I've been selfish and self-indulgent.

That's reasonable. Also, every now and again, I want to kill myself. No problem.

The trouble is, someone whose only moral compass is the mother whom he believes — whom he *has* to believe — is watching over him, is going to find it difficult to walk into a shrink's office and demand to be listened to when he already thinks his mother is disgusted by his self-indulgence.

It will take something else to push me to take this highly sensible and long-overdue step.

It'll come down to love and sex again. Unrewarding sex and unrequited love. Nothing very unusual, but then the privilege of being young is a total lack of perspective. So there could never be a sexier, more gorgeous woman than Lily-the-Goth. And there could never be a more beautiful, more enigmatic man than Mags' friend Sam (the-former-Goth). And there could never be a turn of events more calamitous than my sort-of girlfriend Lily, and my sort-of minor deity Sam, falling in love with each other.

At that point, I can scarcely get out of bed for two weeks. That's what it takes for a boy — for this boy anyway — to seek professional help.

Well, I did tell you I was a slow learner.

CHAPTER
ELEVEN

Men Don't Need Therapy

"Be soft, even if you stand to get squashed."
E. M. Forster, "The Long Run",
New Statesman and Nation, 1938

"So, what brings you here today, Robert?"

Phillip is the head of the University Counselling Service and is exactly the kind of avuncular old chap I was hoping for: grey hair, glasses, loose-knit cardy. This is a first assessment — an "exactly how bonkers are you, anyway?" kind of session, although I suspect these are not the preferred terms.

There was a fortnight's waiting time after booking the appointment. It means that I'm feeling better and it was probably the knowledge that some kind of back-up was on the way that did the trick. That, of course, is not how I see things at the time. Bad things happen; I get miserable beyond belief; I randomly recover. So we don't exactly get off to a cracking start.

"I've no idea, really. I'm absolutely fine," I reply, "I probably should have cancelled." Phillip is already writing something on an A4 pad with a sharp pencil.

"Mm-hmm. Well, you're here now."

"Yes."

"So, what shall we talk about?" He gives me the faintest imaginable smile of encouragement.

I'd quite like to offer a couple of observations about the weather and then get the hell out of there. Instead, I do the sensible thing for once, although talking like this is no less embarrassing than you might think. I start to tell him why I booked the appointment, about being crazy about this boy and having a casual sexual relationship with this girl, about how they're together now, leaving me feeling rejected, abandoned, excluded and generally pulverised. I don't tell him about the suicidal thoughts, because somehow I think that would be a Bit Much. We've only just met, for heaven's sake. This is England.

He looks frankly bored. Oh well, I think, at least I'm not about to be physically restrained and wheeled off to an asylum. Nothing to see here, move along.

"Thank you," Phillip says. "Now, I wonder if you could fill me in on your family background. Your parents, brothers or sisters and so on?"

Oh, OK, this will be easier. At least we don't have to talk about sex any more. I tell him about Mum and Dad, about Dad, and then about Mum, and then about Derek, and then about Dad again. I can't help noticing that his pencil has flown into action. He's now scribbling away like he's got two minutes to finish an exam after spending the first three hours doodling a battleship. At length, he puts his pencil down and reviews his notes. I imagine for a second he's about to slowly remove his glasses, look me in the eye and say, "Who the . . . *fuck* do you think you are?"

He does indeed remove his glasses and look at me. But what he says is this: "There's been a great deal of separation in your life. I think you use those experiences as a model for current adversity and that makes things feel considerably worse than they might do otherwise. I think you've got a problem. And I think we can help."

Those last two sentences. A proper, professional grown-up has just told me I'm not a complete arsehole and I'm not just wasting everyone's time. That helps. That helps a very great deal.

I start going for an hour a week.

As we know, I went to some trouble to get into this university. I mean, really quite a sincere and prolonged amount of trouble. So, given that well over half the reason I wanted to be here in the first place was to be part of Footlights and find someone funny to do comedy with, it came as a bit of a disappointment that no matter how interested I was in them, they didn't seem very interested in me.

The Cambridge Footlights Dramatic Club does three main shows a year at the end of the three academic terms: the Pantomime, the Spring Revue and the Summer Tour Show. In my first year, I auditioned for all three and got nowhere. To be fair, it's unusual for a first-year to strike it big in those shows but I, of course, thought I was deeply unusual.

I watched the Christmas Panto in a reverie of pitiless contempt. The Spring Revue was worse by quite a distance. From that baseline, the Summer Tour saw a marked decline, collecting as it did all of the weakest sketches of the Spring Revue and some new material which wasn't as good as that. I felt like giving the whole thing up and becoming a theatre critic. That's how bad it got.

I hope the young writer/performers involved (some of whom are, right now, among my best friends as well as very successful writers or performers) understand that I wasn't in a brilliant place, emotionally speaking, and that I turned up to watch those shows with a determined attitude of arms-folded indignation and spite. No matter how good they actually were, those students were about as likely to make me laugh as they were to get Professor Hawking to come on and do a sand dance. They also know that what little self-esteem I had, when not channelled into pulling third-years, was focused on what I fondly thought of as my "talent". I wore it like a suit of armour. It felt like Footlights had overlooked just how very shiny my armour was. They were not to be forgiven.

That is until my second year, when they put me in everything.

Along with the big shows, Footlights also do one-off comedy nights called Smokers. You turn up with a bit of material you've written and you perform it — a sketch if you've found people to perform with, or a character monologue if you're me. I did enough of these well enough to catch the attention of the Footlights Committee.

The Committee is the ruling elite, the crème de la clown. Otherwise known as seven blokes and a woman sitting in a basement, trying to run a comedy club. I very much wanted to be one of the seven blokes and a woman.

At the end of my first year, the funny (and outgoing) outgoing president Miles Williams has left me a kind note asking me to give him a ring. I was immediately star-struck not just because the president had noticed my existence but also because he had his own telephone number.

I nervously dial from one of the Robinson phone booths.

"Aah, young Webbington! Thanks for calling, just catching up on a bit of cricket on the telly." Miles has been brilliantly compèring Smokers all year and I'm unnerved by the sound of his voice, as well as by the news that he's in possession of not just a phone number but a television. Jesus, what else do you get if you're president? A speedboat? An annuity?

"Anyway, I just wanted to say that I know you've probably been a bit disappointed this year, but we've . . . NOOO, GOOCH, YOU TOTAL ARSE! . . . Sorry, Robert — Gooch just got out for twelve, the useless cunt. Where was I? Fucking idiot. Not you, Robert. Ah yes, funny. We think you're funny, Webby. Bags of talent. You're obviously going to be in all three shows next year. Has Eddie spoken to you about being on the Committee?"

"Er, no."

"Of course he hasn't, the lazy fucker. Right, well, I'll have a word with him. You and that Tristram Hunt boy. Do you get on with Tristram?"

"Er, I haven't actually met him."

"Nice chap, bit wet behind the ears, bit of a leftie by all accounts but you can't have everything . . . NOT LIKE THAT, ATHERS, YOU FUCKING SPOON! . . . Shouldn't say that, of course, for all I know you're a leftie too. You're not a sinister Marxist, are you, Robert?"

"Erm . . ."

"Oh Jesus, another one. I'm leaving the club in the hands of Communists. Quite right too, probably." He giggles playfully. "Sorry, I'm talking absolute bollocks, no more exams you see, bit pissed . . . THERE IS NO FUCKING WAY THAT WAS A WIDE, YOU BLIND BASTARD . . . Anyway, good luck, make the most of it."

"Yeah, er, thanks."

"I've got my eye on you, Bobbington. Bye."

"Bye."

The Eddie mentioned was the new president and the Tristram Hunt was indeed the future and now former Shadow Education Secretary, Tristram Hunt. He seemed very young to my wizened, twenty-one-year-old gaze and I mean it as a compliment when I say that he was sweet. He had made me laugh doing shows with his Trinity friends, but I was in a competitive mood and I evaluated the threat. Here comes the threat. And . . .

relax. I was the funniest second-year and all was right with the world. The rest of the Committee were older than me and I was keen to impress them.

There are times during the three main Footlights shows that year that I think I did impress them. Sharing a stage with them, moving through the gears of sketches we'd written, I sometimes feel as if I've got them all: everyone in the audience, everyone on stage, everyone in the wings. I know what I'm doing out here, happy and warm under the lights, secure in the laughter of strangers. I wish I could sleep here. I am the benevolent king of their joy. I am recognised and grinned at in the streets of Cambridge. I am the banana-skin god of Footlights and nothing can stop me now.

Except, possibly, the Robinson College Education Committee.

Tick . . . tick . . . boom! *Beowulf* blows up in my stupid face.

Translate this, please.

> Hwæt! We Gardena in geardagum,
> þeodcyninga, þrym gefrunon,

No? What, you mean you haven't spent a year working this shit out? Ah, that's a pity. Because these are the first two lines of *Beowulf* and we've got another 3,180 lines to go. Also minor texts like *The Dream of the Rood*, as well as various fragments. I mean, you've had a year to get the basics, yes? You've taken the language component of your English literature course seriously, I assume? Now you're ready to really get stuck in during those weekly, sixty-minute, one-to-one tutorials, m-hmm? The specialist teacher assigned to you will be a leading academic in the field, of course. This is English at Cambridge University, is it not? Just you and the world expert, alone in a room. It's an immeasurable privilege. It's what you asked for.

Ohhhhh . . . FUUUUUUUUUCCKKK!!!!

A little background — I'll try and be quick. Cambridge English comes in two parts. Part One is your first two years. It's a chronological plod through the canon of literature from Chaucer to the mid twentieth century. At the end of your second year, if you haven't passed Part One then your college won't enter you for the specialist exams of Part Two, which is their way of kicking you out. So the exams at the end of your second year really matter unless you want to go home to Dad in disgrace and then fail to get a job with the *Horncastle News*.

This would all be manageable even on my Footlights schedule if it weren't for the obligatory Part One language component. You have to study a language. As bullshitters go, I've become quite good. But even I can't bullshit an entire language.

If you did, say, Spanish or French at A level, then you could just carry on doing that. But I don't have a modern language at A level so I, in the first week of my first term of my first year, have to choose between

History of the English Language or Old English (Anglo-Saxon).

For once, I can't remember which bastard to blame for my own idiocy. But at some point in my first week at Robinson, some second-year said, "Oh God, definitely do Anglo-Saxon! Definitely! History of English Language is called HEL for a reason! Haha! It's almost impossible!"

Fine, I thought. I'll just learn Anglo-Saxon. I mean, how hard can it be? How many words can they have possibly invented before 1066? Boat? Sword? Rain? This is going to be a doss!

It's with that attitude that I turn up at my first Old English seminar. In front of about seventy students, the Canadian tutor holds up a copy of his book: *A Guide to Old English*. "Read this book," he chortles in an accent that's weird even for a Canadian, "and you'll never need to come to one of my seminars again!" The undergraduates around me chuckle indulgently. Not come back to the seminars! The very thought! My goodness!

I make a note of the title and the author. I buy the book, I ditch the seminars . . . I leave Canadian Laughing Boy's book on a shelf for a year.

So here we are, in one of Robinson's meeting rooms with seven stern-faced academics who are playing tag-team interrogation with the intention of scaring the shit out of me. Cambridge has a college league table based on exam scores. At this time, Robinson was regularly competing with Magdalene to come bottom.

So any student capable of getting a 2:1 but looks as if they're going to do worse is a cause for agitation.

My Anglo-Saxon supervisor has dumped me. She was a massive expert from Trinity Hall. She registered my complete ignorance of Anglo-Saxon with polite alarm. She then noted that I kept not turning up to supervisions, claiming to be ill even though my face was on posters all over town. She then wrote a letter to Robinson, refusing to waste any more of her time on me and predicting a definite fail in my Anglo-Saxon exam. Not a third, you understand, a third being the lowest mark you can get. No, a fail — an almost unheard-of level of academic ignominy.

So I sit there in my oversized navy-blue jumper with my thumbs poking through the holes in the sleeves. One of the firing squad is an SPS (Sociology) fellow who also works at the counselling service. I've bumped into her every now and again and we've nodded at each other. My friend Dora is one of her students. But the University Counselling Service has strict rules about confidentiality. It is my job to mention that I'm in a spot of trouble, as well as trying to cure the trouble through comedy, as opposed to the Tupperware method that I still can't quite take my eyes off. So the Sociology fellow spends the next twenty minutes looking at me sympathetically, but she can't intervene.

It only took me about ten years to stop fantasising about the smart replies and witty comebacks I could have come out with that afternoon. Luckily, I'm completely over the experience now and have no interest in settling scores.

So, Dr Satan Jizzcake is the first to speak.

He looks at me briefly for the first and last time. He will address most of his comments to the ceiling, or to the window, or to his pipe when he takes it from between his thin lips. He's the kind of teacher who tells his third-year History undergraduates that they should spend the whole of their third term playing cricket, because if they don't know what they're doing by now, they never will. He says quietly, as if explaining with infinite patience to a Labrador puppy that it's not OK to shit in Mummy's handbag, "You appear to have structured your life in such a way as to bring shame upon your college. It may be otiose to expect an explanation but I'm obliged to ask for one."

Otiose. Christ.

I mumble, "No, that's fair enough. I'm definitely a bit behind with Anglo-Saxon. But I think I can make it up."

"Make it up?"

"I mean, make up the time. The work."

Dr Jizzcake looks out of the window as if I've just shoved my fingers under his nose and told him to sniff. But that's OK, because Dr Damien Cum-Biggly, a lawyer, is there to take up the baton. "How do you propose to catch up if you haven't got a supervisor?"

"Well," I say, forming the words and knowing too late that this isn't going to go down very well, "you don't always need a supervisor, do you?" The room emits a controlled gasp. What you probably don't do, if you want to ingratiate yourself with a roomful of teachers, is imply that when it comes to learning something, teachers are a sort of optional bonus.

Dr Cum-Biggly slowly scratches one side of his beard. "You're going to study Anglo-Saxon on your own and get a respectable mark in that paper, are you?"

"Er, I hope so, yes."

"But you didn't come to Cambridge to become an autodidact, did you, Robert? You could have done that in —" Cum-Biggly looks down at his notes and pronounces the next word with distaste, "Lincolnshire."

I smile and nod ruefully as if he's made a brilliant joke. He's a big enough cunt to go for it. He looks pleased that I've accepted his obvious point and snooty put-down. Fine, this one's too vain to be a problem, but the other one is talking again.

Dr Jizzcake inspects his unlit pipe. "Even if one were to take your apparent optimism at face value, unsupported as it is by the slightest evidence, your position as an undergraduate *qua* member of this college is nevertheless moot."

I say, "Yeah."

Jizzcake is cooking with gas. "If it is your intention, or even aspiration, to remain an aforementioned member of this college, then one is forced, on pain of repetition, to seek the reasons for your current failure and moreover your implicit lack of respect for your tutors, your peers and your college. Put crudely, you have let everybody down. Why?"

At this point, I'm pretty sure I'm about to leap up, grab Dr Jizzcake's pipe out of his hand and violently jab the stalk into one of his ears. I'm just fighting the impulse when the lawyer adds for good measure, "We know you're in Footlights."

OK, this is getting silly. It's like hearing a Dalek say, "WE KNOW YOU LIKE CUSTARD."

I just about keep it together. What I say next isn't calculated — I thought I should just try telling the truth. But at the back of my mind I am also aware that this is a roomful of repressed old men. Jizzcake himself looks like if he gets up he's going to take that whole armchair with him. I'm just going to have to embarrass him to death. I look as crumpled and unhappy as I can, which isn't much of a stretch because I'm feeling very crumpled and deeply unhappy.

"That's right, I have done some shows with Footlights. I suppose I'm thinking about my future life, but I understand that's causing trouble now. I'll try and work much harder. I've just found it difficult because there've also been some emotional issues."

The Sociologist creases her brow. She doesn't think I should do this in a hostile environment. Dr Cum-Biggly feels no such compunction. "What emotional issues?"

Bingo.

I shift awkwardly in the chair and decide to stop blinking. If you don't blink, of course, your eyes go red and will start to produce tears after about a minute. I don't really need to do this because the emotion happens to be real. Still, "belt and braces", eh?

I look out of the window, just like Dr Jizzcake, and pretend I'm in a play.

"It's all stupid, really. There's a boy here that I fell in love with. I thought he was the best thing in the world. I'd just read *The Picture of Dorian Gray* and then he walked into the bar and I couldn't believe my eyes. But I was wrong to give him my trust." I briefly check if Jizzcake looks like he's about to be sick. He does. Jolly good. You're coming down with me, Jizzcake — all the way down.

"At the same time, I was also fucking this amazing — sorry, I was also having a casual sexual relationship with a really nice girl. Young woman, I mean. I can't explain it . . . sometimes, physically, two people just click, don't they? I probably shouldn't say, but I mean Lily Evans." Dr Cum-Biggly keeps his face static while recrossing his fat legs.

"I'm slightly ashamed of that because it was loveless . . ." (Tears forming; stay on target.) ". . . but the point is that they started going out with each other and then I couldn't do anything. I don't mean I couldn't do any work, I mean I couldn't really eat."

Snot has started to dribble onto my upper lip. I'm going to leave it right there for now.

"So I started going to the Counselling Service and they said it might be to do with my mother dying a couple of years ago. I don't know if that's true . . ." (Bravely wipe eyes with sleeve of jumper, sniff up the snot, wipe remainder of snot with other sleeve and then stare at it.) "But anyway, I've been going there every week for nearly a year. I *think* it helps. At least I've stopped thinking about . . . doing something I shouldn't think about. I don't know, to be honest."

The word "honest" hangs in the air. They're not really going to go for this, are they? I look up, helplessly, and find the light from the window so the remainder of the tears and snot will glisten. Then I look down again.

It's easily the finest performance of my life so far. That's not saying much, but these guys are too busy to watch television or go to the theatre so they don't really know bad acting when they see it.

The Sociologist says gently, "Going forward, we could perhaps agree a realistic work schedule? That you could cover during the Easter break?"

I nod, seriously. "That sounds sensible." I risk a glance at my tormentors. Dr Jizzcake is mortified on several levels. Bad enough he just had to endure an emotional outpouring from a semi-hysterical child, but he has also been made to consider that if there's one thing that would look worse for Robinson than a 2:1 student getting a Third, it's *probably* a 2:1 student lobbing himself off a high balcony. Dr Cum-Biggly, on the other hand, is still in a slack-jawed contemplation of any part of his person "going click, physically" with Lily Evans.

Well, I did tell 15 that 21 was a wanker, didn't I? There again, I hadn't quite lied, I'd just given the truth a bit of a push so that it came to life. The style was questionable, but the content was true. It was real in the story.

They didn't kick me out, for which I'm extremely grateful. My solo efforts with Anglo-Saxon just scraped over the bar and I got a 2:2 for my Part One exams overall. After that, they basically left me alone.

I wish Dr Satan Jizzcake a long and happy retirement.

I never quite got over the fundamental weirdness of counselling sessions. I spent an hour a week doing precisely the thing that, as a man, I am not supposed to do. Talking — at some length — about my feelings.

My counsellor is not the head-guy who assessed me but another man, Michael. He's slightly younger but still reassuringly grey-haired, bespectacled and encardiganned. I turn up every Thursday morning and we go into the kitchen, where Michael makes us a mug of coffee each and we chat about the weather. Then — and this is the strangest part — we go up to his room. Two men, silently trudging up some stairs, carrying their coffees, as if we're about to work on a spreadsheet or plan a bank heist. But no, we're not going to "do" anything, apparently. It seems we're just heading for a comfy office with a carpet and some plants and a couple of armchairs, where one man is going to listen to another man discuss the problems in his brain. There's a part of me, walking up the stairs, thinking, "This is sooooo gaaaay!" It would be almost less gay if we were going to his room to fuck each other. At least that would be sex. At least that would be an *activity*.

Many years later, I met a very nice chap who was a GP. He told me that when men come into his surgery with signs of depression, he would put forward various

296

options including meditation and talking therapy. "Oh, surprisingly, they're quite up for a spot of meditation. At least you can do that on your own. But not talking. Anything but talking."

So look, lads, make of it what you will, but it goes like this.

No, there isn't a couch or a chaise-longue. No, he doesn't have a goatee beard or a Viennese accent. Neither does he hypnotise me or ask about my dreams. I sit down and he says, "How are you?" And then I tell him about my week, keeping an eye on the bits that made me inexplicably sad. Sometimes I end up crying, but not often. I do most of the talking and he does most of the listening. I'm under no obligation to be miserable. But, crucially, I'm under no obligation to be cheerful either. Nor to apologise for wasting his time.

I apologise anyway. One day he says, "Robert, I get this from students all the time, especially the male students. Yes, *of course* there is always someone worse off than you. But imagine you're in a doctor's surgery with a broken arm. The person next to you has two broken arms. The person next to him has two broken arms and a broken leg. This is all very well, but the point is that you have a broken arm and it *hurts*. The others may indeed be worse off. But they aren't here this morning. You are. So . . . tell me about your broken arm."

The judgement-free listening is the main value of it. I like him but he is not my friend and he is not my grandmother. He literally doesn't have anything better to do with his time. Spending the week being able to

297

think, every now and again, "Well, this is a horrible experience going on in my head, but at least I can tell Michael about it on Thursday" makes all the difference.

I stopped going because something brilliant happened. I probably shouldn't have stopped, but I was so happy it felt ridiculous to carry on. How could I possibly take up any more of this man's time when literally no one in the universe had ever been so lucky or so blessed as me?

Her name was Clara.

She was a showgirl. No, she wasn't. She was a student at Robinson. You can overdo it with the word "beautiful" when talking about people in their early twenties, but it's probably worth saying that Clara was funny and charming and had the kind of face I could happily spend a couple of days just staring at, had that kind of behaviour not been considered freakish even in the 1990s.

She had been one of the exotic third-years: friends with Mags, Sam and a few others. There was a whole gang of them that I hung around with in my first year. Now, Clara and some of the others were renting a house on the outskirts of Cambridge trying to work out what to do next. The "sad-grads" they called themselves. I was determined that wasn't going to happen to me, but I was grateful that some of them had stuck around, especially Clara.

This wasn't the first time I was bananas about someone and not the first time someone was clearly bananas about me. And it wasn't the first time I'd had a girlfriend. But it was the first time all three things converged on the same person and HOLY HECK, I CAN VERY HIGHLY RECOMMEND THAT STATE OF AFFAIRS!

Sometimes, in the second-year house I was sharing with Patrick, Joe and Dora, they would catch a look on my face and wonder if I was stoned. Then Dora would squeal with delight, "Nah! He's thinking about Clara!"

Suddenly, I had to go on tour with Footlights. Bollocks. I was one of a cast of five in the Summer Revue, which was exactly what I'd come to Cambridge to do but now I'd found The Love of My Life, it was almost a drag.

The Committee appointed Simon Shingles to be the tour manager. He got the job because of his abiding love for Footlights and also because he had a trust fund and a BMW. It's not that Eddie and the rest of us were impressed by his wealth; more that we were impressed by how much our near-bankrupt club could do a tour without having to buy main train tickets.

Simon was affable enough but tended to wind everyone up by bollocking on about the importance of professionalism and how we all needed to behave like "professionals in the professional entertainment industry". To be fair to Simon, our main objection was that it spoiled the illusion that this was all still just a lark.

It was too scary to take seriously. Not all actors go into the business hoping to be famous, but I did. There are 60,000 actors in the UK *Spotlight*, the performers' directory. So that's 60,000 people who have sufficiently got their shit together to get an agent and a proper photograph of their hopeful faces. If you spent a tortuous week going through those 60,000 faces, how many do you reckon you could put a name to? 300? 400? What I'm saying is, the actors you see being interviewed on TV are the people who knew that the chances of getting what they wanted were approximately half of 1 per cent. And then they got what they wanted anyway. No wonder they all sound mental.

The vast majority of the lucky ones will acknowledge that they are lucky because of luck. There are always some, however, who think they've been lucky for reasons more to do with destiny and their own innate specialness. The profession has its own term for these people.[1]

But despite rolling my eyes with the others every time Simon mentioned "today's cut-throat comedy sphere", I started to concentrate. If I was going to marry Clara — and that, after about four weeks, was my firm intention — then I'd need a good living, wouldn't I? I mean, she was obviously going to get a job one day, but in the meantime someone would have to provide for our many blond children. That was definitely my job.

It didn't occur to me to run any of these ideas past Clara. She was in love with me; I was in love with her. Good. So, that's decided.

I had to be good in this show. I more-or-less had a family to support.

---

[1] See Chapter 12, under "a brief word about cunts".

Simon's finest hour as tour manager was undoubtedly the booking of the Brighton Dome. Mysteriously, he'd managed to secure this huge venue at the last minute for one night only. Sadly this meant we were not in the theatre programme and there were no posters anywhere. By the time we arrived, it became clear how Simon had pulled this off.

What we'd been used to were 200- or 300-seat places which were usually more than half full. That's all you need, really. It doesn't matter how big the room is, you just want the audience to look around and weigh their own numbers, reassuring themselves they haven't picked a dud.

What we got in Brighton was a 2,000-seat venue on the night of the 1994 World Cup Final.

When I asked how many tickets we'd sold, Simon conceded that the pre-sales were "on the disappointing side of brilliant". When pressed, he said that the actual figure, if we "really want to dwell on a literal figure", was "something in the vicinity of fifteen". When he came under some pressure to clarify, Simon clarified: it was twelve. He suggested we might need to go flyering.

I looked out upon the vast sea of empty red seats, disappearing into the distance on three tiers. Everyone called Simon a dick for a while and took their allocation of flyers. I took mine. About 300 expensively printed, glossy, two-colour, A6 publicity leaflets that I was now expected to spend most of the day handing out to the residents of Brighton.

Fuck that. How could I *possibly* be expected to support my family under these conditions? I walked away from the theatre until I knew I was out of sight of the others, binned the flyers and headed for the nudist beach.

What can I tell you? I was seven when I saw a grown-up news report about the opening of Brighton naturist beach in 1980. I couldn't believe what I was seeing. But these people are *bare*! Outside! They don't seem to mind that everyone can *see*!

I suppose 21 wants to show 7 that well-adjusted grown-ups are cool about nudity. More immediately — it's a hot day, I haven't got any swimming trunks and I can't think of anything better to do. I trudge along the beach for half a mile and squint into the distance. Yup, there they are.

I peel off my Footlights Tour T-shirt before I get there. Somehow it won't do to be recognised as a Cambridge revue performer in such an environment. Whatever would Eleanor Bron think?

The clientele appears to be 80 per cent single men who have spaced themselves out with a precise geometry that reminds me of a gents' loo — i.e. if one man takes the far left urinal and the second takes the far right, the third will aim dead centre and the fourth will perfectly dissect one of the remaining spaces. I follow this rule and find a spot. The nearest guy is about three metres away and I carefully position my Doc Martens to obstruct his view of my cock, which is odd because if I didn't want people to see my cock, why did I just take off my underpants in public? I mull this and other philosophical questions over, sitting cross-legged and looking out to sea. I think about Footlights and whether this tour is going to lead to fame and fortune. I imagine the sea as a stadium — the reflections on the water look like a billion fish with flashbulbs, all taking my picture. More exposure, that's what I need, I think, reaching for a cigarette. Much more exposure.

The Zippo has run out of fuel and my lightning attempts have attracted the attention of my neighbour. "Can I help?" he says, holding up a lighter.

"Oh, erm, yes please."

I shape my hands for a catch, but instead of throwing the lighter, he keeps it in his outstretched hand and lights it.

Ah. I see.

I get up and awkwardly step over my boots and across the warm pebbles to crouch down near the man. He's looking right at me, but I don't make eye contact: Little Tart Fauntleroy has now entered Don't Encourage Them mode. It's a new mode and it's not as much fun as I thought it might be. I thank him and scramble back to sit on my clothes. For the next minute or so he tries to talk to me across the little gap, but soon tires of that so just invites himself to come and sit next to me, spreading his towel about a foot away and propping himself up on an elbow. This wasn't the idea.

But then, now that I look around, maybe I shouldn't be surprised. Even without clothes, some of the single men around me are exhibiting what I imagine to be tell-tale hints of cultural uniform (some shaved heads, the odd piercing, a general air of ironic reserve). It suggests to me that Dorothy isn't in Kansas any more, but is certainly among friends. The friend that wants to be friends with me introduces himself.

"Bryan," says Bryan, lighting a cigarillo with his free hand. Bryan doesn't look much like the others. He's about sixty and averagely overweight; he obviously spends plenty of time here since all of him is chestnut brown. In fact, as he offers a hand in greeting, the only tan-line I can see is on his ring finger.

If I spent the first ten minutes on the beach worrying that I might get an erection, the feel of Bryan's firm, sun-creamy handshake leaves me wondering if I'll ever get one again. He starts to engage me in a conversation about local house prices. I nod through this as he puts on a pair of mirror sunglasses. They have the effect, along with the cigarillo, the missing wedding ring and the mortgage chat, of making me think that Bryan is a man with a foot in two camps and not very happy in either.

So there I am, looking at my twenty-one-year-old body reflected in the sunglasses of this porky closet-case who keeps fiddling with his nuts. And I detect the limits of the gay part of my nature as well as the limits of my generosity. I don't feel threatened by Bryan and his interest isn't demeaning. But I don't feel sorry for him either because he's spoiling my morning. And what would it be like if it were every morning? What if being desirable to men meant that I got this kind of attention all the fucking time?

304

It feels, as I make my excuses and get dressed, as if Bryan has taught me some kind of lesson. From now on, whenever I hear a wolf-whistle as a woman walks past a bunch of fat-arsed builders on her way to work, I'll think of Bryan. Yes, I conclude, as I leave the beach, the way I had to put up with that man imposing his presence and boring me senseless while constantly readjusting his balls has taught me basically everything I need to know about sexual harassment.

I was hopelessly wrong about that, of course. I hadn't learnt the first thing about sexual harassment. OK, maybe the first thing, but not the next twenty. There are many exceptions, but on average most men have an advantage in upper-body strength compared with most women. I don't think for a second that Bryan meant me any harm, but if he had, skinny as I was, I could have thumped him harder in the face and kicked him harder in his fussed-over nutsack than most women of my age and weight could do.

Being harmlessly chatted up (never mind groped or attacked) by someone stronger than me . . . that would have felt different. That would have felt very different indeed.

Clara came to stay in Woodhall Spa. Dad was at his most charming. When we visited John and Trudy, Dada was wearing a tie and Tru had made cucumber sandwiches with the crusts cut off.

I sit next to Clara on the swings in the park, talking about our future house by the sea and naming our future children. So far, it's the happiest day of my life. What could possibly go wrong?

A young man may call himself a feminist, but to do so is hardly a test of character. It isn't even a test of feminism. He'll find out how firmly he believes that women have minds of their own when one of them breaks his heart.

At which point, we might all be in for a bit of a disappointment.

CHAPTER
TWELVE

Men Understand Women

"Sometimes you get a flash of what you look like to other people."

Zadie Smith, *On Beauty*

Clara has started a director's course at a small and notoriously twattish drama school in North London. We see each other twice during the beginning of my third year at Robinson and the rest is a grim stutter of awkward phone chats. We're both lousy on the phone and it doesn't help that she hates her course and is utterly miserable. Hers is the kind of hardcore little school that seeks to break down student inhibitions by getting them to wear masks and then violently attack each other. The place is run by over-mighty teachers who've had no one to challenge them since 1968: baby-boom dickwads manipulating go-for-it young people and not an audience in sight. The only thing these particular drama students are going to learn is how to be a drama teacher. Or how not to be one.

I won't pretend this is my first experience of having an unhappy girlfriend, but this time I actually care. I just about grasp that the sentence "I wish you would

307

cheer the fuck up" would be counterproductive, but beyond that I have literally no idea what I'm supposed to do. Never mind: she's coming to see me in a show soon. I'll do some funny dancing. Girls love my funny dancing.

But I know something is seriously wrong. As we've seen, when times are difficult I usually take it out on my girlfriend. Now that my girlfriend is difficult, I take it out on Footlights. I'm now vice-president. The new president is a man called Charlie who is a brilliantly funny writer, but I'm the only writer/performer who has been on tour. Charlie has the title, but to all intents and purposes I'm the goddam star around here.

It is not good for me. It wouldn't make me happy even if things were great with Clara. As things are, I'm at the height, the zenith, the very snow-capped peak of my own arrogant, insecure, minty dreadfulness. Enjoy!

The show in which I expect to do the funny dancing is the Footlights Pantomime that I'm writing with Charlie: *Dick Wittington*.

I inform the director that I'll be playing Dick. Tim Shawl, a Maths third-year, slightly struggles with this and suggests that, traditionally, the principal boy in a pantomime is played by a girl.

I explain that this won't be happening.

Tim also wonders when he might get to see Act One of the script because time is already running short. I tell him, with the obnoxious courtesy of someone who knows he holds all the cards, that this stuff isn't always easy but Charlie and I are doing our very best and the script will certainly be ready when it's ready.

Generally, Charlie is a bad influence and I love it. He has a Withnailish quality, by which I mean he is outwardly clever, posh, rude, very funny and often drunk. What goes on beneath the surface is infinitely more gentle, but not many people will get to see that. Later that year I'll write a sketch called "He's Just Shy" about the world's most appallingly rude bastard at a party whose friend keeps saying, "He's just very shy and vulnerable." You would have to be a saint, or more accurately a clinical psychologist, to see the vulnerability driving mine and Charlie's behaviour that term.

His college have given him a whole flat on the edge of town. I turn up with handwritten scenes and he laughs like a maniac. Some scenes we write together. We sit at his Mac and he touch-types at a speed I find dazzling. There will be an endless supply of coffee and cigarettes till about 3p.m., followed by an endless supply of cigarettes and red wine. We do a lot of laughing, partly about the script, but equally about how late the script is and how we're probably pissing everyone off.

We sweep into production meetings in our long coats, late and emotional, making tosspot pronouncements and generally amusing some people and making others want to stab us.

But there probably should have come a moment when we noticed we were doing nothing more heroic than flying by the seat of other people's pants: the lighting designer with his head in his hands; the musical director frowning his way through a half-written script with no page numbers; the way Tim Shawl can no longer talk without moving his arms like he's being attacked by invisible bees . . . I probably should have turned to Charlie and whispered, "Are we the baddies?"

Which reminds me . . .

I kept hearing this first-year's name and it was annoying me. I knew he had *something*, but people wouldn't shut up. I was going to have to see for myself.

We've hopped back to my second year. I'm in a little performance venue called The Playroom to watch a one-hour non-Footlights revue called *Go to Work on an Egg*. A bunch of mates from Peterhouse and Jesus College have cobbled it together, apparently. Eddie had put me in charge of Smokers and I've auditioned most of them. They're fine but let's not get carried away.

Except for one. As a first-year, he was never going to be in the Tour Show, but he'd been asked to contribute material and I'd written a sketch with him. The sketch was nothing special, but that wasn't unusual. It's just that we'd nearly made each other sick with laughter while writing it. That was both special and unusual.

He's on stage as the lights come up. Come on then, young David Mitchell. Let's see what you've got.

Oh, I see. You've got everything. I spend the hour enjoying the sketches without once taking my eyes off David. He's very funny, which helps. But I've seen other funny student performers. This is different. He's completely committed, but entirely natural. He can afford to seem generous to the other performers because he's going to get your attention just by standing still. It's a precious combination of ease and focus that I conceitedly think reminds me of me. He looks like he lives there.

It's an exciting but also worrying turn of events. What am I going to do about this?

In my head, I hear a version of a conversation I know off by heart from *The Empire Strikes Back*.

Emperor: There is a great disturbance in the funny.

Vader: I have felt it, my master.

Emperor: We have a new enemy: David Mitchell.

Vader: He's just a boy.

Emperor: He could destroy us. The son of . . . er, whoever his dad is must not get on the Footlights Committee.

(Pause)

Vader: If he could be turned, he would be a powerful ally.

Emperor: *(Thinks)* Yes . . . yes! He would be a great asset. Can it be done?

Vader: He will do a two-man late-show at the ADC Theatre with me next year . . . or die, my master.

At the end of my second year, at the Edinburgh Fringe, I'm doing the Tour Show and David's in a patchy play, written by Charlie, called *Colin!*

I pop the question. I don't quite say, "Join me, and together we can rule Footlights galaxy as . . . two blokes", but I do suggest we do a show. He's a polite young man from a minor public school, as well as a first-year being asked out on a big comedy date by next year's vice-president. So I can't help hoping he'll look pleased. What he actually looks like is Charlie Bucket just after Willy Wonka offers him a Chocolate Factory.

In *Dick Wittington*, David plays Andrew the Cat — a fastidious cat who is also a recovering heroin addict. I'm Dick, of course, a fantastically rich and spoilt child who yearns to leave his privileged background and go to London to work in local government. He and Andrew team up with Mr Miyagi, who is played by Matthew Holness (the brilliant future Garth Marenghi). The inclusion of Mr Miyagi is due mainly to Charlie's joyful obsession with Pat Morita's performance in *The Karate Kid*: at various stages in the show, Mr Miyagi defeats his enemies by doing karate on them *very slowly*.

Matt has a reasonable concern about playing a character of East Asian heritage and I try to tell him that the Californian Pat Morita is no more from Okinawa than Matt is. He doesn't really buy that, so then I say that it's a parody of a Hollywood take on Japanese people and he should probably relax. He does not relax. Finally I tell him it's fine because in a later scene which maybe he hasn't had a chance to read yet (this is a fair bet because I'm making it up as I speak), Mr Miyagi will become the victim of racist banter from a Northern club comic played by Tristram Hunt. Therefore we won't care that we've got a white person playing the fictional version of the fictional Mr Miyagi because the joke will be about racism and not about funny foreigners.

Matt doesn't really believe a word he's hearing, but goes along with it. He appreciates that I'm making an effort, probably because he's heard I can be a bit difficult. A bit minty.

He's right.

First, a brief word about cunts. This word for the female genital arrangement is one which some people find unusually challenging for political reasons rather than the usual ones to do with good taste. Or rather, so the reasoning goes, the c-word is unusually powerful because the culture finds vaginas unusually distasteful. Therefore its use is misogynistic and a feminist no-no.

I have some sympathy for this view, and the one and only time I got to work with Rik Mayall he gave me an affectionate telling-off for ignoring it. I used the word in reference to the channel controller who had cancelled *Bottom*. Rik, one of the 1980s pioneers of non-sexist comedy, corrected his idle student. "No no, darling! Cunts are lovely! Cunts are wonderful things! She wasn't a cunt. She was a spoonful of the Devil's cum!"

While I agree with my late hero that vaginas themselves are indeed lovely, I've never quite been able to ban myself from using the word altogether, provided I'm in the company of other men and women who use it all the time. Within my peer group (which inevitably includes a lot of actors), the usage is almost playful and

313

has come to imply a fairly specific kind of arrogance and narcissism. Anyway, Caitlin Moran, Germaine Greer and my wife all say it's OK and that's good enough for me.

So. There's an old adage which actors repeat to themselves whenever they start a new job. "Have a look at the people around you and, after the first week, if you can't tell who the cunt is — it's probably you."

Rehearsing *Dick Wittington*, I don't even bother looking around. I already know. It's like I'm on a mission. It's like I'm starring in the movie *Mission: Cunt*.

I'm keen for everyone to know that, in the words of Sammy Davis Jr, I "ain't the boy next door". Unfortunately, the way I mean to make this point is by a) acting better than everyone else, and b) acting like a cunt.

It will be some time before I realise that in acting, as in many jobs, a) you get better results when you collaborate instead of compete, and b) given the choice, only cunts prefer to compete.

The script is hopelessly late and far too long. In rehearsal, the increasingly frantic Tim Shawl reads out a long list of cuts that are necessary to make the show the length of a pantomime as opposed to the length of a Ring Cycle. Everyone else has their script out, crossing out the excised lines. Since I've given myself title role, a presence in nearly every scene, a five-minute monologue and a couple of songs, these cuts are

314

probably going to affect me, so I should probably also have a script and a pencil at the ready.

Instead, I just sit in the middle of the room in my '94 Summer Tour T-shirt (no one else has one of these, so this is a risible assertion of seniority) and pout at the ceiling. When we get to rehearsing, I start doing my lines, including the ones that have just been cut. The director and the other actors say, "Actually, that's just been cut." And then I frown at the script and say, "Oh, has that been cut? I liked that bit. Why would you cut that?" while staring at Tim with disingenuous confusion. Essentially, for the whole rehearsal process of that show, I give an uninterrupted masterclass in minty cuntiness. Or possibly cunty mintiness.

I still thought that Talent was more important than Practice and did so without noticing that I was using my Talent as a suit of armour rather than as something to be put at the service of a team. I didn't even notice that acting was a team sport. Why would I? I hate sport. And teams. I was the best — other people needed to deal with it.

Inappropriate competitiveness is not an exclusively male trait and neither is swaggering around like a bell-end. But we seem to have made both behaviours sufficiently our own that a woman behaving with equivalent awfulness will have her "femininity" called into question. There is, of course, nothing wrong with wanting to win if what you're involved in is an actual competition. A game of darts, for example, is a competition. But acting doesn't have to be like that and neither does a lot of other work. On the desolate occasions I've found myself watching *The Apprentice*, it's notable that these people are not competing to be the best businessperson, but the biggest wanker. The interaction between the men and women — sorry, that should be "the boys" and "the girls" — is especially surreal. Given that masculinity adds up to little more than the pursuit of not being a woman (not walking like this, not talking like that), it's bizarre to watch "the girls" acting out a version of it in order to compete. You have to pretend to be someone who is furiously insisting that they are not you. Women entering this arena are the ghosts at the circle jerk. All the most harmful and self-harming aspects of masculinity are busily performed: the need to dominate others, the weaselly interest in hierarchy, the confusion between cruelty and strength, an impatience with nuance and the moronic idea that inflexibility is a virtue.

We're not talking about women trying to be men. We're talking about women and men trying to be arseholes. Because that's what they think you're supposed to be like at work. There's a lot of it about.

Into this, Clara arrives at Robinson and gives me a hug at the door just a bit too long and just a bit too tight. Upstairs, she tells me that she's had a fling with a lighting technician called Tony ("Tony the Techie" I call him with the deathless wit of a jilted boyfriend). Clara also says that she doesn't understand how she could be ending our relationship when "we don't really have a relationship".

I've heard this one before — the classic "How could I have just thrown your lovely pudding in the bin when there *is* no lovely pudding?" gambit. But I don't get angry, not yet. I just tell her that this means I'm going back into counselling. I expect that she must understand that she has made this necessary. I'm glad that she's coming to see the show tonight but, naturally, she has made it very difficult for me to do my important job.

She takes it right on the chin. If I were her, I'd get straight back on the train to London. But she's old-school. She says, "Well, I don't have a counsellor so I'm just going to hang around weeping in bookshops until the show. Hope you're in the bar afterwards, though."

It's a two-week run and that night is the first Saturday. It's not my place to say that I'm very good in it, but let's assume for the sake of argument that I massively rock. At the end, as I leave the stage and walk past the rest of the cast in the wings, they hear me say over the din of the applause, "It's not ENOUGH." Dame Fauntleroy is highly displeased.

Clara has been to the bookshop. It's 1994 so she's bought another novel where the main characters can suddenly levitate. She's complimentary about the show, but obviously it doesn't change a damn thing. I should have got on the train more often. We've blown it.

Back at the room, she says, "Now then, am I sleeping on the floor, or in that cupboard? Or whereabouts, exactly?"

I say, "You can sleep with me if you like. I promise to keep my pants on."

She says, "Oh, shush."

In the morning, after a really wonderful night of no sleep and no sex, I make to get up but first say, "Tell me this isn't the last time I get out of a bed that's got you in it."

"This isn't the last time you get out of bed that's got me in it."

It is, of course. And then she's gone.

So I do the thing that sensitive young men like me (whose sensitivity is entirely focused on themselves) do when they find themselves inconvenienced by a woman. They don't shout or lose their temper. Good gracious, no. That's what Dad would do.

No, they just write her a nine-page letter which describes in forensic detail why she's out of her mind. And this is done in the genuine belief that once the girlfriend understands that she is "just confused", "dishonest", "suffering from some weird kind of amnesia" and "completely wrong", why then, she will gratefully fall back into the arms of this gentle prince and relationship bliss will resume.

Clara receives the letter and stops returning my calls.

I go into a miserable sulk of self-loathing. Because that's another thing a sensitive young man would do. Rather than, say, apologise.

There again, once a sensitive young man belatedly understands that he's been dumped, it's only natural for him to start sensitively sleeping around. A whole eight days later, the panto cast party sees me trying to charm all the people I've variously ignored, patronised or insulted over the previous few weeks. One of them is a very nice girl called Jenna. She beckons me over . . .

"Now, Rob, the thing is . . ."

"I know. D'you live nearby?"

"Yes."

"Get your coat."

We run giggling out of the bar, snog in the middle of the street, and then run, giggle and snog all the way to her house. I'll draw a veil at this point, but something must have gone right because we went out with each other for the next eight years.

What I could really do with at this point is someone who isn't going to dump me and isn't going to die. Jenna does an excellent job of both and, as luck would have it, she's also funny and gorgeous. Still, I don't make it easy for her, at least not in the beginning. Little Lord Rebound is going to make her feel romantically short-changed and, as far as lovingly expressed sentiments go, she will wait for some time for an improvement on "get your coat". She doesn't see me gazing at her across the room the way Colin Firth gazes at Jennifer Ehle in *Pride and Prejudice*, and it will be a good four months into the relationship before she suggests I might want to take down the A4 show poster featuring Clara's face from my bedroom wall.

"When's it going to get romantic!!?" is the half-joking catchphrase. We spend our first St

319

Valentine's evening making up the silly cast biographies for the programme of the Spring Revue. Fun, but not romantic. If we go to a restaurant, we split the bill. Fair, but not romantic. One of the happiest days we spend together is in a London park when we find out she is not, despite a catastrophic condom malfunction, pregnant. A massive relief, but definitely not romantic.

I love her. And I love the way my name has changed into "Rob and Jenna". But it never quite gets romantic, not the way it's supposed to. This is where the diary fizzles out because I'm too happy to bother with it any more. But somehow I already know that if I say that to Jenna, presenting it as a massive compliment, she's going to be distinctly unimpressed. "Hey! You've single-handedly turned me from a suicidally lonely and miserable bastard into a complacently content bastard! That's a hell of a thing, isn't it?" Actually, it *is* a hell of a thing. But it's also not Colin Firth with a bunch of flowers and two tickets for the Orient Express.

She's aware of her own conditioning and it pisses her off. She knows she's been sold a dummy about being swept off her feet by Mr Darcy and is annoyed with herself for slightly wanting it anyway.

Thank God I've never been one of those blokes who steers his partner around in public with a hand on the small of her back. I mean, what the hell are they doing? Would it be better if she wore a dress with an actual handle?

But there's definitely something uxorious and protective in my manner towards Jenna. I've gone from preening one-man show to affable husband without having to go through the whole bloody Romeo thing again. It's like I've suddenly noticed how Romeo ends up and I don't like the look of it.

One night, that protectiveness I mentioned pops up in a fairly dramatic way. The venue for this everyday story of sexual harassment and ham-fisted melodrama is, appropriately enough, the bar of the Amateur Dramatic Club Theatre.

It's our last year at Cambridge, and towards the end Jenna is playing Mistress Quickly in a May Week production of *Henry IV Part One*. The poster features her showing a bit of barmaid cleavage, which is fine by her.

However, one night in the bar, a student called Terrance Keble starts making posh, insulting noises about whether Jenna's breasts have been digitally enhanced. He's leader of the student Conservative Association, which doesn't exactly endear him to me, and having started a huge row he walks across the room to rip the poster down, the better to compare Jenna's breasts to those on the poster. He then, for some demented reason of his own, picks up Jenna's bag and starts rifling through her stuff.

I impress upon him, at some volume and not a little perturbation, that these are the actions of "a fucking cock-sucker" and suggest to him with equal warmth that he should return the bag, which he then does. Everyone, including Jenna and about ten angry friends, give him a brief but robust outline of what they find lacking in his moral character. The poster goes back on the wall and things calm down for a while.

But then, just as he's leaving, Keble gives a visibly upset Jenna what I can only describe as a leer, and opens his mouth to say something guaranteed to be insufferable.

That's when I try to hit him.

You've always got more choice than you think. From this one and only experience of actually attacking someone, I can report that, although the clichés about red mist and blind rage have some truth to them, I also know that I definitely didn't have to do it.

I did it anyway — or at least tried to — and I won't forget the look of astonishment on Keble's pink face as Dick Wittington came at him with a clenched fist and a look of murder. My friend Jack instantly put himself in the way, which was lucky for Keble's face and my puny wrists. Jack's a big chap and I didn't get within two yards of Mr Tittystare. Instead he was bundled out of the fire escape by the bar manager and did some shouting about how I "had a fucking problem" and I shouted back that, no indeed, on the contrary, it was he who "had a fucking problem".

This Ciceronian exchange concluded, Jack put me down and Jenna tried to cheer me up by saying I probably shouldn't have done that, but she was secretly quite pleased that I did.

And I really did need cheering up. Because what was the point of it all if it turns out I'm just this normal bloke? I didn't need to be at Cambridge to get pissed up on a Saturday night and lamp a Tory. I could have done that at Coningsby Community Centre.

But the real problem was that this was my low opinion of "normal blokes". I thought normal blokes were violent as well as sexist. For three years I'd surrounded myself with men who, like me, had never been in a fight in their lives, and who were also doing their best to see women as part of a universal whole of humanity rather than some quirky subset.

Despite that, I still insisted I was different. I still had to be the leading Anti-Dad.

It was perfectly clear to me that if I'd decked Terrance Keble and we'd both ended up in Casualty, and if Dr Jizzcake had found that a sufficient cause to send me down in disgrace, my explanation to Dad would have quietly delighted him. He'd have been sorry for me too, of course, but also delighted. His interpretation wouldn't have been that I got into a fight in defence of an anti-chauvinist principle. It would be that I got into a fight because I didn't like the way another bloke was looking at my girlfriend's tits.

And he'd have been dead right. That's what bothered me.

As Finals approach, I start to think about the exam questions that I'd actually be able to answer. I'm hoping for something like:

1. Describe, as loosely as possible, what happens in the first two pages of *Moby-Dick*.

2. Is it called *Prince Lear* or *King Lear*? Feel free to draw a picture if that's easier.

3. What would be an ideal way to stage the play *Arse-bandits in the Round*? You won't be marked down for spelling mistakes, but in case you're unsure, it's "proscenium". Although the answer "do it in a theatre with a proscenium arch" is the wrong answer.

Jenna has somehow got a telly and VCR in her room and she, Jack and I spend a lot of time there working very hard for the Tragedy paper we're all taking by watching videos of *Macbeth*, *Iphigenia in Aulis*, *Beauty and the Beast* and *Aladdin*.

The three of us are also in an unthinkably-close-to-exams production of *Bedroom Farce*, along with David and a few others. And I also do the two-man show with David. Oh yes, and I'm in the Footlights Tour Show again. It's almost as if I'm in denial. I'm pretty sure I'm handling this exam pressure brilliantly by pretending to feel no such thing.

My body, on the other hand, knows otherwise — which is probably why, one day as I get up from my desk, the floor leaps up and smacks me in the side of the head. My heart is beating itself stupid and the silence is roaring in my ears like a Vulcan bomber landing in my brain. I crawl over to the bed and lie still, wondering if I'm about to die. After a few seconds of careful breathing, everything returns to normal. Later that day, Jack tells me that this experience has a name: a "panic attack". Oh, right, that's what that means then. I thought it was just a colourful way of saying you're a bit stressed out. Well, if it appears that I'm more worried than I thought I was about being hopelessly unprepared then the solution is obvious. I go to Jenna's and we watch *The Princess Bride*.

My exam strategy, if you can call it that, turns out to be waiting until I've got an exam tomorrow morning, going to the library to find a collection of essays on the relevant period, trying to memorise about four of them overnight, and then going to the exam. At that point, I find the questions with the least total irrelevance to the essays in my head and write a sleazy opening paragraph explaining why the two things actually fit together quite nicely. I then spew out the pre-written essay, being careful not to include any of the better or more memorable phrases so the outrageous thievery doesn't stick out any more than it needs to. After all, for all I know, the repurposed essays will be marked by one of the academics who wrote them.

Yes, it occurs to me that this is a wretched business and an appalling waste. The panic attack was probably inspired as much by guilt as by anxiety. But I suppose I'm at least consistent. I didn't come here to get an excellent degree. I came here to meet someone like David Mitchell. As it turned out, I met the actual David Mitchell, which was even better.

I wander slowly down Burrell's Walk on the way to the Senate House, where my results will be posted up on a noticeboard. I'm telling myself not to worry. The eleven-plus mattered, A levels mattered. This won't matter.

Still, I have some memory of academic pride (at least with English) and as I look at the board and see that I'm leaving university with a 2:2, I feel a wave of disappointment. It's an outrageous reaction, given what I failed to do. But there we are. The feeling is: "I used to be good at this stuff and now I'm an official mediocrity." It takes all of three seconds for this nonsense to be replaced by profound relief and gratitude. I deserved to fail altogether. This is so jammy they should make me Lord Fluky of Jam, the Bonne Maman Professeur of Spreadable Berries at Robertson's College, Strawbridge.

Mark, Andrew and Dad come to the graduation. The families in the Senate House are specifically asked not to take photographs during the ceremony, which means that Dad, Mark and Andrew all wait until I've seen them before dicking about with cameras, pretending they are about to take a picture. Sometimes I really like men, especially these men.

There's some milling around on the lawn outside and Dad has gone unusually quiet for a moment while I chat along with Mark and Andy. His eyes are quite red and he hasn't even had a drink.

Presently he says to me, "I know you'd rather your mum was here, son, but for what it's worth I'm very proud of you." He looks like he feels lucky to be invited. He's taking up someone else's place.

That's when I forgive him. Right there. At least, that's what I believe in that moment.

I mumble, "Nah, y'all right, mate. I'm glad you came."

I'm leaving home. I left years ago but now it's official. I don't pretend to my family any more that I want to work "in computers". They've gradually absorbed the information that I seriously intend to share a flat in London and try to earn a living as a comedy actor and writer.

I'm growing up in circles. One circle opened when I was thirteen and began with the idea "I want to be funny on TV like in *Home Sweet Home*". That circle, on my graduation day in 1995, is still moving along, looking for its beginning. A sub-circle circle, "I get to be funny on TV by going to Robinson College", is just closing.

29-09-90
Happy 18th Birthday Mr Robert Webb. No, of course I don't feel any different — I can't believe the world now considers me an adult. It probably doesn't if it's got any sense! My party at the Community last Friday was fucking ACE. Everyone came — I mean just the whole country practically.

I picked my Cambridge college — Robinson. They want AAB so I better bloody well pull my socks up.

I've been letting things get me down too often about Mum and should just try to cultivate a sense of inevitable good news. I should start just thinking and walking around like I know that

Robinson will let me in and I know all the rest to come: making a big splash in Footlights, finding some funny people to work with, Edinburgh Festival, Radio 4, Channel 4, BBC 2, plays, novels, Hollywood . . . I mean it's all ludicrous but why not? Ambition is free — this is no time to put limits on it. I'm going to be bigger than John Cleese.

It was a good plan. I'm not knocking the plan. And yes, I do know it looks freakish. "And so, I shall simply write down my life on the back of a postcard and then sort of . . . do it." Well, most of it. I suspect John Cleese is quite safe from my bigness.

The trouble is, it's not a "life", is it? It's a job. A person as young as that can't be expected to know the difference between what he wants and what he needs. This one reckons that if you get the job right, the life will follow. It's not an uncommon view.

If I said that heavily defining yourself by your work might not be a very good idea, then you might react like an American friend of mine. "Worry less about the office . . . that sounds sensible," Matt said. "Although I have to say," he continued, "I've had some pretty cool days at the office."

I've had some pretty cool days at the office too. I just thought they were cool for the wrong reasons.

Let's go to the office. I'm fairly sure I can find it . . .

CHAPTER
THIRTEEN

Men Are Good at Directions

JEREMY: What, so you're going to marry her out of embarrassment?
MARK: There are worse reasons.

> *Peep Show*, written by Sam Bain
> and Jesse Armstrong, Series 4

I'm dancing with Princess Leia in Leicester Square.

I think, "Considering we're completely lost and I've no idea what to do next, this is all going quite well."

A few hours before, Jo, the deputy stage manager, popped her head around my dressing-room door. I'm playing Bertie Wooster in an adaptation of *The Code of the Woosters* at a West End theatre. The curtain goes up in twenty minutes and Jo usually nips in to tell me how we're selling tonight and any other bits of housekeeping. She usually finds me pacing up and down, shouting my opening lines and looking slightly ill.

I say, "Hello, m'love. What's the news?"

"Hi Rob, all good. Nice, full Saturday night. All three levels open and busy." She looks through her notes with a secretive grin. "Nothing else . . . oh yes, Stephen Fry's in tonight and he's bringing a couple of guests."

"Stephen . . ."

"And the guests are his boyfriend Elliott and . . . let me see . . . oh yes, Carrie Fisher." I stare at her.

"So that's just Stephen, Elliott and Carrie. And then they want to come round after and take you to dinner. Have a good show!" She does an evil cackle and goes.

And that's it, really. One minute you're graduating from Cambridge and the next you're playing to a full house in the West End which happens to include Stephen Fry, Stephen Fry's soon-to-be-husband Elliott Spencer and Stephen Fry's pal, Carrie Fisher.

Actually, I might have skipped a few years. This is 2014 so, to be exact, the number of years I've skipped is nineteen. Anyway, a simple nineteen years later . . .

It's a great part in a great show and I've been doing it for weeks. It ought to go well and it does. I change quickly and peer out of the window. The route to the stage door at the Duke of York's is dimly lit, but I'd recognise Stephen's silhouette from orbit. Behind him, a young man and a shorter, older woman. Bloody hell!

And here they are in my room. I've met and even worked with Stephen by now, but it's still surreal to have a TV hero moving around in 3D. He gives me a burly hug and tells me what I did on stage was "fucking masterful". Elliott is reserved and charming. He loves comedy and was at school when *Peep Show* started. I get the impression the 3D thing is happening to him so I'm on my best behaviour. You mustn't let them down:

none of Stephen's generation let *me* down. Dawn French could piss in my trifle and I'd tell her that's exactly what my trifle was missing.

And here is Ms Fisher, five foot one inch in dark glasses, shaking my hand and heading for the window to smoke a fag. She says she loved the show and that the four-minute Charleston that we do at the end is "The best damn curtain-call I've ever seen". That's the daughter of Debbie Reynolds talking there, who may have seen a curtain-call or two. So I'm fairly pleased.

Dear reader, I'm going to take a risk and draw back the curtain to show you the crazed old man with the buttons and levers. Books take ages and the first draft of this chapter was written in the spring of 2016. At that point, Carrie Fisher was alive and well, as was Debbie Reynolds. And so were Prince, George Michael and Victoria Wood. Whenever we lost another eighties icon, I felt sorry for those who knew and loved them, but I also have to admit to the guilty thought of an author's one-track mind. "Jesus," I thought, "the book is sad enough as it is. I'm just sitting here and the book's getting sadder by the bloody week."

But I'm going to leave this little story unchanged because it deserves its own innocence. Apart from being about how rubbish I am at directions, it's all about being present in the present moment. That's where we care least about what's around the corner. And quite right too.

I don't mean to bum you out but . . . we're all going to die. The thing is, very few of us actually believe it. We look at pictures of people who have died and marvel at the pathos. "Ah, there's Jean all smiling. She didn't know she'd be dead in three months." Well, maybe Jean knew and maybe she didn't. But what she didn't do was go around hoping to provide someone else with a satisfying sense of dramatic irony. Nobody lives like that and it's odd that we do it to the dead sometimes. What I remember of Carrie Fisher was that she was beautifully, singularly alive.

Carrie climbs through the window, perching on the sill and sticking her feet up on the fire escape opposite, with a three-storey drop in between. She's in London to start filming *Star Wars: The Force Awakens* and I briefly wonder about Disney/Lucasfilm's insurance arrangements. What's going to happen to me if the tiny star disappears out of the window? I give her a light.

By now I've been around enough famous people not to waste time trying to be cool. If an actor means something to you — just tell them. Ideally, don't bugger around with selfies, but by all means say "thanks" if that's what you feel. I tell her I'm a massive fan of her films and books, and she rewards me with a couple of details about the new *Star Wars* movies that are so secret I start watching the door in case a Disney hit-squad of armed woodland creatures suddenly barge in to make an arrest.

Stephen has kindly booked a table at a super-duper Italian restaurant in Archer Street, where he plans to treat us all. He, Elliott and my Jeeves co-star, the excellent Mark Heap, head off, with Ms Fisher and me following. Outside, the chaps stride ahead and I quickly lose sight of them.

I'm aware that Carrie, at various stages of her life, has been addicted to more-or-less every harmful substance ever invented and she isn't exactly one of those fifty-eight-year-olds who's still leaping around like a gazelle. She takes my arm. Ooh, get me, squiring Ms Fisher around town and nattering about the theatre! This is fantastic.

There's just one problem. I haven't got a fucking clue where we're going.

What have I been doing in London these last nineteen years? What have I been doing, in particular, over the last ten, when my professional life has centred on the theatres, voice-over studios and production offices of Soho and the West End? Why, during those years of under-employment in the nineties didn't I just sit down with an *A–Z* and get some of this shit into my head? Why, more urgently, can't I find my way from St Martin's Lane to Archer Street without three maps and an American?

It's my sitcom flaw. What's the thing about you that you don't mind being teased about? The thing that makes your friends take the piss but which you privately hope is endearing. Maybe you do a certain face whenever you look in the mirror. Maybe you blow the crumbs off a biscuit before dunking it in tea. Maybe you only buy clothes in one colour which you don't even like that much.

Me, I just get lost. I get lost frequently and with distinction. I don't just get lost when walking or driving

— I get lost on trains. I can go to the loo on a train and take ten minutes to find my seat again. I haven't yet got lost on an escalator but it's only a matter of time.

I can't remember the name of the restaurant, but vaguely heard someone mention that you get to it via Chinatown. So I continue to talk to Carrie while cluelessly keeping an eye out for lanterns or pointy roofs. Time is getting on; the other guys will now be waiting for us. You might think, "Hey, it's 2014 — just enter 'Italian restaurant, Archer street' into your phone, you idiot." That, I agree, would have been the rational thing to do. It does, however, assume a reserve of level-headedness that is difficult to find when you've got Princess Leia on your arm and you're keeping General Melchett from his dinner.

Carrie hears the strain entering my voice and says, tactfully, "I guess we're a little lost."

I say, "Yep, I've got absolutely no idea where we're going. Sorry. I'm really shit at this."

"No problem, I'll call Stephen."

We're in Leicester Square and she calls Stephen and I call Mark Heap. There's a salsa band playing just outside Burger King. While we're waiting for an answer, she takes my free hand with hers and stretches away. I pull away too and then, moving back, I lift her arm, beneath which she does an elegant twirl.

We're still dancing when she gets an answer message. She yells, "Stephen, you asshole! Where the hell are you, you giant prick?" She then lets go of my hand and pulls her shades up to squint at her phone. "Oh my," she mutters with amusement, "that may have been the wrong Stephen."

We found them in the end. On the way, I was determined not to panic. I thought: come on, this stuff doesn't happen. I don't know if I'm ever going to meet this person again, but I do know that I am never, ever going to have Carrie Fisher all to myself on a balmy evening in the middle of London. At the end of *Star Wars*, Princess Leia gives Luke Skywalker a smile and a medal. But even Luke doesn't get to dance with her.

Anyway, this wasn't getting lost; this was a minor navigational hiccup. To get really lost we'll need to go back to 1998 and the six days I worked as a truck driver.

In 1998 I supposedly live in a flat in London's Kensal Green with some friends, but in fact I spend most nights with Jenna in London's Swiss Cottage. The downside is that Jenna shares a flat not only with our friend Sally Watson, but with our friend David Mitchell.

David and I are two years into the business of creating a career in comedy and we do so with the quiet hysteria of the chronically obscure and stonily broke. We write together, we travel together to meetings, we travel back from them, we perform fringe stuff together, we watch TV, we stop watching TV and go to the pub, we walk home from the pub, we say goodnight. He is the first vertical person I see in the morning and the last at night. We're annoying each other and I'm not helping the situation by living in his flat without paying any rent. But the flat for which I *am* paying rent seems a long walk away and contains a cat that isn't house-trained. So I can either live with David, or I can live with a load of piss and shit. He doesn't seem as flattered by my preference as I might have hoped.

Sally's boyfriend Richard offers me some work. He's the warehouse manager of a company that supplies events lighting. For example, if an incredibly wealthy person is having a wedding reception in a marquee in their vulgarly enormous garden, some company will have to supply all the pretty lights, lasers and star-cloths, as well as the less pretty cables and generators. And that company will need someone to deliver all the stuff on time and to the right place. That driver had better know what he's doing.

That's where I come in.

Eighty pounds a day. That's the stupendous and irresistible offer. The twin novelties of having a break from David (while giving David a break from me) and actually getting paid mean there's nothing to think about. Unfortunately, the thing about decisions where there's nothing to think about is that they're usually worth at least a quick think . . . half a think . . . a thought's-worth, at minimum.

I have a standard driving licence which means that — in 1998 — I'm allowed to drive a seven-and-a-half-ton truck without a moment's tuition. Yes, that surprised me too.

Outside the warehouse, Richard shows me the truck. You know those massive articulated lorries? Well, it's like that but slightly shorter and minus the bendy bit at the front. So I guess it's about ten metres long.

Richard sees the way I've gone very still. He offers a bit of cheerful South London reassurance. "Yeah, basically just think of it as a very long car. And obviously a bit wider." He nods to himself, looking at it. "Also quite a lot taller, obviously, so watch out for low bridges!" He hands me a piece of paper with the delivery address. I can't help noticing that the last line of it says "Gloucestershire".

The truck is still being loaded. I'm twenty-five and the other company workers are my age or a bit younger. I light a cigarette because I think it will make me look like I'm still working class. After a couple of glances from the lads I stub it out again, having quickly remembered that, when working, a defining characteristic of the working class is doing some bloody work.

I try to help them load the camlocks. What is a "camlock"? It's a two-inch-thick insulated copper power cable. It needs to stretch from the pretty lights where the party happens to the noisy generator, placed as far away from the party as possible. The camlocks are coiled neatly into a large loop and secured with industrial-sized cable ties. If you stood in the middle of such a loop, it would come to the middle of your shins.

I suppose what I'm trying to tell you is that each coiled camlock weighs about as much as your average fridge, assuming your fridge is where you keep all your gold bars.

I try to lift one of the coils but unfortunately this one has been nailed to the floor. I try another, but apparently someone has nailed them all to the floor. One of the lads politely waits for me to get out of the way and then hoists the coil onto his shoulder like it's made of firmly cooked linguine. I half expect him to drop it onto a hip and stare unsmilingly back at me, doing a hula hoop.

Richard introduces me to Gabe and Jonno, two Australians who will be riding in the cab with me to somewhere in Gloucestershire. They're both about nineteen: Gabe is square-jawed and muscular, Jonno is rounder and mixed race. A flash of liberal guilt makes me want to ask Jonno if he's descended from the Wise Aboriginal Peoples but decide this probably isn't the moment. Gabe says, "All right, mate?" and Jonno says, "How y'going, Rob?" Neither of them is big on eye contact. I reply with a hearty Lincolnshire "Now then!", which slightly baffles them, but I think they get the general goodwill.

Jonno sits near the window with Gabe in the middle. I take the driver's seat, for — yes — I am the lorry driver. The Yorkie bar that Jenna gave me as a good-luck gift is sticking in my right thigh. We laughed at the time but now it feels like the unwanted lipstick smudge on the cheek of a little boy. I grapple it out of my jeans and chuck it in the door slot. Here be man-time!

Right. Three pedals all in the usual place. Super. Here's a manual gearstick with most of the numbers still on. Good. This, of course, is a steering wheel. Check. So that's . . . where's the fucking handbrake!? Oh I see. The handbrake is this plunger that comes out

338

from the dashboard. And the lights, indicators and windscreen wipers all seem to be operated from stalks coming out of the steering column with no discernible markings. Fuck me, it's the TARDIS. But the boys are waiting so I almost shout, "Righto then, off we jolly well go!" I'm nervous. I'm veering wildly between Paul Webb and Gussie Fink-Nottle.

I drive carefully out of the warehouse car park and turn left onto Wood Lane. Of course, that involves using the brakes. When you're driving something heavy enough to crush a Sherman tank you need some quite fierce brakes. Jonno and Gabe are amiably bantering about how the truck is "obviously overloaded" and "definitely illegal". What I was used to with Chesney was sticking my foot down hard and waiting for Chesney to get the idea that I wanted it to slow down. You can drive in absolute safety like this as long as you don't have to go down hills or around corners.

The truck, however, is fitted with air-brakes. That means the moment your right foot even starts to think about hovering over the middle pedal, the effect is one of slamming head-on into a mountain. "Sorry, lads," I say, as the three of us bounce around the cab like ping-pong balls in a prize draw. "No worries," says Gabe, expressionless and looking straight ahead. "Air-brakes — total killer."

I've consulted an ancient road map and I'm pretty sure that the next thing that happens is that I turn right onto the A40. At this time, "sat-nav technology" is something that only people with tin hats and every back issue of *Conspiracy Tomorrow* talk about. "Okey-dokey!" I say with petrified jauntiness as we approach the junction with the Westway. I stop at the lights. I can just make out BBC Television Centre in the distance, a building in which I'm yet to set foot. What the fuck am I doing here? Why doesn't someone just put me on the telly?

The lights turn green. I stall. I start the engine and we lurch forward and stall again. I reach for a handbrake that isn't there. Cars behind start beeping. Gabe and Jonno are instantly livid on my behalf. Gabe shouts "Fuck off!" to no one in particular. Jonno winds his window down and sticks his head out. "FUCK OFF! He's doing the best he can!"

I get the truck started again and commit to the turn just as the lights go red. The trick here, I think, as I keep a grip on the steering wheel despite all the sweat, is to go forward and then turn at the last moment. It's the right idea but I do it half-heartedly and too early. Looking in my wing mirror I can see that on the present trajectory I'm going to take out two sets of traffic lights. The truck stalls again. "Think I should reverse and try that again," I say, peering at the gearstick and looking for an "R". Gabe is quietly putting his seat belt on. He says, "I don't know if reversing would be altogether wise in this situation, mate."

I say "Quite right" and put the truck into first and stall. I'm now blocking three, possibly four, lanes of traffic. The cacophony of beeps and horns has left

340

Jonno quite beside himself and he's now having an actual argument out of the window with another driver.

"It's his first day! *Of course* he doesn't know what the fuck he's doing! Oh yeah? Well, you come and try if you're such a fucking genius! You prick!"

Gabe has correctly surmised that the time for respectful silence has passed and that my male pride could now withstand some guidance. He says to me, "Just go straight and then give it a hard right turn when I say so." I could kiss him. Gratefully, I do exactly as he says, moving the truck straight at the concrete wall of the far left of the road we're turning onto. "Now!" he says, and I turn the wheel hard to the right as far as it will go. As we turn, Jonno's side is going to come mightily close to that wall. He reaches out to retract his wing mirror but it's not that kind of wing mirror. I look out of my own and see I've missed the traffic lights by centimetres, but we're mounting the kerb of the central reservation and crushing a bollard. Jonno winds his window up to avoid the sparks now flying up as his wing mirror makes slow-motion contact with the wall. "You doing fucking great, Bob!" he says. Gabe is smiling too. We clear the wall and straighten up. The beeping stops.

I have successfully made a right turn. I only caused a medium-sized tailback and destroyed one piece of road furniture. Jonno says, "Now we're cooking with gas!" and turns on the radio. I love these guys.

I got better at driving the lorry but no better at driving it in the right direction. In all, during my lorry-driving career, I took it out six times and got lost twelve times. At least on that first trip to Gloucester and back, I had Gabe and Jonno to navigate. More usually I was on my own, getting lost in Plymouth, getting lost trying to find Spitalfields Market, and on one night, randomly ending up in Cambridge and having to perform a twenty-three-point turn in the car park of Queens' College.

That first night, coming back from Gloucestershire, the bastard thing even broke down. The three of us spent the night in the cab. Every time I was close to the impossible destination of sleep, Jonno would suddenly remember how annoyed he was and randomly yell, "I am so fucking cranky about this!"

It's only called "male pride" when it's being challenged; the rest of the time it's just pride. I'm not indifferent to taking pleasure in traditional areas of male competence on the rare occasions that I actually show any.

As part of the writing process for the Footlights Tour Show, the club used to splash out on a writing week in a holiday cottage in Bacton, near Great Yarmouth. One of the best things about the place was a real fire in the front room, and Eddie and I quickly set to work lighting it. We had both watched our fathers do it in exactly the same way. A clean grate, of course, then a layer of tightly scrunched newspaper, on top of which you place a lattice of chopped sticks and then just a few initial lumps of coal. The two of us worked in a reverie of contented silence. We were definitely enacting some kind of rite.

A similarly happy man-based memory comes from Le Touquet in France. It was 1999 and the first time we'd all got just about enough money to have a holiday. Le Touquet was just a stopover on the way south for a week in a villa. As it happened, Jenna and the other women opted for an early night, leaving me, David, Jack and two other friends, Tom and Ellis, to go to a pool bar.

There's something to be said for exclusively male company from time to time. That might strike you as ridiculous if you are, or you're close to, a man who prefers male-only company *all* the time. But for me, playing pool and having a pint in a friendly bar with just "the boys" was fairly novel. We were a mixed bunch anyway. But I'd been relying heavily on Jenna, and Clara before her, to be basically all my friends at once. It's quite a bad idea.

In the bar, the five of us didn't suddenly fall into a chauvinistic orgy of braggadocious machismo, and neither did we get more than usually pissed. It was just five blokes enjoying each other's company. What I really liked was that we were all playing pool as skilfully as possible while not giving the slightest fuck about winning.

How come I had enough money to go on holiday? It's a two-word answer: Michele Milburn. Two things happened in May 1997: Britain elected its first Labour government in eighteen years and I got an agent. Tony Blair was, of course, extremely popular at this time, as absolutely nobody likes to be reminded. New Agent! New Britain!

★   ★   ★

Before then, for the two years after leaving college, I'd lived on Super Noodles and toast. I tried to avoid opening letters or answering the phone in case it was the landlord, the bank or the DSS. I was claiming housing benefit and taking whatever part-time work turned up. I worked as an usher in a theatre; I drove a lorry; I worked in a photo-library for a magazine about buildings (that's *Buildings Magazine*).

Jenna had a credit card and would occasionally bail me out. I tried to get my own credit card, but was refused. It was the Co-op offering a card to Labour members that turned me down. I must say, I thought that took the biscuit.

The credit report I subsequently ordered made for interesting reading. Fed-up with gang-mastering, Dad had opened a fruit and veg shop in the middle of Woodhall. For some reason he needed me to sign a few papers to get it started, but assured me that it wouldn't affect me in the slightest way. I vaguely understood I was going to be some kind of sleeping partner in the business. It seemed a painless way of doing him a favour and I'm quite sure he believed what he said. After all, no one starts a business thinking it's going to end in bankruptcy, even though, in this case, that's obviously what happened almost immediately.

It was an excellent shop, but a financial failure for two reasons. One was that Dad would undercharge his friends or insist on giving away stuff for nothing. Since he was on first-name terms with about 80 per cent of the village, that was quite a lot of apples. Second, what profit he did make, he immediately spent in the pub. A fine example of a small businessman supporting the local economy. Sadly, the shop went bust and my credit rating fell through the floor.

So it was with a shaking hand that I held the letter that Michele Milburn had sent to the Etcetera Theatre in Camden in 1997. Eddie had come up with the idea of doing a schools tour of a play that was on the A-level syllabus. He found a translation of Molière's *The Miser* and cast me in the title role, with himself, David and Colly (Olivia Colman) playing all the other parts. Together with Tom and Charles (a sort of upmarket Gabe and Jonno), who had organised Footlights tours and were also brilliant lighting and sound technicians, we became the Juggling Fiends Theatre Company.

The plan was simple. What you did was, you wrote to lots of private schools that you suspected of having more money than sense. You used headed notepaper and kept mentioning Cambridge University. Charles worked out a budget that would not only allow us all to get weekly wages (money for acting!) but would leave enough cash to fund a four-week run in a small London theatre.

Dear Robert,
    I'm sure you already have representation but in case you're still looking . . .

Michele was an agent at Amanda Howard Associates and Amanda didn't want me. They came to see me and David doing our first two-man show in Edinburgh and

345

Amanda didn't want David either. But she reluctantly allowed Michele to take us both on. Michele got us a string of meetings with producers and the part-time jobs started to fall away as we slowly began to earn a living as comedy writers. I started to open letters and answer the telephone. I even got a credit card.

By 2002 I was nearly thirty and living with Jenna in a tiny flat in Belsize Park. David and I were writing for other people's shows and had even been in a sketch show for BBC2 called *Bruiser*. During a failed attempt to make a team-written sitcom, we'd met and really liked another pair of writers called Sam Bain and Jesse Armstrong. They got in touch to say that a producer called Andrew O'Connor had come to them with an idea for a clip show where two flatmates watch TV and misinterpret everything — a kind of live action *Beavis and Butt-Head*. Sam and Jesse thought it would be cool if we saw everything from the characters' points of view and sometimes heard their thoughts. The five of us had a meeting and Andrew got some money from Channel 4 to make a fifteen-minute pilot which would be called *P.O.V.*

So the plan I wrote in the diary on my eighteenth birthday is starting to fulfil some of its freakish ambitions. Robinson, yes; find someone funny to work with, yes; Edinburgh Fringe, yes . . . the job is looking up. The life, though: I'm not really thinking about the life. The life is surely fine until somebody tells me it's not fine. That's life, isn't it?

346

I buy a copy of *Men Are from Mars, Women Are from Venus*, feeling immediately very pleased with myself that I'm man enough to read a popular book about relationships.

The slight downside to popular books about relationships is that all of them are wrong. Wrong because they all start from the premise of difference: that men and women are so fundamentally, innately, mentally and culturally different that they might as well be considered as two different species from two different planets. If you start from there, you give yourself permission to accept every stereotype you've ever heard about men and women. So books like the one mentioned — as well as its imitations with titles like *Why Men Don't Listen and Women Can't Read Maps* (Orion, 2001) and *Why Women Talk and Men Walk — How to Improve Your Relationship without Discussing it* (Vermilion, 2007) — are there not to question the different expectations placed on men and women: they're there to excuse and reinforce them, usually with a truckload of hokey metaphors and dodgy-looking science.

For example, in *Men Are from Mars, Women Are from Venus*, John Gray suggests that men and women react in different ways to stress. Women want to talk about it with close friends, while men want to go into their "cave", i.e. retreat to the shed or games console. Rings a bell, surely? If the sales of his book are anything to go by, Gray has indeed rung more than fifty million bells.

That's how you make serious cash at this gender lark. Make a generalisation and then explain it with horseshit theory that lets everyone off the hook. If Gray had a couple more jokes he could be on *Live at the Apollo*. "Men and women, eh? Eh? They're different, aren't they? Eh? Why can't men wrap presents? C'mon, fellas, you know it's true! There you are, Sellotaping your fingers together! Why can't we wrap presents? Eh? Ladies! You have to come and do the wrapping for us, don't you!? Eh? Ladies? You have to do the wrapping. Sometimes, we've got you a present and you have to wrap it! I'm saying you have to wrap your own presents! Exactly!"[1]

And it seems to Jenna and me, as once again she goes glumly to bed and I stay up with a bottle of wine to play *Civilization II* for another two hours, that yes, Mr Gray is definitely onto something. I'm not rejecting Jenna — I'm just "in my cave". And when Jenna wants to talk about how our relationship doesn't seem to be much fun any more, that's just because she's from Venus. Luckily, Venusians only want to be listened to; there's nothing a Martian can actually do to help. In fact, if a Martian tries to "solve the problem" then he's just showing that he doesn't get that she's from another planet. So I make a big show of "listening" because, conveniently, that is now the maximum requirement.

It doesn't occur to me that the reason why Jenna wants to talk about our relationship is that it really is looking quite peaky. Neither do I consider that, as a girl

---

[1] Men really do seem to be worse at wrapping presents and I suggest that's because they've had less practice. As to why that might be . . . John Gray is about as interested as John Bishop.

and then a woman, she has been told about five times an hour that care of personal relationships (wrapping presents, among other things) is her job. I, on the other hand, am quite certain that care of personal relationships is basically none of my business. I wouldn't know where to start. I mean, I'll read the stupid book and everything, but the stupid book just gave me a massive pass. So, if you don't mind, I'll just do my "listening" and then play *Civilization II* because that's precisely what I feel like doing with my time. Men don't have "me time", you understand: they just have "time". And now, rather marvellously, spending large portions of it alone doing something enjoyable isn't being selfish, it's fulfilling the basic psychological needs of my people: the Martians.

Jenna gets a job and goes on tour in a production of *Charlotte's Web*. It's a Theatre in Education tour, which is where you do a show for schools and then follow the performance up with some kind of workshop with the children. It's an established route for making-it actors to get work and maybe an agent. Given that *The Miser* was nothing if not a TIE tour, I have absolutely no right to be snooty about Jenna's job, but I manage to be snooty anyway.

Partly I'm jealous. Almost all the work I'm doing with David is writing. *Bruiser* had vanished in the same way it had initially surfaced — without a trace. It seemed like we were going to subsist as writers (which was something) but not as actors (which was everything).

Also, even eight years on, the memory of what happens when your girlfriend goes away for weeks on end was still rancid enough to make me feel sick. I completely trusted Jenna not to shag Tony the Techie. But still, even I could see the relationship wasn't in great shape and the last thing I wanted was for Jenna to break out and Get Some Perspective.

And third, despite *The Miser*, I was snooty about TIE for the sake of being snooty. I remembered a company visiting QEGS and doing an amazingly shit play for the fifth-years and sixth form about the dangers of alcohol. The shouty but turgid performance of the patronising and humourless play was greeted by the audience of Lincolnshire teenagers with giggling incredulity, replaced gradually by sullen resentment. I'm pretty sure that UKIP recruited about a hundred future voters that day. Typical Metropolitan Elite! Who *are* these London cunts? Who do they think they are, telling us there's something wrong with getting smashed on Thunder bird before we go to a barn-dance? One of them has a red-label bottle of Thunderbird as a prop when everyone knows that the blue-label stuff is much stronger. And this bloke — the one doing the workshop — is he *even* Rik Mayall? He isn't, is he? He's an actor from London and he isn't *even* Rik Mayall.

Sixteen years old, I was out of my mind with envy. Despite how badly it had all gone, these guys were in their mid-twenties and professional actors. Look at their proper facial hair. Look at the way even Tiffany and Zelda are excitedly waving them off as they get back in their bloody Transit van.

I say goodbye to Jenna as she gets into a Transit van. I decide I need to up my game. What, after all, is the problem? Well, I think to myself, I've just turned thirty, and Jenna is about to turn thirty, so she's probably worrying about children. That's it! She probably wants to know whether or not I'm going to marry her. Am I going to marry her? Hmm, tough one. Er . . . yeah, why not? Jenna's great! I mean, it's not brilliant ALL THE TIME but what relationship is? I'd definitely be sad if we broke up or she died . . . Soooo . . . Yeah! I'll just ask her to marry me. That should do the trick.

My friend Ellis is well travelled and I ask him to suggest a romantic city where I might pop the question on an away-break. He says "Milan". Cool. Milan, then. This'll show her! Sure, it's been a bit nothing-y lately, but once we get married and have children, that's when the romance really starts, my friend! This is where it gets romantic!

Jenna comes home in a break from the tour. We're walking on Primrose Hill and I drop a heavy hint about how she shouldn't make any plans for the next weekend . . .

She bursts into tears and moves in with her mother.

It didn't cross my mind that she would say no. I don't know whether to be relieved or annoyed that she said no before I'd even asked the question. It turned out that she had indeed Got Some Perspective on tour, but I think she was well ahead of me anyway. She told me that she'd been waiting for me to ask her for a long time, but that the moment I did, she realised it wasn't something she wanted any more.

That day, we go to the pub and I make lots of soothing noises about how she probably just needs to have a proper think. I'm still kidding both myself and her. I won't need to cancel the flights to Milan because I didn't book them.

She doesn't move out straight away. There's a surreal limbo period of out-of-body weirdness. Neither of us can believe it's happening and we talk to each other quietly like we're both stoned.

The pilot called *P.O.V.* has been commissioned for a whole Channel 4 series and the new title is *Peep Show*. I do the first week's filming and Jenna even leaves me some warm food for when I get in at night. On the Saturday morning, we're watching MTV when "The Scientist" by Coldplay comes on. Oh great, thanks lads.

She looks at me. "This isn't going to be our break-up song, is it?"

"No," I say decisively. I immediately like "The Scientist" but I've also heard that Coldplay are massively unfashionable, so I add, "We deserve a better song." It's just more bullshit.

She moves out four days later.

Yes, let's go back to the start. Let's ask our questions and tell our secrets and run out of the theatre bar and kiss in the street.

I've got a job to do. But at the weekends, I go back to playing *Civilization II* on my tangerine iMac. Except now, I do it with two bottles of wine instead of one.

CHAPTER
FOURTEEN

Men Know Who They Are

"A child of five would understand this. Send someone to fetch a child of five."

Groucho Marx

"Mummy?"

"Yes, sweetheart."

"On non-uniform day, if I go as Spider-Man instead of as a princess, will I get laughed at?"

"I suppose you might. What will you say if they laugh?"

"Shall I tell them that they're laughing because of The Trick that makes boys unhappy and girls get rubbish jobs?"

"Yes, sweetheart. I think that would be a very good answer."

It's 2015 and the person asking the question is a five-year-old girl called Esme. The person answering is her mother, Abigail. Abbie is my wife; Ezzie is our eldest daughter. We also have Dory (for Dorothea), who is three.

"The Trick" is the family code-word for the incoming tide of gender bullshit that Ezzie, Dory and their friends (including the boys) will spend their lives wading through. The idea that boys and girls, men and women, have different roles to play in life according to the different contributions they make to a shared reproductive system is one they are going to have to deal with whether we like it or not. So they might as well have a name for it.

You may think that introducing the idea of "the patriarchy" into the minds of small children is the ultimate in liberal overkill. You may even think that it's cruel. In my view, you might as well say it's cruel not to let them have a teddy-bears' picnic in the Dartford Tunnel. The Trick is dangerous for girls. And if I've tried to say anything in this book, I've tried to say that it's dangerous for boys too. Feminism is not about men versus women; it's about men and women versus The Trick.

I met Abbie in 2003, recording a Radio 4 comedy show called *Concrete Cow*.

After a long wait, the first series of *Peep Show* was about to be broadcast on Channel 4, so among this unknown cast of six I'm equally unknown but have a kind of "pre-celebrity something-or-other" going on. David and I have had too many setbacks for me to treat this the way I would in my *Dick Wittington* pomp. By which I mean, I try not to lord it around like a golden penis. I make everyone tea in the green room; I carefully note that Abigail says her brothers call her "Abs" and drop it in casually when asking if she wants milk; I laugh immoderately at everyone else's jokes and make suggestions for script improvements with elaborate courtesy. I am doing my impression of a good company player. But I don't do such a good impression as to leave them in any doubt that it's an impression. My every deliberate gesture is there to scream: "You're bloody lucky to have me, but I'm being VERY HUMBLE ABOUT IT."

Abbie's having none of it. Over a cast lunch I say that my friend Emma was talking to a colleague at work about how I had a part in a sitcom. The colleague had said, "What, like a shopkeeper or an extra or something?" and Emma had replied, "No! He's one of the main ones!"

Abbie takes this in for a beat and says, "So that was a story about how you're one of 'the main ones'?" Then she opens her eyes madly wide and cries in a cod Californian accent, "WHAT ... A GREAT ... STORY!!!"

Her reaction to me in general is evenly divided between thinking I'm an idiot, and thinking I'm an idiot that she might want to shag. But then, along with my deliberate gestures there are my undeliberate gestures, like the way I pull my T-shirt up and jump around in front of her. Or the way I go up to her face and yap like a dog.

"I think that Cambridge boy might fancy me," she says to her friend Brede. Brede is in the audience during the first recording and confirms that whenever Abbie goes to the microphone at the front of the stage, I spend the whole sketch staring at her bottom. Yes, it's possible.

Abbie went to a single-sex boarding school and her own flirtation technique is equally mature and straightforward. When she hears me say that none of Shakespeare's comedies are actually funny, she starts singing a made-up song called "Pretty boy is a fucking moron".

We spend the end-of-series cast meal talking to each other. Sadly, Auntie Trudy just died and I tell Abbie about her and she tells me about her Auntie Elsa. We quietly lose the others on the way to the pub and snog in the taxi all the way back to my flat. When we get out, the driver says, "Please invite me to the wedding!"

Three weeks later, we're in a pub in Clapham called the Eagle. We're having a chat which turns into me explaining slowly and carefully all the reasons why I'm hopelessly in love with her. She replies, with a smile and a shine to her beautiful eyes, "My heart is full."

Three years after that, we can't invite the taxi driver because we forgot to get his number. But we pack St Paul's Church, Covent Garden — "the Actors' Church" — with lots of other family and friends. "This room," says my best man, David Mitchell, "is full of very nice people."

Indeed it is, including David himself. Here are Abbie's cool friends from UCL and drama school. Here's Jenna with her smashing future husband, Nick. Here's Heather Slater from QEGS and Carole Plumb from the Dower House. Here's Patrick, Joe and Dora from Robinson. Here's Eddie and Jack and my Footlights friends. Here's Will and his lovely wife.

Absurdly, magnificently far-fetched vows are exchanged, along with gold rings and a kiss. It's late December and the hymns are replaced with Christmas carols. We sing "Good King Wenceslas" with men and women taking alternate verses, to the amusement of both. Jack brilliantly belts out Sondheim's "Being Alive" and Eddie beautifully reads "[i carry your heart with me(i carry it in]" by ee cummings. That song and that reading: it's not as if Abbie and I don't have the right ideas about what marriage might be.

It's just that — now — I look at pictures from the wedding, and although I remember a fantastic day, I also see something else: it's "Jean all smiling", the one who doesn't know she's dead — and I feel an unwanted irony. Look at this young couple enjoying their wedding. They don't know, do they? They don't know they're walking straight back into The Trick.

But first, one last word from Mr Paul Frederick Webb.

. . . *forsaking all others* . . . If you're going to swap a promise like this, it's probably a good idea to know what you're asking the other person to forsake. Obviously Abbie, who spent her hen night toasting her former lovers (that took quite a few refills), knew all about mine.

So did Dad.

He bangs his hand on the table. "I knew it! You like a bit of both, boy! Fair enough, mate. You just like shagging and you're not fussy! It's not my scene, but

God knows, with women, even *I've* sometimes nearly put it in the wrong hole, so to speak. Good old boy."

Well, he did ask.

We're back in 1994 and I'm home from Cambridge and missing Clara. She came to stay for a few days and Dad seems delighted that I've got such a clever, posh, blonde girlfriend. In fact, now that the evidence is in that I'm somehow capable of making this happen, it's like he's emboldened to ask a question that seems to have been bothering him for some time.

We're watching *Channel 4 News* over tea as usual. There's a report about teenage suicide among boys who've been subjected to homophobic bullying.

"It's not bloody right," Dad says angrily into his pork chops, sausage, bacon, leeks, mash and cauliflower cheese, "they're only little old boys. They can't help it if they're shirt-lifters, bless them."

He can do this, our dad. He can come out with statements so fantastically wrong and fantastically right in the space of one sentence that all I can do is prepare the next forkful of sausage, bacon and cauliflower. "Not bloody right at all," he repeats. He's gearing up for something; he's getting himself cross enough for some kind of announcement. He clatters his knife and fork down on the sides of his plate. Christ, what now?

"I mean, I've always said that if you — or Mark or Andrew — ever thought you might be — or Mark or Andrew — that you might be *that way inclined*, I'd have no problem. No bloody problem whatsoever."

"Right," I say, helplessly.

359

"I mean, there's some blokes who'd chuck their sons out on the streets, but they're twats. In my view. I'd never do that with you. Or Mark or Andrew."

"That's . . . good."

His expression softens slightly and he picks up his knife and fork. The next question is addressed to his food. "So what's the score then, boy?"

Fucking hell, you're joking, aren't you? What, here? Now? OK, honey. Here goes.

"Well, you know I'm with Clara, obviously."

"I do, mate. Lovely girl. Lady, I should say. Lovely young lady."

"And obviously, when you're with one person then you're with one person and that's it." Given Dad's historical approach to monogamy, I worry that this came out as an accusation, but he's still listening. "But before her . . ." I take the Michael Portillo line because, it happens to be true, "as a teenager and a younger man . . ."

"Go on, boy. None of my business. Go on."

". . . not all the people I had, erm, relations with were girls. In fact, one or two of them were boys."

He goes into his jubilant table-banging routine.

A year earlier, my brother Andrew had said, "If you ever tell him, it'll break his heart."

No, mate, it didn't break his heart. Mainly because he managed to turn it into an example of a typical Webb who needs to put knobs in holes. That and family loyalty. That and the fact that he loved us. There were times when any of the three of us could have told him that we'd just set fire to a hospital and he'd have found a way of saying that those hospital wankers probably had it coming.

Ultimately, we're not talking about much sex with many people. But I was right to treat it as a big deal generally, just as I was wrong to think that Dad would have some kind of fit about me individually. This is the thing about villages: sooner or later, everyone knows everything about everyone else. There's always "the score". Person A drinks too much. B had an affair with C and they eloped to Cleethorpes. D had a breakdown when he lost his job and E and F are thinking about changing to *The Guardian* but seem normal otherwise. G's garden is overlooked and everyone knows he deadheads his geraniums in the nude. I, J and K have all done time for ABH, but only L and M are on HRT. O, P, Q, R, S, T and U all have cancer. V cheats at golf.

Which is partly why, despite the stereotype suggested by the *Daily Mail* — a stereotype they collude in by buying the bloody thing — rural Conservatives are not the monsters of bigotry that I and some of my friends on the left have occasionally found it convenient to assume. In fact, they are some of the most tolerant people I've ever met. Not because they're inherently nicer than city-dwellers, but because they don't have a choice.

For twenty-five years I've been made to feel welcome in Woodhall Spa Conservative Club: drinking there and playing snooker with Dad, Mark, Andrew and their friends. My public support for Labour has been discreetly overlooked. It's recognition that community is more important than politics, even as the best political disagreements are often about how best to maintain a community.

Dad made exceptions for me just as I made exceptions for him. His views on snooty, Champagne socialist, metropolitan, formally pan-affectionate, middle-class Oxbridge luvvies had to take a step back when he noticed he had one for a son.

And my views of baby-boomer, non-college-educated, slightly racist, deeply sexist, angry white working-class Tories were tempered by having one as a dad. This is the kind of forced empathy that villages, not just families, are rather good at. Given the divisiveness of the Brexit vote and the Trump presidency, I think it's worth saying that it's precisely these exceptions, these accommodations we have to make with each other, that create cracks in the wall of mutual suspicion and make possible a politics of civility — cracks which the algorithms and self-policing identity groups of Facebook and Twitter hastily try to paste over.

Well now, dear reader. I think it's about time we had a look at the place I've so far managed to avoid, the place where we find this particular Webb, to put it mildly, not at his best. Time to go to the ending.

Imagine a child's drawing of a house. This one is thinner but taller than the first one. It has a chimney, but no smoke comes out because the house is in London instead of Lincolnshire, and in London the fireplaces are pretend. Upstairs there's a bedroom for the Big Sister and Little Sister, one for the Mummy and Daddy, and other rooms where the Mummy and Daddy go to look at their computers.

Downstairs, the Daddy is standing outside the back door of the kitchen with a cigarette in one hand and a can of beer in the other. He is waving at the Mummy. The Mummy is inside the kitchen and pointing at the Daddy while talking to him through the door. A speech bubble comes out of the Mummy's mouth and there are lots of long words including, "disappointment", "certifiable" and "alcoholic".

All this time, The Trick had been lying in wait. You can spend your twenties believing in equality, but if you were raised in an averagely Tricky family then you're going to need a very careful and realistic plan when you start your own. Otherwise, all your talk of liberation is going to count for dick once the nappies hit the fan. There are many ways to be a dad, but instead of making up my own way, I just let the original model reassert itself. Unfortunately the original model was no beauty. Unfortunately, it was Dad.

So you work and you're tired and you come in and the baby is crying and sometimes your wife is coping brilliantly and enjoying life and sometimes she's obviously got postnatal depression and can barely stand up for exhaustion. Either way, you can make sympathetic noises, but it's really none of your business because you're working and if you're not working you deserve a beer.

The promise I'd made was to be a 50/50 husband and father. I would do half the house and half the kids.

It was a good promise. Abbie was working; I was working: there would be a bit of rebalancing but it would be no sweat. Obviously, I just needed to be a bit more fussy about the work I said yes to.

Instead, I said yes to everything. I'm a father. I have a family to support. I'm not going to be famous for ever. I need to make hay. A man works. You'll thank me later. I'm tired. I need a drink. I changed that nappy, didn't I? I did the bottles and the steriliser, didn't I?

I look at my CV over those years and there's persuasive evidence of breadwinning panic. *Great Movie Mistakes, Argumental, Robert's Web,*[1] *Pop's Greatest Dance Crazes, Young, Dumb and Living Off Mum,* and almost any ad or voice-over going. I did all this stuff as well as I technically could, but my heart wasn't in it and the audience noticed.

What's worse is that when I wasn't working, I was just sitting outside, drinking, smoking and talking to myself. Fantasies of violence, usually. That time I had to blow my cover as an MI5 agent by shooting a terrorist. That rapist I beat up. That time Jonathan Ross got me to admit I'd served in *a certain regiment* of the British Army. David, of course, only really established himself on panel shows for want of something to do while I was in Kosovo. I stayed up late to rehearse these make-believe conundrums. It was desperately important without being much fun. The Guy-Buys weren't fun

---

[1] A TV show about the internet which would have been a terrible idea even if I'd got my way and called it *World Wide Robert.* Some producers have no sense of adventure.

364

any more. They were all constantly pissed. I wished the Guy-Buys would pull themselves together.

Either that or I was picking a fight on social media. Twitter was the Coningsby Community Centre I never had. It's like I was making up for all those punch-ups I previously had the sense to avoid. I charged bravely into the fray, armed with nothing more than a four-pack of Kronenbourg and a block button. And then charged away again when suddenly everyone seemed terribly cross.

I was like the bad driver to whom everything comes as a surprise. What zebra crossing? Ooh, that roundabout came out of nowhere! Why is everyone beeping? Why am I in the *Daily Mirror* just because I said I couldn't stand Jeremy Corbyn? What's wrong with having a pointless scrap with Julia Hartley-Brewer?[1] Oh, hello Abbie. What's that you say? It's three in the morning? Is it? Oh, so it is. I was just coming . . . Yes, if you'd *listen*, I was saying that I was just coming in. I'm not shouting. Why would I shout? Fucking hell, it's only a couple of beers . . .

Me and a spot of alcohol dependency, then. Who could have *possibly* seen that coming?

How bad did it get? No idea, I was mainly drunk. Not falling down drunk, never drunk when filming or before a show; I never got the shakes or had to do a *Leaving Las Vegas* with a bottle of vodka. On at least two occasions I remember putting a cork back in a wine

---

[1] Katie Hopkins with adverbs.

bottle that wasn't empty. I'm no doctor, but this doesn't sound to me like most alcoholics. It doesn't even sound like most doctors.

I was, however, being a relentless pain in the arse. Mostly absent, often slurred and forgetful: there was no conversation worth having that I didn't need to have twice. Certainly never violent, but much quicker to take offence. Slow, pompous, chippy. You've met this guy, this woman. A dick. A boring, drunken dick. Not all the time, not every single day. But some of the time, most days. Eventually Abbie just wrote me a letter telling me how much she missed me.

What was going on in my head now that I had children?

What do I remember about houses with small children in them? Actually, let's not remember.

What do I remember about the fathers of small children? Let's not go there either.

But mothers! Mothers are great. And what mothers do eventually is that they . . . ooh. Let's just pop open another lager and be somewhere else. The future, preferably. The future where I get it together.

But for now, there's Daddy in the picture, standing outside, waving at his two daughters through the kitchen window. It's as if he prefers it. It's as if young families make Daddy sad.

Chapter 14 Quiz

Yes, it's time for the traditional Chapter 14 pub quiz. As with society, you don't have to be a heterosexual male to join in, but it has been created mainly with that in mind. The subject of this week's quiz is: Gender, Sexism and Masculinity in the Half-Changed Liberal Mind. Yes, this is quite a weird pub. Here goes!

1. Your girlfriend is getting ready to go out to the pub and is wearing make-up. Do you:
   a) suggest she puts on a bit more make-up
   b) ask her why she's wearing make-up when you're only going to the pub
   c) tell her she looks best with no make-up
   d) shut the fuck up about make-up because it's not your face

2. Your girlfriend is unusually irritable today. You figure it's about a month since her last period. Do you:
   a) triumphantly tell her she's being an arsehole because she's got PMT
   b) suggest gently that it's possible that she's being an arsehole because she's got PMT
   c) make her a cup of tea and say it can't be much fun having PMT, especially when it turns you into such an arsehole.
   d) make her a cup of tea and don't fucking mention PMT. If you knew your cock was going to start bleeding tomorrow and it was going to be very painful and extremely inconvenient and this has been happening every month since puberty and it isn't going to stop until your fertility disappears, presaging your own death and

forgoing the miraculous opportunity to carry another living being inside your body and then give birth to it like having a snooker ball pushed out of the end of your cock — not a melon out of your arse, but a snooker ball out of your jizz-sprinkler — then you'd be a bit fucking cranky too

3. A man who sits down to do a wee is:
   a) nearing the end of his useful life and should be given a one-way ticket to Switzerland to get Dignitased
   b) some manner of pervert
   c) clearly just back in from a night on the lash and urinating in the only way viable but doing so with shame
   d) just a guy having a wee. Possibly because he lives with three other people who do sit-down wees and this saves a bit of loo-seat admin. However, he remains a man because he doesn't locate his self-respect in wee posture

4. A bar stool is:
   a) an item of pub furniture for ladies and students
   b) somewhere to put your coat if it isn't occupied by a lady or student
   c) something to lean against with a straight left arm, holding your pint in your right hand (reverse this for left-handers and homosexuals), while cocking your left foot over your right with

the left-foot toes pointing at the floor
d) somewhere to sit, but not as good as a normal chair

5. On average, women earn less money than men over their lifetimes because:
a) they tend to be a fair bit lazier and stupider than men
b) they're just as clever and hard-working as men but their brains aren't really suited to certain well-paid professions and this is because of science and their being from Venus
c) they're just as clever and hard-working as men and their brains are equally suited to any profession, but they lose out when they choose to start a family
d) give me a break. For about 500 discriminatory reasons, including: they're just as clever and hard-working as men and their brains are equally suited to any profession, but they lose out, not because they choose to start a family, but because society chooses to impose a financial penalty on them for starting a family in a way that it doesn't for men

How did you get on? If you scored 5,634, then congratulations because . . .

That's Numberwang! If you didn't get 5,634, commiserations. Also, if you answered anything other than d) for any question, then you have been

Wangernumbed and must now be taken out to be gassed.

On with the show!

I'm with Dada (my granddad, John) in his care home. He's ninety.[1]

I'm sure we've all seen it, the Care Home Kaleidoscope Synecdoche (I expect this phrase will catch on): a house concentrated into a single, glittering room. Trinkets, ornaments, pictures in frames — the mementos that survived the downsize. They stand for all the treasures — including the people — left behind.

The horizon is narrowing and the pathos is there too in John's conversation. The man who did his bit to destroy the Third Reich tells me once again that the food here is good but, if anything, they tend to put a little too much on his plate.

It's 2012 and I'm there with Abbie, Esme (three) and Dory (a few months). Dory needs a nap and Abbie apologises, taking her out for a ride in the buggy. The tea lady just came and gave Ezzie a couple of chocolate biscuits which she has eaten with all the care and precision you'd expect from a three-year-old. "Sorry about the mess, John," I say, picking crumbs off the carpet and madly putting them in my pocket. One of the first things you learn when you have small children is to just go with the mess, embrace the mess. This doesn't mean that you expect everyone else to embrace it too.

---

[1] I'm sorry, John, but I'm afraid that is *not* Numberwang.

"Don't worry about it, mate," John says.

Esme is restless and asks for a story. I look at my granddad. "Would that be all right, John? If I read Ezzie a story?" I slightly project my voice at his massive ninety-year-old ears while trying to avoid the patronising sing-song that seems to get professional care-workers through their day.

"Ooh . . . yes please. I'd like to hear a story too," he says, with a slow-motion smile starting to form. "I mean, you've already heard all mine!"

I rifle through the bag that Abbie has made up of stuff to distract the kids. John's smile is disappearing as slowly as it formed and his glazed blue eyes are searching through the past. He adds, not unhappily, "I wish I'd read y'mother a few more stories."

I swallow hard. "I'm sure you were busy, mate. Don't worry, she got the knack in the end."

"Well, yeah . . . she was a great reader, our Pat. By guy!"

"By guy" is the way John softens "By God" when in the presence of women or children. It reminds me of something, but I don't follow the thought: before me is the great pleasure of reading to my daughter and grandfather at the same time.

I open *Zog* by Julia Donaldson. Zog is an infant dragon who goes to dragon nursery school to learn how to do dragon-like things. About halfway through, Ezzie asks, "Are dragons real?" I wrestle with this for a moment, but decide not to lie.

"No, sweetheart. There are no real dragons."

Ezzie takes this in and looks again at the pictures in the book. "But they're real in the story."

Gosh. That's a good way of putting it. Must remember that one.

"Yes, my love. They're real in the story."

We are storytelling animals, us humans.

"By guy . . ." John had said. By guy . . . Guy-Buy? Is that where I got the name, all those years ago? The name for the Guy-Buys, my gang of twelve disciples, by God?

I doubt it, but it's tempting to think so. Life is a mess and the desire is always to try and straighten it out instead of embracing it as it is; to unpick the cobweb into its silvery thread.

What if Mum hadn't died? What if I hadn't had to go back to school for a year? What if I'd got ABC grades the first time and had gone to Leeds? There were funny people at Leeds but I wouldn't have met David. So, no Mitchell and Webb. Which means we wouldn't have been an off-the-shelf double act ready for *Peep Show*. Which means I probably wouldn't have been cast in *Concrete Cow*. Which means no Abbie. Which means no Esme and no Dory.

That's a hell of a silver lining. For me to make sense of Mum's death, all I have to do is dispose of the best parts of my working life, unmeet Abigail and essentially bump off my children.

Abbie, understandably, finds this way of thinking completely insane. And her talking me out of it — this big-screen narrative I'd made for myself — was the beginning of my becoming a better husband and a better father. We create these stories for ourselves. But some stories we just grow out of.

And more than that, gradually it starts to dawn on me, I'm just this . . . bloke. Not just any old bloke, but one who has invested so much pride and energy into believing I am not a bloke that I've been acting like one of the worst blokes I've ever met. All the anxiety I'd felt about not being a proper boy had found an opposite reaction in avoiding my dismal definition of a proper man. Dad had given me such a frightening early exposure to traditional masculinity that I thought I had life-long antibodies. I thought that it was impossible for me to be an abrasive, hard-drinking bloke who takes his wife for granted because I'd seen what that looked like and it sucked. And the story in which I awarded myself a starring role — the sensitive young man whose Mum died, who got up and out of death and Lincolnshire, who can't be sexist because he doesn't like football, who can't be sexist because he's read *Man Made Language* by Dale Spender and votes Labour, who can't be sexist because he once had a secret boyfriend, who can't be sexist because he's been writing anti-sexist comedy sketches since school and now gets paid to perform them on TV — that guy can't possibly be in the grip of sexism. That guy might quietly notice that he's broken his promise to be an equal partner in the home but . . . OK, fair point. Soon, Abbie. I'll put this right soon.

"You are not," Abbie would say for the umpteenth time, "about to amaze everyone by jumping on your

373

horse like Prince Hal." I'd spent years thinking that *literally any minute now* I was going to suddenly transform into a present, reliable, sober, responsible, fun and loving parent and partner. In other words, an adult.

Instead, I was playing the "man-boy" Jeremy Usborne while scarcely doing this man thing any better myself. It was all provisional. I would get round to it right after this job, this beer, this cigarette and this daydream.

The final nail in the coffin of the "provisional" mindset came in the form of several nails in several coffins. In short, everyone died — John, Derek, Dad.

What do I want? What is my idea of a mature masculinity or an earned adulthood?

For a start, let's not give it capital letters and make it a "thing".

"Well, honestly, nude zorbing, who'd have thought it? And now on *BBC Breakfast*, Robert Webb is here to explain Mature Masculinity."

I mean, fuck off. Fuck off, baldy *Peep Show* dick.

As soon as it enters the zeitgeist it's over. Anyone remember the New Man? This was a half-hearted attempt in the mid 1980s for guys to feel that they were in touch with their "feminine side". It was largely to do with eyeliner. That and an attempt by Athena to shift another load of black and white posters featuring shirtless gay models holding babies.

The New Man died in 1985 when Lofty in *EastEnders* had an asthma attack after Michelle jilted him at the altar. Lofty was in love with single mum Michelle and had offered to become a "house-husband". On the morning of the wedding, Michelle had a secret meeting with her child's secret father, "Dirty Den", a manipulative liar and adulterer with links to organised crime. So obviously Lofty didn't stand a chance.

Mr Rochester has a lot to answer for. Charlotte Brontë's original Fifty Shades of Moody Twat is the direct precursor of Dirty Den and the accompanying notion that only a tall, dark emotional car-crash can make anyone come.

The New Man was pathetic, but sufficient to provoke a backlash: the New Lad. *Loaded, Zoo,* Britpop, comedy was the New Rock and Roll! The only thing new about it was the chippy insistence that young men stop apologising about beer, football and promiscuity. I hadn't noticed the apology (none was required anyway) and didn't like being told that there was something wrong with me because I didn't sit around obsessively compiling top-ten lists. And the bloody football again. Again with the bloody football.[1]

Culturally, we just lurch from one wonky stereotype to another. We're all meant to be Rambo. No, we're all

---

[1] Obviously, I have a reputation to defend as a leading "white knight cuck libtard feminazi" but it's worth saying that I have no problem with anyone enjoying football. I'm not down on all competitive sports just because I was shit at them. And living in your body, enjoying your own physicality, is a fun thing to do, despite also being physically and mentally healthy.

meant to be Nick Hornby. No, we're all meant to be Ed Sheeran in an ironic Rambo T-shirt listening to a Nick Hornby audiobook while perusing a catalogue of Grayson Perry ceramics. While crying and wanking.

I want the same thing for boys, men, girls, women and anyone who grew up feeling that none of these words held any meaning for them. I want them all to have the freedom to express their individual and contradictory selves with confidence and humility. Feminism has had some success in challenging the restrictive stereotypes of what a girl or woman is supposed to be like. What I'm after is extending that awareness to the half of the population who might still be under the impression that gender conditioning didn't happen to them because they've got a Y chromosome.

Gentlemen, it did happen to you. I don't blame you for forgetting because forgetting was part of the deal. I've been remembering for you.

It was forward of me I know, but I'm terribly modern like that.

If I claimed today to have made it as a 50/50 husband and parent, I think Abbie would either die laughing or just strangle me in my sleep.

But I hope I'm at least no longer the pompous dick I was in 2009 when I said to her, "I can't get this done in one generation."

Balls to that. It's a change of attitude, not the evolution of gills.

Reimagining masculinity is worth doing for its own sake, but in my case I know Ezzie and Dory are watching me. I don't assume that either will end up sharing their lives with a man, but if they do, I want them to expect good things. They know whether or not I'm taking responsibility for my own health; they know how often I walk them to school and pick them up afterwards; they know who's emptying the dishwasher, who's taking them to the dentist, who's making his wife laugh and who's arguing with her respectfully.

The Persil is the political. There are several steps to male enlightenment if he aims for equality of unpaid domestic labour. At first, he puts a wash on and expects a medal. When the medal doesn't appear, he may give up. There again, if he has steel in his heart, he may try again. This time he puts a wash on and then takes the clothes out. He may even attempt to dry them. Still no medal. Finally, and this only took me five years, he may eventually put a wash on, dry the clothes, fold them up and put them away.

To be honest, I still find this last part quite challenging because, for the sake of speed and efficiency, Abbie has severe rules about which clothes go in which drawers. In fact, she has fairly strong views on what happens *within each drawer*. But she has encouraged me not to fear the System and I have been left with the impression that she prefers my getting the job slightly wrong to my refusing the job. It's weird that I was ever in a position to refuse the job.

At home, I keep a close eye on my temper. Obviously, I'd rather chew my own arms off than hurt

377

the children, but I also try to catch an oncoming mope or sulk: the Mood Tyrant can be just as scary as the guy throwing crockery around. I don't drink alone and I've quit smoking. It remains a sexist world and I can't change it for my daughters the way I would like to. But I can try to improve the situation one man at a time. Starting with me.

You can write a pop song about changing the Man in the Mirror: it's just hard to get that message to stick if lots of people think you're a child molester. Still, it's a good idea. It's never too late to try, especially because we only have so much time. As Johnson in *Peep Show* said at Gerrard's funeral, "The scythe is remorseless. I hope the scythe's remorseless swing can bring some comfort to you all. OK."

I don't know if I mentioned this, but we are all going to die.

There was a two-year period in my early forties when I lost Dad, then Derek, then my last grandparent, John.

Saying goodbye in the care home, I'd got used to the idea that it might be for the last time. This time, while Abbie and I are ushering the girls out of the door, I hear my ninety-two-year-old Dada say: "At least we had some good holidays, mate!" I turn back and reassure him that we had some brilliant holidays, which we did.

But what does he mean, "*at least*"? I think I know: he felt a deficit. And so did Derek, and so did Dad. None of them spent their last words with me saying: "I wish I'd spent less time with my children, I wish I'd dominated more men, I wish I'd cried less, I wish I'd shrugged and walked away more often when I upset the women I loved, I wish I'd spent less time saying what I was really afraid of and what I really wanted." No, they ended their lives saying that they'd missed out on too much of the good stuff: friendship, understanding, family and love. And that they'd caused too much harm. That's where I was heading until a few years ago, and there are boys whose bicycles still have stabilisers on that are heading in that direction right now.

I would save them the trouble. I mean to offer them a wider understanding of what it is to be a boy. That it's OK to cry. It's OK to talk about what's wrong. It's OK to play with girls if you like them, to dress like girls if you want to, to like the colour pink if you like it, to want to hang out with your mum if you love her company, to not be all that bothered about football if you're not all that bothered about football.

But small boys know that already. They don't invent these gender rules as they get older. We teach them.

It's difficult to give an honest performance when you've been handed a lousy part. You stare at your lines, wondering how you're supposed to make sense of them. You learn them and stumble through the show anyway, tripping up, getting in the way of yourself and the women you're sharing the stage with. They're having the same problem with their own part, except they also have to do all their moves backwards in high heels, with you talking over them and the spotlight shining on them too fiercely or not at all. The whole thing is a bad dream.

Some people forget that they ever expected anything else. Others get lucky. They're the ones who remember being handed the script in the first place — the one that said BOY, or the one that said GIRL — and remember how disappointing it seemed when the only part they were born to play was the one called INSERT NAME HERE —.

Once you've remembered, it's hard to go on with the show. It's time, in fact, to write yourself a better part.

In St Peter's Church in Woodhall Spa in 2013, I delivered the eulogy I'd written for Dad. The place was packed and another forty or so people were standing outside. I got a few laughs, remembered some of his unremembered acts of kindness, and ended it like this:

> The sadness that we feel now, we can afford to hold close; safe as we are in the knowledge that grief is love's echo. We only have to listen and it's there. Today is a heavy day, but this is just an aftershock. The earthquake, the main event, as usual, was love.

He had three grandsons. When I told him, in 2008, that Abbie was expecting a baby, he said, "It'll be a boy, boy. The Webbs only do boys." And then when we turned up with a girl, followed by another girl, he was delighted and said, "Robert has to be different, doesn't he?"

Yes. Robert has to be different.

At the same time, Robert is completely typical . . .

380

"Don't let Nana or Trudy see you cry."
"You're wearing girls' socks!"
"Do you want some of my beer, boy?"
"I regret to inform you . . ."
"Your behaviour has been deplorable."
"When's it going to get romantic?"
"Fuck off! He's doing his best!"
"My heart is full."
"You let me down."

There are probably lots of men who haven't had their lives marred or pointlessly complicated by the expectations of gender, but I've yet to meet one. You had to bury your pain; you had to conform to the tribe; you had to grow up faster than you wanted; you had to have sex as early as possible and with as many people as possible, even if that made you a liar; you weren't romantic enough and you felt bad; you failed to do manly tasks with competence and felt bad; you made promises you couldn't keep.

If you want a man of a certain age to go a bit quiet and stare into the middle distance for five seconds, ask him about his relationship with his father. Then expect the word "complicated" to feature quite heavily in his next sentence.

The Trick is a stupefying waste of everyone's time. It creates barriers, not just between men and women, but between mothers and daughters and fathers and sons. To oppose it has been the cause of feminists for many years. It's a cause I share.

Just before we got married, Abbie wrote this:

Wedding Day

This, they say, is the best it gets —
this glorious day, so let's
have this glorious day and kiss Goodnight,
and wake up hungover, and fight.
And make up and kiss Goodnight,
and wake up and make jokes:
some good, and make plans
and kiss Goodnight and sleep
and hold hands.
And wake up and insist and be wrong
and laugh like monkeys, without understanding,
  and be right.
And then let's kiss
and kiss
and kiss
and kiss
and kiss
and kiss Goodnight,
and sleep
and keep each other warm
and wake up
and take up each other's cause
and forsake all others, for as long as the light
  lasts.
And then let's kiss our last Goodnight
And oh! Christ let me dream of your sweet face
  then.

Those of us who are loved have no excuse. I was right the first time when I tried to protect my bee in her roofless castle. All along, I had the information in my back pocket: I knew I was loved from the moment my mother picked me up at the bottom of the purple stairs. And when she died, I had the right idea as I sewed the badge back onto my school blazer.

"He needs to be a friend to himself."

Men will struggle to treat women as equals if we haven't learned to look after ourselves; to recognise our feelings and take responsibility for our actions. We should remember what we knew all along: that we are allowed to be fully human, fully compassionate, fully alive in the moment and fully committed to friendship and love.

Self-respect and kindness to others: that's it. That's how we restore freedom to the galaxy . . .

You won't be surprised to hear that some of my early enthusiasm for *Star Wars* might have leaked out and Ezzie and Dory are now big fans. We sometimes chat about those brave, beautiful rebels. Han and Luke, of course; how even Darth was a rebel in the end. And especially Princess Leia, the best kind of princess. Such conversations are not uncommon while we're out playing in the garden.

Football, usually. We often play football. I'm starting to quite like it.

Acknowledgements

Huge thanks to my editor, Francis Bickmore, especially for his attempts to get me to calm down. His occasional emphasis on generosity and humility have not necessarily created a kind and humble book, but it would have been less kind and less humble without his wise brain on the case. Thanks to Jamie Byng, Jenny Fry, Anna Frame, Vicki Watson, Pete Adlington, Neal Price and the whole lovely team at Canongate. They have given me the strong impression that the publishing world is full of bright, collaborative and committed people. A bit like TV but with more knitwear.

Thanks to my literary agent, Ivan Mulcahy, for his usual brilliance; for his help in shaping the original proposal and in particular for the advice: "Make it 15% funnier." I did at least attempt to comply with his wishes.

Thanks to Michele Milburn who has been my theatrical agent for twenty years and has helped to coordinate all the publicity hullabaloo for the book as well as being my ever supportive collaborator and friend. Thanks too to her excellent assistant, Tara Lynch.

Thanks to Henna Silvennoinen for her commitment to the book and everyone at Audible for making the recording of the audiobook relatively painless. Thanks especially to John Ainsworth, the audiobook's producer, for his patience and kindness as I fluffed, laughed and occasionally sobbed my way through the reading.

Thanks to Helen Lewis at *New Statesman* for her patience as one of her contributors went AWOL for two years and for commissioning a long article, the original HNTBAB, which was the genesis of the present book.

Of friends who have helped, my thanks go to Tom Hilton for his best guess on the length of that particular seven and a half ton truck; to Jason Hazeley for his suggestion of a chapter quote and his early encouragement; to Molly Ker Hawn for her advice on the book world; to Jonathan Dryden Taylor for advising on certain matters of presentation; to Toby Davies, Robert Thorogood, Katie Breathwick, Heather Slater, Nick Dunham and Mark Evans for their general enthusiasm (this stuff helps); to "Jenna" and "Will" for their generosity and double thumbs-up, and to David Mitchell for helping me to remember what happened and when. His excellent *Back Story* was a useful resource for the university section of the book, but I pestered him about chronology all the same. Without wishing to turn this into a mawkish BAFTA acceptance speech (if you're standing in a bookshop and you turned to this page first, the rest of the book is nowhere near this . . . "luvvie") I wouldn't be in a position to write this book without the partnership that I formed with the gentle and brilliant David Mitchell.

Thanks and apologies to my brothers, Mark and Andrew, and to my sister Anna-Beth. You will not have found this an easy book to read at times. I have felt the steady warmth of your love and encouragement as I worked.

Nearly finally, thanks — and again, sorry — to my daughters, Esme and Dory, for all the fun that we missed while Daddy was looking cross because he had a deadline. "Have you *still* not finished your book?" said Dory (5) one day. Yes, my love, I have finished it. You and Esme won't get to read it till you're both . . . hmm . . . fourteen (if your mother and I have anything to do with it) but I hope by then you will think that it was worth the time. You have my second name and you didn't ask for it to be a famous one. The least I can do is to try and make it mean something good.

Which brings me to the dedicatee of this book, my great love, Abigail Burdess. Thank you, Abbie. Without your support I couldn't have written *How Not To Be a Boy* and without your influence it wouldn't be worth reading. I think you must be from the future. Where you come from, people aren't judged or told how to behave on the basis of whether they've got balls or boobs. I imagine that being from the future can get lonely. I've been trying to keep you company but this time I also invited the rest of the world. They seem like a nice bunch. If you put the kettle on, I'll go to the shop and get some Pringles.

THIS IS GOING TO HURT

Adam Kay

Welcome to ninety-seven-hour weeks. Welcome to life-and-death decisions. Welcome to a constant tsunami of bodily fluids. Welcome to earning less than the hospital parking meter. Wave goodbye to your friends and relationships . . . Welcome to the life of a junior doctor. Scribbled in secret after endless days, sleepless nights and missed weekends, Adam Kay's diaries provide a no-holds-barred account of his time on the NHS front line. Hilarious, horrifying and heartbreaking by turns, this is everything you wanted to know — and more than a few things you didn't — about life on and off the hospital ward. And yes, it may leave a scar.

THE REAL PET DETECTIVE

Tom Watkins

Any pet owner knows the agonizing panic when their beloved furry family member suddenly goes missing. Fear no more: Tom Watkins, former policeman turned true-life pet detective, is on hand to reunite animal companions with families across the nation. From recording the owner's voice to lure cats from their hiding place, to organizing a flyover and a *Crimewatch*-style reconstruction of a dog-snatching (for Toby the Terrier), Tom will do whatever it takes to get the nation's pets home, safe and sound. This is the story of twenty years of missing pets and their owners, and the adventures of Tom's team of expert pet investigators.